'What a journey this is! This book has empowered me by informing me about an important history that I'm connected to, from my experience of having my lyrics used against me to the work that I do with young people.'

Roachee, Roll Deep

'Placing sounds, songs and beats in the midst of the structures of empire, Lambros Fatsis reads Black music and music-making as radical resources – modes of learning and knowing that hold in them rhythmic, sonic and rumbling resistance practices. *Policing the beats* is an essential text for music lovers and music makers.'

Katherine McKittrick, author of
Dear Science and Other Stories

Policing the Beats

Manchester University Press

Policing the Beats

manchester university press

Policing the Beats

Black music, racism and criminal injustice

Lambros Fatsis

Manchester University Press

Published by Manchester University Press
Oxford Road, Manchester, M13 9PL

www.manchesteruniversitypress.co.uk

British Library Cataloguing-in-Publication Data
A catalogue record for this book is available from the British Library

ISBN 978 1 5261 7140 5 hardback
ISBN 978 1 5261 7141 2 paperback

First published 2026

The publisher has no responsibility for the persistence or accuracy of URLs
for any external or third-party internet websites referred to in this book,
and does not guarantee that any content on such websites is, or will remain,
accurate, accessible or appropriate.

EU authorised representative for GPSR:
Easy Access System Europe, Mustamäe tee 50, 10621 Tallinn, Estonia
gpsr.requests@easproject.com

Typeset
by Cheshire Typesetting Ltd, Cuddington, Cheshire

Contents

Foreword   *page* vii

Introduction   1

Part I: Is it even music? Policing Black music as 'out of tune'
under British colonial rule

1   Cop-italism and slavery: Excavating the colonial origins
    of British policing   17
2   Crude noise of a 'vile race': The danger of Black music(s)   26
3   Policing 'dangerous noise' one beat at a time   34
4   'Salvation 'tis a joyful sound': A concluding coda   48

Part II: Does it belong here? Policing Black music as 'out of place'
in post-war Britain

5   'If you brown, they say you can't stick around': Policing
    and (cr)immigration in post-war Britain   63
6   (Don't) Welcome to Britain   66
7   Racism runs riot   73
8   'It gets me 'fraid when Babylon raid'   87

Part III: Isn't it criminal? Black music as 'out of order' in contemporary Britain

9   To be Black is a crime   109
10 Looking for 'crime' in grime   118
11 Blaming Drill for making people kill   128
12 But isn't Rap violent and misogynistic?   144

Part IV: Sounds radical: Black critique(s) of White reason

13 Who feels it, knows it: Black radical thought in sound   165
14 Who knows it, feels it: Learning about criminal injustice
    from the policing of Black music(s)   175
15 Listen to this book: An annotated playlist   194

Postscript: Of skinfolk and kinfolk: A rap on 'Whiteness'   212
Glossary   216
Abbreviations   225
Acknowledgements   226
Text acknowledgements and permissions   230
Notes   232
Index   303

Foreword

Paul Gilroy[1]

People interested in racism are accustomed to hearing the word
'criminalisation'. For decades it has been a fundamental explanatory concept that overflows the governmental archives of inequality
and injustice. Its power spans the twentieth-century discussions
that began with Du Bois' timely, fatal question: 'How does it feel
to be a problem?' Its usefulness continued into the twenty-first
century when the culture of impunity constituted around the murderous violence of police forces in the overdeveloped countries,
sparking a worldwide response of dissent and refusal, especially
among the young, the vulnerable and the racialised.

This is a valuable book. It explores the patterns of opposition
and resistance constructed around the plural vitality of modern
Black music in numerous locations. It presents the archives of black
Atlantic musical culture and situates them in the wider histories of
capture, enslavement, escape and autonomy. Transformative protest, rooted in oppressive confinement, yielded gradually to affirma-
tions of freedom that did not admit European distinctions between
politics and culture.

The text is brief and readable. Lambros Fatsis has produced a
publication to be read. It will even be read on phones! His style

is clear and crisp. Difficult works of history and sociology have been distilled into an open, popular format that will resonate far beyond campus bubbles. Secondly, this book is ambitious, not just in its breadth of reference and the sheer volume of historical and interpretative material that has been assimilated, processed and reworked to form Fatsis' original contribution. It is ambitious also in identifying and filling a little-known space that may have been previously detected but has not been explored in the systematic way that is on offer here. The reader is walked through a large body of introductory and contextual information and then steered towards the issues of power, government, class, racial hierarchy and sexuality that are pending in the policing of Black music and its spaces of manufacture, use and re-creation.

The regulation and control of the resulting music cultures is recognised as significant. It is endowed with the capacity to determine and shape important social and economic relationships rather than simply reflecting them. Fatsis' line of inquiry thus reveals insightful things about power, government, cities and the racial ordering of the world. Thirdly, this work of theory and history is infused with the insurgent spirit of 'abolitionism' but it has been produced by a self-declared music lover, somebody who knows black music(s) intimately and whose appreciation has been transmitted in every paragraph.

The deep love of music and its lore evident here means that the appeal of fatalistic responses to bleak political predicaments gets tempered by joy and appreciation of all the remarkable creative and solidary processes enabled by cultures of organised sound. Syncopated rhythms, wild notes, and the Bass Culture's characteristic low-end signature, are all part of a formation that has repeatedly articulated politics and aesthetics in unprecedented mutualities. Art and artefact, text and performance, artist and collaborative audience, blend, meld and mix. They conjure hidden underground spaces, public spheres where dissidence is played out.

Overdetermined by the political movements that oppose racism, these sounds have summoned, enacted and systematised alternative possibilities, not only for art and culture, but for social living and critical thinking. Across the centuries and against the odds, they have maintained ethical, ontological and epistemological dimensions deriving from, but not quite reducible to, their African sources.

This culminates in a creole planetarity which has unfolded and proliferated even in the most inhospitable of circumstances. Its contagion is not so much a result of the poetic words and philosophical sentiments associated with seductive rebel musics and healing bass cultures, it is an effect of the phenomenology of music as organised sound. The orphic traditions that result surpass simple repetition. The music of the enslaved floated out of the places of their suffering to envelop the plantations and their deadly surroundings. It was heard by everybody and its defiant complexity could not be dismissed. More than that, this music acquired the power to alter the functioning of the words that were paired with it. Humanising tactics were at work. Rapturous tones could be associated, disturbingly, with pathetic sentiments and vice versa.

Frederick Douglass's famous autobiographical narrative inaugurated a new discussion of the power of music and its special significance to slave-descended populations. Commentaries encompassed exploration of the profound problems of aesthetic value and cultural interpretation that arose from analysis of slave song: musical art made from suffering and its transcendence. The same difficult objects drew the repeated attention of people seeking the bloodlines of a black aesthetic. Recently, they have been pored over by others seeking the circulatory system of what is sometimes called the Black Radical tradition.

The liquid ecologies of the black Atlantic made the night time the right time. The noisy capacity to play with time supplied a grounding practice. The tools that could accomplish time's suspension and subordination were being refined. In overcoming it, celebrants could begin to build an orphic system in which common pleasure could be derived from the artful command of time's mutability. James Baldwin, who may be the best guide to the profundity of this history as it appears in north American territory, made astute observations that are relevant to the expanded, comparative dimensions of this book. His pointed meditation on the history of black music and the failure of US jazz critics adequately to come to terms with it, identified the special power of music:

> Music is our witness, and our ally. The "beat" is the confession which recognizes, changes, and conquers time. Then, history becomes a garment we can wear, and share, and not a cloak in which to hide; and time becomes a friend.[2]

Baldwin's observations invite additional inquiries into the conditions that made music into a witness and an ally, and helped time itself to 'become a friend'. In his formulation, musical time (the beat) actually subdues historical time. Thus the friendly relationship with the passage of historical time that he seeks is preceded by its subordination to the beat. Music can transform the way that duration and historicity are apprehended.

These vernacular operations mean that, in its turn, history acquires some of the properties of an object. For Baldwin, it is less a tool of liberation than a chosen sign or perhaps a prop in the larger drama of dissent, opposition and freedom-seeking, to say nothing of what he might have meant by presenting the beat as a 'confession'.

Fatsis follows these signposts in revealing that these musics have been much more than either allies or weapons. They have provided means of healing and recovery. They have promoted the distant possibility of 'empathic repair',[3] and offered therapeutic, hermeneutic, and aesthetic instruments. They have supplied mirrors as well as welcome lubrication for the evolving, sympoietic excursions of the untrammelled human self. Organised musical sound conjures with the material, cymatic prefiguration of alternative worlds that are being summoned, can sometimes be rehearsed and, occasionally, even shared.

Utopian mentalities have frequently been nurtured and augmented by the musical performances and collaborations that compose this tradition of freedom-seeking dissent, flight and re-creation. They have seeped into the arguments made here and reshaped the book's critical contours. It rapidly ceases to be a body of writing about the power of music and musicking and becomes, instead, a larger historic projection of how life could have been lived differently: how life, law and labour might, even now, be reconstituted so that more chances to become fully human will arise.

Here, music is heard not merely as a series of soundtracks to other more important varieties of oppositional creativity and political action. It emerges as an existential and historical agent in and of itself. It is shown to be capable of facilitating and intensifying political mobilisation, collective refusal and acting in concert.

It can do this because it has promoted and amplified meaningful, relational life amidst a general haemorrhaging of meaning and the technological stultification of even well-intentioned opposition to the eugenic racial order. Against those spectacular resources, Fatsis shows that in the depths of estrangement and loathing, this music celebrates and reproduces connections that are as resonant as they are reparative.

Introduction

They want to licen' me foot they no want me to walk. They want to
licen' me mouth they no want me to talk.

– King Radio, *Sedition Law*[1]

It's Friday night and people are dancing to the heat of a steady beat
that shakes minds, bodies, buildings and even the liquid content
of revellers' drinking glasses. The tune is Louis Jordan's *Saturday
Night Fish Fry*, an infectious jump-up rhythm 'n' blues party gem
that describes the legendary rent parties in New Orleans – where
hosts entertained their guests with soul food and food for the soul
(= music), at the price of a small admittance fee used to pay the rent
(not unlike shebeens/blues dances in Britain). Everyone's having
fun, but then we hear Louis Jordan sing:

> Better get out of here, this is a raid. Now I didn't know we was
> breakin' the law. But somebody reached up and hit me on the jaw.
> They had us blocked off from the front to the back. And they was
> puttin' 'em in the wagon like potato sacks [...] When the policeman
> said: 'Where you goin' there, bub?' Now they got us out of there like
> a house afire. Put us all in that Black Maria.

What are cops doing in the lyrics of such an upbeat party banger?
Why is the party raided in the first place? Before an answer to these
questions is attempted, please allow me to leave these questions
hanging and the suspense going. In exchange, I will regale you

with a few more stories. Without leaving New Orleans, think of a young boy parading down Royal Street with a sign around his neck which reads: 'I was arrested for playing music.' So he was, for violating the city's noise ordinance and taken to a Juvenile Detention Centre. Unlike the Louis Jordan story, this is a real incident involving Sammy Wilson from Trombone Shorty's Brass Band who was the boy in question.[2] A similar fate awaited the To Be Continued Brass Band, who received a cease and desist order at the corner of Bourbon and Canal streets accompanied by the threat of a court summons – should they refuse to sign a form acknowledging that they had violated Section 30 – 1456 of a city ordinance. Returning to fiction, without losing sight of the reality it describes, let us now turn to the words of Harlemite Jess B. Simple, a persona invented by Langston Hughes, in a story about the birth of bebop music as a response to the way it was policed:

> 'You must not know where Bop comes from, [...] Everytime a cop hits a Negro with his billy, that old stick says "BOP! BOP!! .... BE-BOP! ... MOP!! ... BOP! And that Negro hollers, "Ooool-ya-koo! Ou-o-o-!" Old cop just beats on, "MOP! MOP! ... BE-BOP MOP!" That's where Be-Bop came from, beaten right out of some Negro's head into them horns and saxophones, and guitars and piano keys that plays it. Do you call that nonsense?'[3]

Despite the fact that this is *not* how bebop emerged as a modern(ist) style of jazz music, Simple's narrative is not altogether false especially if we remember how bebop was policed around the 52nd Street in Midtown Manhattan, where bebop relocated after its birth in Harlem's smoky clubs – like the iconic Minton's Playhouse.[4] Away from NYC, in Salvador, Bahia capoeira pioneer Mestre Bimba recalls how penal codes in colonial Brazil legislated corporal punishment or forced exile for the practitioners of capoeira. He writes:

[T]he police persecuted a capoeirista like you chase after a damn dog. Just imagine, one of the punishments they gave capoeiristas that were caught playing was to tie one wrist on a horse's tail, and the other to another horse. We even used to make a joke, that is was better to play *near* the police station, because there were many cases of death. The individual couldn't support being pulled at high velocity along the ground and died before arriving at his destination.[5]

If you need an image for all this, look no further than Tam Joseph's *The Spirit of the Carnival*, which graces the cover of this book and depicts a wall of riot shields and a snarling dog, forming a circle around a Carnival masquerader at the centre of the scene. From North America and South America to carnivals in the Caribbean and its diasporas, the question of why cops saunter along with their truncheons to take a swing at jazz, clamp down on capoeira, or contain Carnival goers refuses to go away. What is it about such music(s) that exposes them to such harsh policing? That is the question that this book grapples with, as a study of the policing of Black/Afro-diasporic music(s) from the era of imperial–colonial slavery to the present day. Much of this (hi)story resembles the plot of Adal Maldonaldo's protest dance piece *La Mambopera*, which depicts the criminalisation of African rhythms. A dancer is brought to trial for allegedly causing a heart attack with her ancestral movements. But why would African rhythms have such a dangerous impact on white audiences? Could it be that they were perceived and policed as a threat to the sensory, cultural and political integrity of white, mainstream society? To answer such questions, we must turn to the history of policing against Black music(s). But we must also reckon with, confront and expose the racist ideologies and the imperial–colonial context that made associations between Blackness and danger possible in the first place. That is exactly what this book does, by tracing the policing of Black music(s) to its imperial–colonial origins – in order to explain why news stories about 'criminal' (drill) rappers sweep the nation's media and political discourse and fill the respectable, law abiding 'public' with dread. If anyone wishes to understand why the latest rap subgenres are tainted with the stain of 'criminality' today, a closer look at the long history of the state-sanctioned, racialised criminalisation of Black music(s) is needed. And this book provides it, by discussing how the music(s) of the African diaspora have been silenced in Britain's colonies and 'at home' too.

Focusing on Britain might sound odd, encouraged as we usually are to look elsewhere for evidence of racist violence and criminal injustice – especially in that former British colony: America. The choice to account for Britain's foundational role as a pioneer in imperial-colonial statecraft is therefore deliberate. It is as deliberate as the attempt to ignore, deny or excuse the legacy of imperial-colonial violence that comes with seizing a 'quarter of the world's landmass'.[6] In singling Britain out, I am not ignoring how other imperial-colonial powers also put a padlock on Black musical expression. I am merely filling a sizeable gap in the existing literature on the policing of Black music(s) in Britain and the lands and people it captured by force, as a partner in a pan-European, inter-colonial, transatlantic network of oppression that spread racial terror at sea, in the plantation and the imperial metropolis too. This international dimension explains the striking similarities in the policing of West African Àsìkò music,[7] Brazilian samba,[8] Afro-Cuban music,[9] South African marabi music[10] and blues music[11] – to mention a few. The emphasis, therefore, may be on Britain but not without recognising or acknowledging the diasporic nature of the music(s) that this 'island nation' continues to suppress. Such 'jewels brought from bondage' travelled everywhere Black people went, creating a 'counterculture' of Black expressive traditions.[12] In so doing, elements of African music, religious and cultural rites were fused with European instruments, creating diasporic forms of Black music-making. African they certainly were, but *diasporically* so – as cultural nodes of a Black Atlantic network that connected people, politics and music(s) too.[13] In discussing the ways in which Black/ Afro-diasporic music(s) were and continue to be policed, therefore, I am never denying music's right to speak back and talk Black. On the contrary, it is by drawing on Black music that insights on how it has been policed emerge – as a critique of the history and political ideologies that made such policing a reality to be resisted. And resisted it was, socio-culturally and politically too as readers will discover as they thumb through this book. In fact, I could stop here and let you read on in peace. But I would be a terrible host if I didn't give you a tour of its contents first, so you know where to go looking for more information and details of all the above.

Part I traces the ideological and historical contours of how Black music genres became branded, stigmatised and policed as 'criminal', by looking at how they are first dismissed as 'noise' that is aesthetically *out of tune* and therefore inadmissible as music in the minds of nineteenth-century thinkers and colonial legislators alike. The four chapters that comprise this section of the book argue that in order to ban, restrict and contain the performance of Black music, it was necessary to dismiss it as 'noise' produced by people who were assigned a status of cultural inferiority. Defining Black cultural traditions as devoid of artistic merit and creative imagination coincides with the origins of European racism as an ideology that portrayed the enslaved as lacking intellectual abilities and therefore deserving their subjugation as a colonised population. This is clearly seen in a variety of legal and other texts that justify the banning of drumming and dancing as a spectacle of unbridled sensuality that symbolises moral depravity and breeds disorder. Such openly racist views on the rich cultural traditions of the African diaspora were not mere ideological justifications of slavery that assigned the enslaved to an inferior or inhuman status. They were also deceptive rationalisations of how prohibitions on Afro-diasporic music were designed out of fear of the music's potential as a form of communication to incite rebellion. To illustrate how Black music was policed both as a source of dissonance and as an instrument of dissent, Part I focuses on the suppression of African drumming and dancing traditions in Britain's colonial outposts in the Caribbean and West Africa, while also discussing the policing of Trinidadian calypso/*kaiso*.

Drawing on historical research, song lyrics and musicians' auto-biographical testimonies that expose the policing against Black music under colonial rule across the Atlantic, what is offered here is a glimpse of the colonial history of policing against Black music, which is overlooked, if it ever features, in discussions of the criminalisation of Black music(s) today; notable exceptions notwithstanding.[14] Such contextualisation is important as a way of setting the scholarly record straight. But it also allows a closer and different look into the ideology of colonialism, beyond narrow economistic interpretations. With music as our guide, colonialism is reframed here not merely as an economic model that is premised on expropriation of land and the exploitation of (un)free labour. It is also approached as a form of violence on intellectual, cultural and public life. Using music to dramatise the violence of colonial rule, offers a unique and hitherto lacking insight into the long and disreputable history of policing against Black music(s), which educates us out of the puzzled reaction that the policing of Black music genres generates today.

Part II looks at political and legal processes that targeted Black people and their music(s) as 'suspicious' and 'dangerous' in post-war Britain. This part of the book focuses on the policing of reggae soundsystems as an example of how citizenship is policed by defining Black lives out of it, through tactics that subjugated, monitored, controlled and curtailed the movement and expression of Black Britons. Exposing the racist imagery of 'Black criminality', it will be argued that Black music becomes the main stage where such unequal power relations play out loud. To do so, Part II documents the targeting of UK soundsystem reggae to demonstrate how *order maintenance* assumes the guise of *cultural evaluation* to designate *political belonging*, by establishing who and what fits the frame of white mainstream culture. Perceived as a form of sonic and social disturbance, reggae dances in the UK were energetically pursued by police officers who often violently raided such events, turned soundsystems down, damaged sound equipment, attacked partygoers and made arrests for disorderly behaviour. To contextualise the violence that was reserved for soundsystem reggae, Part Two traces the history of postwar migration to Britain to expose the British state's hostility and suspicion towards those whom it perceives and polices as culturally *out of place*. Drawing on calypso (early–late 1950s) and reggae recordings (early 1970s–late 1980s) that document and critique the policing against Black Britons, Part Two attunes us to Black music as a rich and stimulating resource with which to understand how national belonging is policed through culture; with soundsystem dances featuring as examples of what and who has no place in Britain, even in a supposedly post-colonial context.

Part III brings us to the present, turning to the criminalisation of rap subgenres like UK grime and UK drill music – to show how they became stereotypically associated with violent crime and social disorder. Not unlike their musical parents, rap subgenres have seen the full force of the law used against them in quite unprecedented ways – although the discriminatory logic that makes crimes out of rhymes today is cut from the same historical cloth that the previous parts of this book unravel. The main bulk of this section chronicles how rap became indelibly linked to 'Black criminality', as a form of cultural pathology that is ostensibly responsible for the glorification, glamorisation and growth of 'gang culture' and violence in Britain's major cities. Much of this discussion draws on my experience as an expert witness for the defence – in criminal trials that rely on rap 'evidence' to bring charges against defendants. To do so, a rebuttal of frequently recurring arguments about, or rather against, UK drill music is offered – aiming at doing away with mythologies that stand in for the truth. This involves arguing against simplistic and hypocritical charges of misogyny and violence in rap, by showing the selectivity with which rap is blamed for what is otherwise normalised in white, patriarchal mainstream society and culture. In so doing, I point to the ways in which 'race' is seen as an active ingredient in, or the cause of, heterosexist violence – turning Blackness into a criminal category through the policing of rap. Approached as such, the latest rap subgenre – UK drill music – is decriminalised by moving away from criminal justice rhetoric that likens it to a source and site of social and political disorder. It is instead seen as a cultural artefact that offers us an alternative conception of 'criminality', not as what one *does* but who one *is*. Racialised as 'crime', it becomes what Saidiya Hartman describes as a 'status offense': an act that is 'deemed illegal only for a particular group of persons', but not others.[15] Such a realisation helps us understand how and why Black music genres are policed as politically *out of order*, as noisy interference that disrupts a dominant social order marked by hierarchies of 'race'. Part III concludes by exploring patterns of continuity and change in the multiple ways in which various Black music genres have become the object of state regulation and social control from the era of colonial slavery to the present day. Looking at the fate of contemporary rap subgenres like drill at the hands of the law, this section challenges readers to confront the racist ideology that clamped down on Black music in Britain's colonies and reflect on the ways it still plays out as a normalised and legitimised feature of contemporary society and its criminal justice institutions; that are anything but 'postracial'.[16]

Part IV offers an intellectual and political provocation that invites readers to rethink music as an under*mined* (unused and unappreciated) resource for thinking about the social world around us. Without limiting the discussion to specific genres of music as in the previous sections of this book, Part IV reintroduces the music(s) of the African diaspora as a different and exciting register for redefining what intellectual thought and cultural production *are* and what they *can be* or sound like, away from and beyond the white mainstream. This is a necessary move which aims at a more positive and constructive vision than the previous sections have allowed. In response and in opposition to the very ideologies that have dismissed and policed Black music as *aesthetically out of tune* (Part I), *culturally out of place* (Part II) and *politically out of order* (Part III), Part IV makes a case for thinking *with* Black music as a rich repertoire of radical thought that is rarely approached *as thought*, arguing that Black music is uniquely placed to function as a counterpoint to white intellectual traditions and the violent social and political institutions that have criminalised Black music since the heyday of European colonial rule. Black music(s) are therefore presented as a radical epistemology: an intellectual, cultural and political instrument that attunes us to the importance of *listening* as an intellectual faculty/aptitude/possibility; to *sound* as a non-verbal form of information; and to *knowledge-making* as a commitment to carving out spaces where public and political culture can be made, improvised and experimented with. Part Four also invites us to rethink police racism and criminal injustice *through* Black music, as a vital resource for understanding criminal injustice institutions – as guardians of a social and political order that is *ordered* by and through racial hierarchies, whose roots lie in the imperial-colonial ideology that created 'race', racism, policing and police racism. Bringing this book to a close, Part IV ends with an annotated playlist, which 'phonographs'[17] the main arguments made in this book. Each selection is followed by a brief paragraph to contextualise and sound out an interpretation of the message that each tune or record carries within, between and beyond its grooves.

In addition to the four parts that provide the bulk of this book, you will also find a Postscript on whiteness – which functions as a positionality statement in all but name. This was deemed necessary as a way of recognising my social *location* as someone who is racialised as 'white' yet listens to, thinks with and writes about Black culture – while also pointing to my ideological *position* as someone who is committed to anti-racism and anti-colonialism; ethically and politically too. Finally, this book includes a Glossary that defines new words that are invented for this book and expands on other terminology that is frequently used throughout the book. The Glossary also contains a short note on the way certain words appear capitalised (or not); e.g. Black/white and marked by single quotation marks (e.g. 'crime', 'race'), while also alerting readers to newly coined words (e.g. cop-italism) and specific uses of words (e.g. 'British' and 'liberalism') – which acquire more critical interpretations than are usually reserved for them. This is essential as this book draws on language that doesn't obey the protocols of standard usage, committed as it is to abolitionist and Black radical thought rather than social science – which I consider mainstream even when it presents itself as critical. In so doing, the thinking and language that shapes this book – directly or indirectly – comes from mode(l)s of thought that owe a debt of gratitude to Black studies in general and Black radical feminist thought in particular: as an 'intellectual and political tradition' and an 'ethical intervention'[18] that sees 'the forces of sexism and (trans)misogyny, classism and racism' as 'inextricably linked in a mutually constitutive web of oppressions and domination'.[19] Indeed, my version of abolitionist thinking and practice is wedded to the intellectual work and organising activity of Black women: from nineteenth-century figures such as Ida B. Wells, Mary Prince, Sarah Parker Remond, Sojourner Truth and Harriet Tubman to twentieth and twenty-first-century protagonists such as Assata Shakur, Angela Davis, Ruth Wilson Gilmore and Mariame Kaba and many others, like Pauline Hopkins, June Jordan and Toni Cade Bambara and groups like the Organisation of Women of African and Asian Descent and the Brixton Black Women's Group. Their writing and organising may not necessarily assume the mantle of abolitionism, but their thinking betrays an abolitionist imagination. Central to such an abolitionist imagination, and the radical Black feminist spirit that runs through it, is an approach to thinking and activism that sees both as connected and cross-pollinating as vital ingredients in transformative change to which this book is dedicated.

As you have probably guessed already, the book you are holding is a mix, if it is not a mixtape! It contains a lot of historical detail, but it is not a history book. It pays tribute to Black studies, but it is not a book on Black studies. It brims with (Black) music, but it is not a work of ethnomusicology. It discusses policing, 'the law' and criminal injustice, but it is not a criminology book or a treatise on legal studies. It is published by an academic press, but it is not an academic book. It is written with a broader public in mind, but it is not a trade book. It should therefore be approached as a DJ set in print form, which contains a *selection* of material that is pieced together by a person rather than coldly, dispassionately and arranged by an 'objective' robot, or the latest AI tool. As such it is not 'the' definitive account on the policing of Black/ Afro-diasporic music(s) in Britain. It is *my* version of it, as I know and understand it. My aim therefore has been to present what *I* think about what I know and how I know it too, by listening to Black music *first* and then reading from sources that are faithful to the music(s) and culture(s) of the African diaspora. To impose or expect other angles, approaches, ambitions and material is to miss the point and make the book something other than it is. I therefore cannot apologise for not writing the book that someone else wants to read or write, just as I don't expect others to write the books I want to read. It is also written so that it can and *should* be read in full, including endnotes and supplementary sections. Being a book, it does not compress the information it contains like a journal article, or a blog post. It expands on the topic it discusses. As such, it is not an isolated MP4 file but more like an LP that needs to be listened to *in full*, while also reading the liner notes and details of who plays, or what is sampled on the album. Consider this a frank disclaimer and a friendly warning that I feel duty-bound to include, to establish an honest relationship with my readers at the outset. So that's what this book is all about and I hope you will find something that interests you in it.

PART I

Is it even music? Policing Black music as 'out of tune' under British colonial rule

> The conquest of the earth, which mostly means the taking it away from those who have a different complexion or slightly flatter noses than ourselves, is not a pretty thing when you look into it too much. What redeems it is the idea only. An idea at the back of it; not a sentimental pretence but an idea; and an unselfish belief in the idea – something you can set up, and bow down before, and offer a sacrifice to.
>
> – Joseph Conrad, *The Heart of Darkness*[1]

Policing. Slavery. Racism. What's *music* got to do with any of that? Not a lot, if we insist on thinking with our mind's eye alone. Once we start thinking with our ears, however, a different picture emerges – drawing our attention to a view of British policing that situates it in the historical, ideological and political context of colonial slavery.[2] Seen this way, the policing of Black/Afro-diasporic[3] music(s) serves as the keynote for understanding the imperial-colonial history of British policing, as one of the most violently suppressed forms of cultural expression under British colonial rule. Indeed, it would be almost impossible to properly trace the origins of British policing other than *through* the policing of Black music(s).[4] Far-fetched though such an assertion may sound, this section is nevertheless written with a steadfast commitment to such a position – defying conventional police mythistories that cover up the imperial-colonial roots of British policing, by insisting that it was immaculately conceived in Victorian London; making police racism look like something that suddenly reared its ugly head in the 1990s with the murder of Stephen Lawrence at a bus stop in Eltham, South London.[5]

Contrary to dangerous myths and comfortable untruths that dominate the white, criminological mainstream, much of what follows invites us to think about the unholy alliance between instruments of social control (= policing), forms of political (mis)rule (= colonialism) and ideologies of oppression (= racism) as intimately related and directly applied to the policing of Black cultural expression – with music as the prime suspect. How else are we expected to understand how Black Britons remain the proto/stereotypical targets of British policing, or why contemporary Black music genres – like UK drill music for example – are policed in such a heavy-handed manner? We could of course pretend that police racism is somehow disconnected from the legacy of imperial-colonial rule, by treating all evidence of its existence as incidental, accidental and exceptional, just as we could reject the term institutional racism altogether.[6] Or we could dig deep into the long and ignoble history of imperial-colonial statecraft, by demonstrating how political domination is exercised through cultural suppression, with a little help from racism as the political ideology that justifies and legitimises the whole operation.

The following pages attempt to ink such thoughts into our consciousness, as a way of 'rememory[ing]'[7] and 'restor(y)ing'[8] the way we understand policing, the policing of Black (music) culture(s) and the violent legacy of British imperial-colonial rule as partners in crime. Starting with policing, its often neglected and often denied imperial-colonial history will be unveiled to (re)introduce what policing is and does as a disciplinary tool at the hands of imperial-colonial statecraft. We then move on to see how the origins of British policing as colonial 'violence work'[9] coincide with the policing of Black/Afro-diasporic music(s) in Britain's plundered territories along the Atlantic, while also demonstrating how and why Black cultural life was suppressed as dangerous 'noise' and therefore evidence of both the assumed and assigned inferior status of the enslaved and the colonisers' fear of insurrection: a puzzling contradiction that will also be explored. The policing against Carnival and calypso/*kaiso* is then discussed at length, as an example of the racist criminalisation of Black music(s), before a coda allows us to catch a glimpse of Black resistance to imperial-colonial rule – often with and through music, as an essential corrective to racist, imperialist mythistories that denied the enslaved the ability to fight for freedom from bondage.

1

Cop-italism and slavery: Excavating the colonial origins of British policing

The usual history of British policing follows a familiar refrain that goes like this: the police in Britain emerge as an institutionalised force with the formation of the London Metropolitan Police in 1829 by Sir Robert Peel, after whom the proverbial 'Bobbies' are named. The story quickly gains momentum, by adding a familiar plot line, which informs us that this 'new' police force was founded in response to public unrest,[1] rising crime[2] and as an instrument of discipline[3] to keep the industrial(ised) working class in check. More sophisticated accounts go further, offering some context into how the advent of industrial capitalism required the suppression of non-productive or leisurely pursuits.[4] Such accounts point to how the English working class was beaten into submission to conform to the demands of industry – not just as a productive force which keeps economic activity alive, but as a moral imperative too. Industriousness, therefore, was not just productive and profitable for the industrial capitalists. It was also a sign of propriety, restraint and other straight-laced Victorian values of prudishness and high-toned moral superiority. This being the socio-cultural and historical context in which policing became professionalised, the social 'unrest' that policing was born to suppress was a response to 'deskilling' as a result of industri-alisation. The 'crime' was the recreational use of public space and the 'discipline' administered mostly took the form of preventative beat patrolling, to root out 'inappropriate' (read: non-industrious) behaviour in public. More severe measures, however, were not uncommon, which the Peterloo Massacre of 1819 demonstrates fairly clearly. In fact, it became '[t]he signal event that showed the need for a professional police force'[5] to clamp down on the politi-cal activity of rebels like the Luddites – who destroyed their tools to protest against the replacement of skilled work by industrial machinery – or the Chartists, who advocated work reform for the impoverished and exploited English workers. What the '[o]riginal police force' – as Vitale[6] calls it – was created for, therefore, was to police the unproductive occupation of public space by working-class people (the proletariat). This involved making them work for a living in factories, coercing them into accepting their lower station in the emerging capitalist social hierarchy and removing any obstacles to the efficient operation of mass-produced manufac-tured goods and the profits made by trading or selling such goods commercially.

While this rendering of British policing is not entirely false, it amounts to a near-total erasure of the imperial-colonial context within which all such economic, socio-cultural and political activ-ity emerged. What is neglected is the fact that the policing of the English white working class was modelled after the policing of colonial (surplus) populations in the British colonies of Ireland, the Caribbean, the Indian subcontinent and the Middle East too.[7] Even when the role of the police as 'domestic missionaries'[8] is acknowledged, their pre-professional colonial predecessors are seldom mentioned in mainstream narratives. This produces a con-fusing and confused police historiography, which sees Britain as an industrial(ised) capitalist nation that is somehow disconnected from the ways in which industrial growth in English cities was 'financed by profits from the triangular [slave] trade'.[9] It is therefore worth remembering that the iron industries, railways as well as the systems of banking and insurance that made capitalism possible, largely relied on the colonial economics of the slave trade.[10] Karl Marx stated this plainly enough, in a passage that is actually intended as a tribute to 'the good side of slavery'.[11]

'Direct slavery', Marx noted, 'is just as much the pivot of bourgeois industry as machinery, credits, etc. Without slavery you have no cotton; without cotton you have no modern industry. It is slavery that gave the colonies their value; it is the colonies that created world trade, and it is world trade that is the pre-condition for large-scale industry. Thus slavery is an economic category of the greatest importance'.[12] It is therefore no exaggeration to claim, as Erin D. Somerville does, that: '[t]he triangular shipping route of the slave trade largely formed the banking industry in England'.[13] Indeed, the 'insurance market is believed to have begun at Edward Lloyd's coffee house in London' as a space where 'sailors, shipowners, and merchants ... met to discuss private insurance arrangements' and a place where 'runaway slaves could be returned'. Even familiar high-street banks like Barclays Bank and the Bank of England had their 'capital tied to sugar and slave merchants'.[14] The connection between the slave trade and Britain's banking and insurance system could not be better or more callously demonstrated than by the fate of the *Zong*, the British slave ship that carried '132 African slaves that were thrown overboard for insurance money' that ship-owners could claim on 'slaves dying of unnatural causes, including drowning to prevent rebellion or to ensure the safety of the ship and crew'.[15] *This* is the very context in which capitalism developed and whose interests policing served, justifying perhaps a playful neologism: 'cop-italism' to tie together the economic and political system of capitalism and the police force that serves and protects it.[16]

Separating the history of policing in mainland Britain from the history of such policing in Britain's colonies, therefore, can only be thought of, rather charitably, as a case of cognitive dissonance or, less forgivably, as an unpardonable blind spot in police scholarship. Besides, as Fryer[17] notes, 'the emerging industrial working class in Britain was exploited [and policed] by the same capitalist class that exploited [and policed] black slaves'. Or as that diligent student and critic of capital(ism), Karl Marx himself reminds us: 'capital comes dripping head to toe, from every pore, with blood [...] turning [...] Africa into a warren for the commercial hunting of black skins'.[18] It is therefore impossible to trace the birth of British policing to 1820s London without connecting what happens in mainland Britain to what is happening in its colonies, unless we are to willingly (mis)take imperial Britain for a non-imperial nation. Alas, it is not possible to have an empire without colonies, or colonies without colonising land(s) and people. It is also not possible to do any of this without violent force, which is why it makes sense to set up a colonial police force that would violently enforce the imposed imperial-colonial order 'out there' in the colonies, for the sake of all of us 'right here' in the metropole. This is why the dominant, liberal historical copaganda doesn't make any sense – other than as a wilful exercise in denial(ism). When the Met was founded in London, the slave trade may have ended, but the (racial) capitalist cistem[19] of slavery itself was still alive and well – a decade *after* the official origin story of British policing. While the slave trade was made illegal after the British Parliament passed relevant legislation in 1807 – with effect from 1 January 1808 – slavery itself would have to wait to be (nominally) abolished with the Abolition of

Slavery Bill and the Emancipation Act, which initiated the process in 1834.[20] However, although '[a]ll slaves under the age of 6 were freed immediately', 'the rest became "apprentices" for up to six years, working most of their time (for free) for their ex-owners'.[21] In short, what started as the abolition of the slave trade in 1808 only signalled the abolition of slavery itself three decades later.

This observation serves as an important reminder of the fact that it is impossible to discuss or think about developments in Britain's internal affairs, like the formation of a professional police force, for example, without recognising that all this happens in an imperial context. It should therefore come as no surprise to hear that the Metropolitan Police force that we know as the Met is in fact the reincarnation of pre-professional colonial, slave-catching militias, with the plantation *overseer* being the forerunner of the metropolitan *officer*. As mainstream police historians remain dishonourably silent on this fact, it is interesting to note that rappers were quick to draw such parallels. Besides, not unlike the enslaved, rappers also become 'police property' in our supposedly 'post-racial' times.[22] A case in point, is KRS-One's (1993) anthemic *Sound of Da Police*, which makes that connection between the 'officer who patrols the nation' and the 'overseer who rode in the plantation'. This detour, with old school hip-hop as our guide and our soundtrack too, may seem fanciful. Yet, it treads where police historiography barely treads water; exposing an unwillingness to connect policing in the heart of the empire as 'an all-purpose lever of urban discipline'[23] to how policing England's working-class poor has its prehistory in the 'slave-hunting gangs hired by the West India sugar planters'.[24]

To separate the one from the other is to divorce the history of British policing from its historical background. The history of British policing cannot be anything other than imperial-colonial in nature – emerging, as it did, in *that* very context. Contrary to conventional wisdom and mainstream criminological historiography, therefore, policing was not immaculately conceived in nineteenth-century London. It was founded during colonialism and slavery. The models and styles of policing that emerged in the metropole, derive from pre-professional, informal militias that were formed to patrol, capture and control fugitive slaves and colonial subjects in Britain's overseas 'possessions'. In fact, as Elsa Goveia succinctly argued, 'the experience of the British colonies makes it particularly clear that police regulations lay at the very heart of the slave system and that, without them, the system became impossible to maintain',[25] echoing W.E.B. Du Bois' flat assertion that 'the system of slavery demanded a special police force', with the 'overseer, slave driver and member of the patrol system' functioning as the imperial-colonial model for metropolitan police forces.[26] The antecedents of the London Metropolitan Police in 1829, therefore, exist not just in the Royal Irish Constabulary – also founded by Robert Peel in the former British colony of Ireland – but in the plantations of the Caribbean and the Indian subcontinent too. Even the River Thames police, which was founded by Patrick Colquhoun in the beating heart of the Empire, was also an imperial-colonial police force – formed, as it was, to protect the profits amassed from the spoils of colonial plunder, like coffee, tea and sugar – which were 'the basis of the industrialization of England'.[27] The Thames functioned as the 'jugular vein in the British Empire', connecting 'the workshops of Bengal, the plantations of the Caribbean, and the forests of North America',[28] and the River Thames Police was set up to accept 'direct responsibility for the payment of wages to lumping gangs of the West India fleet'.[29] As Linebaugh stresses, '[t]hrough these waters passed the wealth of the Empire'[30] and Colquhoun profited personally by working as 'the London agent for the planters of St Vincent, Nevis, Dominica and the Virgin Islands'[31]– much like Peel acted as a colonial governor, managing the colonial occupation of Ireland. As such, British police forces – metropolitan and colonial alike – started their life as instruments of suppression – wielded by slaveholders and colonisers to maintain a form of discrimination, dehumanisation and violent subjugation (racial slavery) – before evolving into professional institutions that serve and protect the state from those who are seen as undeserving of its protection. Originally designed to brutalise and terrorise slaves and colonial subjects, pre-professional colonial policing transitioned into professional institutionalised policing, targeting the same 'suspect populations' though comparable methods of 'penal excess'.[32] None of the above suggests a smooth, linear and uninterrupted progression from colonial to metropolitan policing.[33] Alas, the violent legacy and 'afterlife'[34] of racist logics and tactics that made colonial policing possible endures and informs Britain's institutionally racist police forces today.[35]

This chapter has hitherto attempted to reintroduce the police as 'the bloodhounds of capitalist law and order'[36] by connecting the historical origins of British policing to the political (racial capitalist) economy of imperial-colonial slavery. Showing how policing has blood at its root(s), we also saw that 'Vagabonds, Beggars, Pilferers, lewd, idle, and disorderly Persons' who loitered around nineteenth century London[37] were not the only targets of police oppression. A similar but much worse fate awaited those who were enslaved, herded, trafficked and traded as human cargo, property and source of (un)free labour in Britain's colonial plantation archipelago.[38] The chains that link together capitalism and slavery however keep us on a rather short leash, if we discuss imperial-colonial slavery as a 'crim[e] of dollar blood' alone – to borrow June Jordan's arresting phrase.[39] Imperial-colonial rule was always 'more than an extractive commercial operation'.[40] This urgently reminds us, as Frantz Fanon did, that 'Marxist analysis should always be slightly stretched every time we have to do with the colonial problem',[41] given that colonial imperialism did not just revolve around 'the *organization of production*'.[42] Rather, it was based on and demanded 'the persistence and *organization of oppression*'.[43] Sylvia Wynter's description of racial capitalist coloniality as the embodiment of 'emporio–imperio' is crucial here. Wynter points out that 'the forces of the *emporio*' (= emporium/trade) 'were the forces of the *imperio*' (= imperial rule), in a politico-economic cistem where 'the plantation' served as 'the unit base' of 'emporialist' and 'imperialist' histories, politics, ideologies and practices of capture, exploitation, expropriation, subjugation and control.[44]

Even with such important clarifications and qualifications, however, this is only half the story. This 'half-story' tells us that the enslaved were policed as 'walking manure hideously proffering the promise of tender cane and silky cotton',[45] to secure the political dominance and economic super-exploitation that overdeveloped Britain and 'underdeveloped' its imperial-colonial outposts.[46] What is missing, however, is an account of what else was policed, beyond the labour power of the enslaved – or what ideological justifications made 'covert[ing] the accumulation of life-times [...] into labour time' possible in the first place.[47] To fill in the blanks, the following section focuses on the policing of Black music(s) as a casualty of imperial-colonial governance – aided and abetted by racism as the ideology that enabled colonisers to violently dismiss and aggressively police Black expressive culture as crude, uncivil(ised) 'noise' to be eliminated, rather than as artistic achievement to be appreciated.[48] In so doing, we move away from the strictly economic-material dimensions of racial capitalist colonialism to consider the racist ideological-political war against the cultural life of the enslaved. With Black/Afro-diasporic music(s) as our guide, what follows is a discussion of how colonialism, as 'the White Man's difficult [but necessary] civilizing mission',[49] armed with racism as its ideological manual – detected in the music(s) of the enslaved a clear sign of intellectual, aesthetic and cultural inferiority *and* a source of trouble; as an expressive outlet for rebellion. Policed both as a *source of aesthetic dissonance* and as an *instrument of political dissent*, Black/Afro-diasporic music(s) will therefore carry us to an understanding of imperial-colonial policing as a *cultural* institution that orchestrates social, cultural and political life through regulation and social control – punishing those who do not, could not and should not belong to the civilised, white Western world, other than as 'outlaw[s] of humanity' as Nazi jurist Carl Schmitt[50] so chillingly put it.

2

Crude noise of a 'vile race': The danger of Black music(s)[1]

So far, we have unwrapped slivers of British imperial-colonial history by focusing on the predatory or 'cynegetic'[2] policing of the enslaved for material gain and political dominance. We now turn our eyes to how such political dominance is achieved through the policing of Black culture(s), vindicating Cedric Robinson's[3] re-reading of Marx's claim that, in the context of ideological-political oppression, 'the first attack is an attack on culture'.[4] Starting with a discussion of why the music(s) of the enslaved was and could only be perceived as 'noise' by the colonisers, we then explore how Black-music-as-noise was policed against through legislation that sought to suppress it – before looking at specific examples of affected genres, as indicative case studies that vividly illustrate the racist criminalisation of Black music(s) under British colonial rule. In short, the following section aims at unmasking the logic (= racism) and tactics (= laws) behind the policing of Black music(s) – drawing primarily on the banning of African drumming and dancing and the policing of calypso/kaiso[5] and Carnival celebrations in Trinidad. In choosing those examples, I am by no means suggesting that these are the *only* Black musical culture(s) to be policed this way. I am merely directing our attention to them

as powerful evidence of how and why Black music(s) have historically been policed the way they have, while also inviting us to think
about what exactly is policed when Black music(s) are policed.

If music were the 'food of love', as the Old Bard claims in
the opening line of *Twelfth Night*, it is shocking to see how
much hate is directed at Black music(s) by colonisers, missionaries and scholars (to say nothing of the police, prosecutors and
judges today – as we will see in Part III of this book). But then
again, everyone knows that anything that does not conform to
the standards and established principles of European traditions of
music composition, must be derided as 'noise'. That is certainly
true of Black/Afro-diasporic music styles during the era of colonial
slavery, attracting the sneering condescension of European white
supremacists as proof of intellectual, aesthetic inferiority, cultural
backwardness and 'otherness'. From Hegel's denunciation of the
'negro's' music as 'detestable noise' that is 'meaningless and ugly',[6]
Lady Nugent's[7] repulsion towards the 'noise of rude music' and
Benjamin Latrobe's irritation at the 'incredible noise' and 'uncouth
songs' that 'screamed a detestable burthen on one single note',[8]
complaints about how 'heathen negroes on the estate began to beat
their drums, to dance and to sing in the most outrageous manner'[9]
fill the minds of plantocrats, colonial governors and other apolo-
gists of slavery. Such 'barbarous concert of vocal and instrumental
music', however, didn't just cause 'great inconvenience and annoy-
ance'[10] at a purely aesthetic level. It also ignited feverish conceptions
of African or Afro-diasporic music(s) as offensive music to the very
core of a Western-European self-image as the epitome of cultural
superiority, turning 'tonality' into a 'colonizing force'.[11] In contrast
to Western criteria of music-making that prize 'melodic perfection,
correctness of pitch, finish or purity of tone',[12] the polyrhythmic,
antiphonal qualities of Afro-diasporic music could only signal the

demise of 'centuries of culture' that 'end with the Negro jungle tom-tom' – as Horkheimer and Adorno[13] put it, at their racist best.

Nothing exemplifies the perceived gulf between Western-European music and 'noise' better than Grenadian poet and writer Jacob Ross's short story *Song for Simone*, which satirically pits Beethoven's *Minuet in G* against steel pan music – making even pannists themselves question the musical nature of their art. In a characteristic passage Mr James, a steel pan virtuoso, asks Simone – the story's protagonist: 'You call steelpan music, music?', only to inspire a retort that finds Western music-making lacking for not having 'guts': 'No drums, no real riddim, no bassline.'[14] What this exchange in Jacob Ross's short story exposes is the ideologically imposed divide between the assumed virtues of melodious, harmonic Western music and civilisation and the presumed vices of percussive, (poly)rhythmic African 'noise' and 'wilderness'. Never mind the fact that 'African music is rich in melody, timbral variety, and even two- and three-part harmony', even though 'rhythm is often the most important aesthetic parameter'.[15] What is noteworthy here is the realisation that what counts as music involves 'the moral evaluation of noise'.[16] What counts as music then, becomes a culturally loaded decision-making process about the normative value of sound. And what counts as noise also falls prey to definitions of pleasantness, politeness, civility and their polar opposites – namely: rudeness, disturbance and incivility. Unlike music, 'noise' is the sonic equivalent of dirt: 'matter out of place' and a 'threat to good order' that is 'regarded as objectionable and vigorously brushed away'.[17] And much of the above depends on the 'unlistening ey[e]'[18] of the beholder, if the latter thinks and acts within the 'folklore of white supremacy'[19] as the mythology of a 'Superior Race' that made 'Europe ruler of the world'.[20] What we see in the devaluation of Afro-diasporic music, therefore, are the same arguments that were applied to the denigration of the enslaved more broadly – denying their humanity and their ability to produce thinking and create civilisations and culture(s), as a way of justifying the violence that was reserved against them. *We* Europeans are enlightened and intellectually advanced, *they* remain 'in the vicinity of African stupidity' and 'barbarous sensuality', forever consigned to 'the land of childhood, which lying beyond the day of self-conscious history, is enveloped in the dark mantle of Night'.[21] Whites are culturally elevated, '[t]he Negro', however, 'exhibits the natural man in his completely wild and untamed state. We must lay aside all thought of reverence and morality – all that we call feeling – if we would rightly comprehend him; there is nothing harmonious with humanity to be found in this type of character'.[22] Besides, 'Africa is no historical part of the World; it has no movement or development to exhibit. What we properly understand by Africa, is the Unhistorical, Undeveloped Spirit, still involved in the conditions of mere nature.'[23] Unlike us, '[th]ey have no culture, no system of writing (nor do they) preserve monuments of their history; they have the vaguest obscure memory of facts recorded in certain pictures, they lack written laws and have barbarous institutions and customs.'[24] Indeed, as the primary author of the American Declaration of Independence, the third president of the United States and slave-owner Thomas Jefferson[25] testified: 'never yet could I find that a black had uttered a thought above the level of plain narration; never seen even an elementary trait of painting or sculpture'. Aren't *they* 'inferior to the whites in the endowments both of body and mind' after all?[26]

Christened by Sylvia Wynter as 'the Sepulveda syndrome', after the racist-humanist theologian Ginés de Sepulveda, such 'mythology of the inferiority of the non-white'[27] distinguished 'the civilised races of man' from 'the savage races' who would, after all, be 'almost certainly exterminate[d] and replace[d] throughout the world' by the former.[28] Yet, this barrage of racist bile is only a glimpse of the prevailing 'racist humanism'[29] or 'murderous humanitarianism'[30] of the wild, white West. Absent are similarly nauseating comments by Immanuel Kant and David Hume[31] among others – who traded in demeaning and abusive caricatures of African people in their learned treatises, even as they extolled the virtues of liberty and criticised slavery; other than when it was imposed by Europeans on the 'darker nations'.[32] Such a selection nevertheless brings to our attention 'the racial order of manichaean colonial domination',[33] a snapshot of which can be found in a bitingly sarcastic passage from Toni Cade Bambara that deserves to quoted in full below:

We are ordained	You are damned
We make history	You make dinner
We speak	You listen
We are rational	You are superstitious, childlike (as in minor)
We are autonomous and evolved	You are shiftless, unhinged, underdeveloped, primitive, savage, dependent, criminal, a menace to public safety, are needy wards and clients but are not necessarily deserving
We live centre stage, true heroes (and sometimes heroines)	You belong to the wings or behind the scrim providing the background music[34]

The dualisms that Bambara so concisely and incisively exposes and explodes, with her characteristic lacerating wit, are not just illustrative of how imperial-colonial(ist) worldviews function as the ideological weapons that made slavery possible. Bambara's shopping list of racist stereotypes also helps us understand how the aesthetic, the cultural and the political join hands to determine who is worthy and who is not. Racism and colonial slavery, therefore, come to be understood not just as purely political–governmental projects, but as cultural–civilisational expeditions too. The two are in fact indistinguishable. At the hands of colonial imperialists, culture was *how* political domination was to be achieved: by installing European civilisation as a sacred commandment that would divine how life was to be lived, while attacking as profane the already existing 'primitive' civilisations of the exterminated Indigenous people and the enslaved Africans who were trafficked in Europe's brazenly hijacked territories along the Atlantic. Seen this way, the '[c]heerful [...] myth of the civilizing mission of colonial imperialism'[35] takes on a more sombre meaning: as a form of disciplining the enslaved into the ways of the West, by imposing 'superior' linguistic, religious and cultural traditions to replace and destroy the insurrectionary potential of existing but 'inferior' ones. Why? Because such cultural wealth was a source of life-affirming, community-building, socio-cultural and political activity that had to be stamped out to make room for Europe's dominion over the four continents and the seven seas.

What is perceived as aesthetically or culturally *offensive* is what is pursued as an *offence* not just to the realm of intellect or the senses but to colonial order itself. That which is *aesthetically discordant* is also *culturally dissonant* and *politically disorderly*, making Black music(s) 'suspect' as the polar opposite of artistic expression, Western civilisation and socio-political harmony. What is punished as offensive (literally, as an offence), therefore, is an(y) attempt at participating in cultural and socio-political life away from, outside and beyond the order dictated by imperial-colonial regimes. And *that* is exactly what makes 'Black noise' so 'dangerous' to the ideological, cultural and political project of white domination. It is a cacophonous attack on imperial-colonial harmony that must be quelled to defend an imposed cultural and political order that *orders* people, both by classifying and ranking them in hierarchical order and by disciplining, coercing, subduing them by force. The two meanings of the word 'order' (from Latin *ordo* = rank) converge here, referring both to order-as-hierarchy and order-as-discipline – by positioning people on a social scale that measures and grades their humanity to determine their access to power. The 'difference' that is announced by the sound of 'Black noise', therefore, must be policed as alien, inadmissible and threatening to the established social order. As Edward Kamau Brathwaite puts it:

> [T]he necessary assumption [was] that slaves, since they were brutes could produce no philosophy that 'reach[ed] above the navel' – their music was dismissed as 'noise', their dancing as a way of (or to) sexual misconduct and debauchery. On the other hand, the 'political' function of the slaves' music was quickly recognized by their masters – hence the banning of drumming or gatherings where drumming took place' – often on the excuse that it disturbed the (white) neighbours, or was bad for the bondsmen's own health.[36]

Such supposedly unthinking, uncivilised, hypersexual and rebellious people would have to be treated with the 'brutality, cruelty [and] sadism'[37] that was reserved for them by 'the cult of the gun, famine, drought and economic destabilization'[38] that 'Western-bourgeois industrial/techno-economic'[39] colonial rule brought in its wake. So they were, with legislation that was created to silence the music(s) of the enslaved and crush any prospect of rebellion that music, as an instrument of insurrection, was (rightly) suspected of being. Having hitherto looked at portrayals of Afro-diasporic music(s) as 'utterly without meaning' and as 'queer haphazard noise',[40] we now turn our gaze to how the music(s) of the African diaspora were policed as a way of policing the enslaved: mind, body and soul. Starting with a compilation of relevant laws and police powers – an account of how some music styles like calypso/*kaiso* were targeted is also given – the chapter ends with the question of just what was policed when Afro-diasporic music(s) were policed.

3

Policing 'dangerous noise'
one beat at a time

'After the dance, the drum is heavy'/ *Aprè dans, tanbou lou* (in Haitian kreyòl). So cautions a famous Haitian proverb, made even more famous by Edwidge Dandicat's acclaimed travelogue *After the Dance*. But what does it mean? In general terms, it means that after even the most joyful experiences, like carnival in the streets of Jacmel for example, there are consequences that weigh heavily on the revellers' bodies and minds – not unlike a hangover. In our case, however, the heaviness of the drum comes from the knowledge that every beat that vibrates from the drum's skin is met with the clamour of the police patrol. It is no accident therefore that specific legislation was enacted to make the drum(s) fall silent – across Europe and North America. Indeed, in the US slave patrol legislation was introduced to 'prevent all caballings amongst negroes, by dispersing of them when drumming or playing',[1] resembling similar prohibitions under colonial rule in Africa, the Caribbean and Brazil.[2] Such legal codes or 'slave laws' were essentially 'police measures [...] concerned with the slave, first and foremost, as a potential threat',[3] often taking the form of bans on 'noisy instruments',[4] 'drums of African origin in all types of public meetings'[5] and prohibitions on 'playing objectionable native tunes' or 'obscene songs'.[6] Here comes the charge of lewd and (c)rude music again, coupled with the political imperative to assert dominance and exert control over 'the unregulated movement and assembly of black folks' as 'a matter of public safety', especially when '[g]atherings were too loud or too unruly'.[7] Just like a 1731 Law for Regulating Negroes and Slaves at Night Time, which declared the 'playing or making any hooting or disorderly noise' a 'crime' – whose punishment was delivered in the form of twenty lashes from the master's whip.[8]

It should be stressed here that the geographical terrain where such colonial legislation left its bloody footprint may differ, as well as change hands, but the legal(ised) oppression that colonisers relied on is virtually identical. This is true whether we think of the French *Code Noir*, the Black Codes in the American South, or the various English slave codes that were drawn up to ensure the 'better ordering and governing of Negro Slaves', as the subtitle of the Jamaica Slave Act of 1664 has it.[9] This seems important to note, to end silly and insulting debates over which imperial-colonial power was better, kinder, softer. Indulging such arguments would amount to little more than a pitiful exercise in moral superiority – in a scenario where *all* parties are guilty of the *same* horrors, regardless of the varying levels of devastation they left behind. In fact, there was often overlap and borrowing as evidenced by similarities between the legal codes that ruled 'the rearguard garrisons of European and American imperialism'.[10] This is especially true if we look at Britain and its former colony, the US for examples. Just think of slave codes in Barbados and Virginia. In the 1660s, 'plantation owners in Barbados created a series of "slave codes" that regulated the behaviour of slaves and made the local community, not just individual slave owners, responsible for them', just like in 1723, when the governor of Virginia introduced 'a strong militia [that] became responsible for chasing down runaway slaves, inspecting slave dwellings, disrupting large gatherings, and ensuring order during festivals and funerals'.[11] What makes such legislation similar and comparable to each other is not just the fact that both are clear about what the governance of the enslaved looks like, what it entails and who ought to be enlisted to carry out the task. What they also share is the same ideological parentage with John Locke's liberalism-for-the-liberals and slavery-for-the-enslaved philosophy. Besides, Locke penned much of such slave legislation in his capacity as a senior administrator of slave-owning colonies by drafting instructions to colonial governors in Virginia (then a British colony) and writing the constitution of Barbados, based on slave codes that justified chattel slavery.[12] The same John Locke also sat on the Council of Trade and Plantations of Carolina, as secretary from 1673 to 1675, and authored the Fundamental Constitutions of Carolina – a characteristic passage of which, states that 'every freeman of Carolina, shall have absolute power and authority of his negro slaves'.[13] *This* is the inter-colonial context within which slavery developed and justifying it was the role that European philosophy played, as its ideological accomplice.[14]

With this thought in mind, a deeper dive into the laws that outlawed Black music(s) in Britain's colonies in the Caribbean is in order. Aimed at 'the pursuit, capture, suppression and punishment' of the enslaved, such slave laws-cum-police regulations were introduced to forbid the enslaved to 'beat drums and blow horns, since these were means of communication which might be used to help runaways'.[15] Seen as 'activities [that were] dangerous [...] as means of concerting uprisings', the music-making practices of the enslaved became 'another reason for the existence of these laws' – as pioneering Caribbean historian Elsa Goveia reminds us.[16] A characteristic example is the 1787 Consolidated Act (especially Clause 21),[17] which was introduced in Jamaica to enable the 'government of slaves' and prevent 'rebellions concerted at negro dance'.[18] So heightened was the fear of the insurrectionary potential that the music(s) of the enslaved posed that even 'overseer[s]' and 'any other white person' would also be punished if they 'shall knowingly suffer any slaves to assemble together and beat their military drums or blow horns or shells [...] Every white person so offending shall suffer six months' imprisonment.'[19] Heavier penalties were to be exacted by a 1774 law which 'prescribed the death penalty' to musically tinged religious worship like Jamaican Myal,[20] coinciding with the banning of other 'religions of the dispossessed' like shango, pocomania and cumina.[21] It is interesting to observe here the similarities between Myal and other forms of West African Vodun (also: Vodou, Voodoo), which was also banned in Haiti even *after* the revolution.[22] The first three rulers of independent Haiti, Toussaint Louverture, Dessalines and King Cristophe, 'totally banned voodoo assemblies' and 'Toussaint banned all sorts of African dancing as well' taking a cue from the colonisers' sweaty panic over the 'threat of the cults' to 'law and order'.[23] In another corner of 'the Caribbean cradle'[24] – namely, eigteenth-century Trinidad – a 'British law passed two months after the 1797 capitulation[25] and amended in 1808 required the large colored population in the island to secure police permission to hold dances or entertainments after 8pm'.[26]

Among other symbols of danger and signs of trouble, the African drum exercised the plantocratic imagination as a cursed object endowed with powers to liberate the mind, body, spirit and soul of the enslaved. The drum therefore became a recurring target of legislation that forbade it 'because [it was] used for war in Africa', as Sir Hans Sloane remarked.[27] Indeed, as Errol Hill observes, 'the drum was the principal musical instrument at all slave festivities, and to outlaw its use, as was done in Jamaica in 1792, in Tobago in 1798, could only result in a state of permanent hostility between master and slave'.[28] Yet the drum was not simply outlawed as a weapon that could shorten the shelf life of colonial slavery. It was also blamed for the dance movements or 'drum dance[s]' it provided the beat for, as 'licentious and deserving to be prohibited'.[29] And prohibited they were in 1883, demanding that our analysis of the policing *against* drumming and dancing does not lose sight of how inseparable the political, the aesthetic, the sensual, the spiritual, the moral and the cultural are in any discussion of colonial statecraft. As Sylvia Wynter teaches us:

> With both the Jamaican Jonkunnu[30] and its parallel, the Trinidadian Carnival, the accusations of 'bawdiness', 'lewdness' and being 'dirty' constituted the chief accusation of the official Christian society. The secular aspect of both was attached on these grounds, but their religious aspect was attacked on far graver grounds – that of initiating and inspiring revolt. The circumstances of African transplantation to the New World caused these 'bawdy' rites to take on a new purpose and meaning – resistance and response to an alienating situation.[31]

As such, the banning of drumming was a ban on pleasure, worship, consciousness-raising and community-building too. 'The ban on drums' may indeed have been 'a ban on the gods', because '[d]rums were sacred to the gods, Ananja [and] Dya Shango'.[32] Beyond religious belief, however, 'the gods continued a world view which was subversive to the planter economy' as a whole.[33] This is why slaveocrats had such 'fear of the central part the drum played in the planning and psychological preparation of the slaves for revolt'.[34] As Wynter adds '[n]ot only were drums part of the whole ritual of revolt; so also were dances'.[35] What made the music of the enslaved a 'subterraneally subversive [...] counter-poetics',[36] therefore, must be seen as an affront on many levels: ideological, political, economic and cultural alike. Ideological because (re)claiming one's autonomy in and through music and dancing rejects racist ideologies that assume and assign the enslaved to a subordinate role that was scripted for them – however momentarily. Political because the music-making of the enslaved undermined the laws that institutionalised colonial rule. Economic because drumming and dancing was an 'assault' on and a 'freeing of time from a market process', recapturing 'time as a life process',[37] rather than as an industrious pursuit in the interests of profit-making from (un)free labour. And cultural because, no matter how loudly Europeans would denounce the cultural practices of the enslaved as incomprehensible 'noise', it was still a clear sign of life-affirming activity and a celebration of agency that slavery *must* deny – to justify its reason for existing. When the enslaved assembled to play drums and dance, they stepped out of the state of passivity, obsequiousness or 'mere nature' that racist views of them demanded. In so doing, they retained and adapted 'black performative practices' as 'sousveillance acts' to 'escape and resist enslavement',[38] while also building 'communal activity, providing a cathartic release from the traumas of plantation life' and honouring intellectual, cultural, religious and political practices through music, dancing and oral traditions – that helped the enslaved speak in coded messages that showcased 'their cunning, intelligence and linguistic wit',[39] by communing with their trickster-gods (e.g. Esu-Elegbara/Exú) and transmitting words of wisdom found in the trickster figures of their tales (e.g. the Anancy/Anansi stories).[40] What could be more frightening and dangerous to an(y) ideology and a practice of political rule?

Moving beyond slavery but remaining in the grip of colonial rule, which stood firm in the anglophone Caribbean well into the 1960s, 1970s and 1980s, we now turn our attention to the policing and criminalisation of Trinidadian calypso/*kaiso* and Carnival – as an illustrative case study of how the political vagaries of colonial rule worm their way into the cultural life of the colonised.[41] Indeed, as

Sylvia Wynter notes: '[t]he struggle of the Trinidad Carnival and calypso music against the forces of law and order, not only during but after slavery, is the cultural history of the island'.[42] Calypso/*kaiso* and Carnival are drawn together here not as identical or reducible to one another, but as cultural traditions that nevertheless coexist. While Carnival has its own characteristics as a festival that includes masquerading (*mas*), dancing and mostly steel band music, calypso/*kaiso* is also a part of it. Were this not so, calypsonians would not sharpen their minds, flex their muscles and ready their tongues to showcase their musical poetry in calypso tents during the Carnival season. Indeed, Carnival can prove to be a real testing ground for the calypsonians' popularity – depending on how their tunes are received. If they become hits, the calypsonian will bask in the glory of their success. If they flop, there is always next year's Carnival. Nothing could be worse, however, that the attempts of the colonial authorities to police or even ban the Carnival. The 1881 Canboulay riots are a testament to that, a good example of the fraught relationship between the police and the policed, the law and the outlawed, the state and the people. It is to such riotous occasions, therefore, that we attune ourselves to in turn.

Starting with the (in)famous Canboulay riots of 1881, which have been described as 'a "major armed clash between the Trinidad colonial police and the "local" … population',[43] it might be best to let a calypso verse do the talking first – giving, as it does, a full but bitter flavour of this momentous event:

> Can't beat me drum
> In my own, my native land
> Can't have we Carnival
> In my own, my native land. …
> In me own native land,
> Moen pasca dancer, comme moen viel' [I cannot dance as I wish][44]

Although there is little historical information about it, this 'sharp lament', 'potent with the protest venom'[45] is thought to have been composed during or around the time that the Canboulay riots erupted.[46] But what happened? After years of police repression against Canboulay/torchlight processions (from: 'cannes'; sticks/ torches and brûlées; burned),[47] things came to a head in 1881 when Inspector-Commandant Arthur Baker enforced previously existing legislation (an 1868 ordinance) to stop Canboulay torch-bearing. In the early hours of J'Ouvert (also: Jour ouvert, Jouvay, or Jouvé, where 'jour' means day and 'ouvert' means open/the opening of Carnival Day), on 27 February 1881 – Baker and 150 armed police clashed with torch-bearing masqueraders in a battle of *balata* truncheons against bottles, sticks and stones.[48] The charge? A threat of 'public nuisance' and 'riotous assembly', fortified with the targeting of 'bandsmembers [*sic*] as habitual criminals (after one, rather than the customary three, offences)',[49] as Susan Campbell informs us.[50] These charges were essentially a mix of whatever previous laws colonial police officers like Baker could concoct, to suppress Carnival celebrations – not unlike modern-day cops and the Crown Prosecution Service (CPS) in Britain.[51] Another account gives a few more interesting details alerting us to how the rioting lasted for two days, with reinforcement from the military, '[s]oldiers from a visiting man of war ship'[52] and additional police from Barbados.[53] But, as Wynter notes, 'the riot went on' and '[o]nly when the troops withdrew could the Governor persuade the people to stop'.[54] So grave were these disturbances to the authorities that a Colonial Office envoy (R. C. G. Hamilton) was sent from London to investigate. So he did and dutifully wrote a report entitled: 'The Causes and Disturbances in Connection with the Carnival in Trinidad', which was essentially a dispatch to the Secretary of State for the Colonies in London.[55] In his report, Hamilton noted with much dismay that 'bands of men in procession passed in front of the police barracks carrying lighted torches and jeering at the police. They sang in chorus reflecting on the police of which the chief burden was: "The police can't do it", and they held a mock funeral of Capt. Baker,'[56] It is a testament to the 'deeply-rooted strained of resistance within the West Indian psyche', as Kevin Le Gendre puts it, that Trinidadians were 'prepared to fight the police for their place in Carnival'.[57] Which they did. Even when the rioting stopped, it concluded with 'a rite': an anti-police rite. The torch-bearing Canboulay revellers 'carried effigies of Baker, the police captain, and buried them in a ceremonial fashion'.[58]

It should therefore not come as a surprise to note that despite Hamilton's recommendations that 'Carnival would be regulated but not stopped', the authorities did not back down. In fact, '[g]radually torchlight processions were declared illegal. The drum was banned' and more attempts were made to interfere with Carnival, leading to the 1891 Arouca riots 'in which the Sergeant who led the police was killed'.[59] Arouca, a town in the East–West Corridor of Trinidad and Tobago, was apparently 'the center of the great Kalinda stick fighters' who came under fire following the riots and 'were jailed even more frequently'.[60] Erroll Hill recounts what happened as follows: 'One of the last battles in defense of a drum beating was the famous Arouca riot of 1891. Constables broke up a drum dance and were beaten off by stickmen. When reinforcements arrived the whole village attacked with sticks and stones. Then an armed squad was dispatched by special train to quell the rioters.'[61]

Such episodes were of course not scattered, sporadic or isolated events, but flare-ups in a permanently explosive political atmosphere forged in the crucible of colonial rule. Such attempts to stop the Carnival, as the popular calypso: *Don't Stop the Carnival*[62] goes, were so influential to the island's cultural and political history that they largely determined the evolution of its music. Trying to escape the ban on drums, 'presented the carnival bands with a serious problem of finding a substitute instrument for their tent practices and masquerade processions'.[63] The solution was found in the development of string bands which also signalled the rise of the calypsonian 'as the foremost entertainer of the carnival season'.[64] Starting their musical life as small ensembles where the *cuatro/quatro* (a small four-stringed guitar)[65] dominated, the jazz vogue of the 1920s imposed more elaborate orchestration – including saxophones, trumpets, trombones and clarinets. Deprived of access to such lush orchestral arrangements, working-class musicians found another solution in the forms of the tambour-bamboo band, where bamboo stems became a percussive instrument until the arrival of 'the "pan" era in carnival music'.[66] Alas, even the beating of metal drums exercised the punitive imagination of the colonial authorities, inspiring special regulations that would prohibit street processions: a 'ban [which] led immediately to a renewal of the old struggle between police and masqueraders', especially in '1942 [when] carnival was banned as a wartime measure'.[67]

Even as carnival music changed, the colonial state's animus towards the music(s) of its subjects lurched back into gear. From the skin drum to the string band to the rise of the calypsonian, to the tambour-bamboo band and the steel band, '[t]he history of Trinidad carnival is the history of a common people's struggle for freedom of expression from the misguided paternalism inherent in colonial rule'.[68] It is therefore a testament to Trinidadians' creativity and perseverance in the face of oppression that they kept innovating and inventing ways to make music, circumventing and defying the restrictions that were imposed on them. The use of tin oil drums is a characteristic example that demonstrates how discarded oil drums, as 'the rejects of the white economy[69] were humanized as instruments on which to make music'[70] – not unlike the use of old boxes or bits of metal as thumping, percussive instruments to keep the spirit of the Carnival moving.

But we have barely said anything about calypso which, like steel pan music, continues to reign supreme at Carnival and beyond. Described as 'both blood-relation and life-blood of the Carnival as a 'politico-cultural institution' and an 'important tributary that flows into the stream of Carnival',[71] calypso also attracted the attention of the police at the service of the imperial-colonial British state. This was especially the case when calypsonians would dare speak truth to power, as the following tune did, decrying the appalling 'treatment meted out to the panmen by unfeeling officials':[72]

> While he, at night, to loitering must repair;
> Outlawed his bands, his music, everywhere
> Repressed with fury and so great hubbub
> His crime was poverty with pride invest
> Your lack of sympathy provoked the rest.[73]

Such radical critiques of (colonial) state power hardly went unnoticed and in another wave of repression calypso music became the problem genre of the day. Key among them was a Theatres and Dance Halls Ordinance which set up the 'benighted police force and alien high-ranking [colonial] officers as the supreme authority over the kaiso' with powers to 'ban records' and forbid calsypsonians to 'sing in [calypso] tents without a license duly signed by the police officer superintending the district',[74] on the grounds that the characteristic *picong* (piquant mischief): 'barbed wit, biting satire and ridicule'[75] that are essential characteristics of the genre, can be 'insulting' to individuals and certain section of the community, 'whether referred to by name or otherwise'.[76]

Attempting to 'cleanse' Carnival festivities from what the authorities perceived as lowly, vulgar and perverse lyrics, the police and the colonial secretary, who had the power to enforce such regulations, could effectively determine *who* could sing and *what* they could sing about, while also imposing sanctions that put calypsonians in a position of legal and economic disadvantage – through the banning of their live performances and records. Worse still, such judgements were made by people with a questionable understanding of 'the subtleties, innuendos, insinuations and nuances connected with this art medium'.[77] Raymond Quevedo, who is quoted here as an authority on calypso and a renowned calypsonian to boot (Atilla [*sic*] the Hun), spoke against such police regulations in the Trinidad Legislative Council, lambasting amendments to the original Theatres and Dance Halls Ordinance as 'wicked', 'nefarious', 'perverse', 'pernicious' and 'dictatorial',[78] on the grounds that: 'the police arrogated to themselves the right to decide what calypsos should or should not be sung – a responsibility for which they lack the necessary ability and even appreciation', in an attempt to 'suppress the calypsonian from expressing his views'.[79] Raymond Quevedo, aka Atilla the Hun, would know a thing or two about such iron-fisted policing – having been charged with infringement of the Theatres and Dance Halls Ordinance and the banning of records.[80] A characteristic example is his 1938 tune *Banning of Records*, which was itself banned. As Atilla sang:

> Imagine our records being banned from entering in our native land.
> That they are obscene I must deny, but all things look yellow to the jaundiced eye.
> I think they're ungenerous to attempt to take our music from us.[81]

Lest this is seen as an exceptional case of a political agitator, although Quevedo was involved in *realpolitik* as Deputy Mayor of the Port of Spain City Council,[82] Errol Hill reminds us that

[t]he 1930s also witnessed the return of police censorship of the calypso. In 1868 a law was passed prohibiting the singing of any profane song or ballad, and several people had been convicted in the past for infringing that law. But the burden of proof that a song was offensive lay with the police, and there was no attempt to censor or prohibit a song before it was rendered. Censorship began when singers were required to submit the texts of their compositions for approval before presenting them in public.[83]

Here's Atilla again:

> There are police spies sitting around
> Taking shorthand notes of my song
> But I can tell them independently
> That they can never tell their masters for me
> Nevermind whatever measures are employed
> Kaiso is an art and cannot be destroyed
> And centuries to come I'd have them know
> People will still be singing kaiso.[84]

And here's Lord Protector, lashing out against class and 'race' (or rather race as 'class' and class as race)[85] oppression:

> Class legislation is the order of the land
> We are ruled with an iron hand
> Class legislation the order of the land
> We are ruled by an iron hand Britain boasts of democracy
> Brotherly love and fraternity
> But British colonies have been ruled in perpetual misery.[86]

What both Atilla and Protector describe are clear and unmistakable instances of the criminalisation of dissent. Would it come as a surprise, though, to note that calypso was also derided as noise, not unlike the many examples we saw in the preceding pages? Atilla recounts an incident involving a 'famous Austrian professor' who found it impossible to 'score [Lord] Executor's music' due to the idiosyncrasy of his style, complaining that: 'This is not music. This is something else ... there is no respect for metre ... he breaks the metre whenever he likes ... he does all kinds of things that are not permitted in music.'[87]

What is and isn't permitted in music cannot of course be decided by our incensed Mitteleuropean ethnomusicologist. But it is indicative of the arrogant suggestion that it *should* be, treating any deviation from the colonising force of the dominant 'Euromodern'[88] 'Occidentosis'[89] as deviant noise – which violates aesthetic, socio-cultural and political standards established by 'the En-whitenment' and its ideological progeny. It is rather telling that a single 'tempestuous outburst'[90] against calypso/*kaiso*, provides a neat summary of how and why Black music(s) have been historically policed as dangerous noise to be silenced and replaced by the great symphony of the white intellect. There is therefore no better way to segue into the next chapter, than by reminding ourselves how aesthetics and culture are inseparable from politics in the long and disreputable imperial-colonial history of policing against Black music(s). The history of the liberation struggles of the enslaved does the rest. So let us listen attentively to how the enslaved rose up against those who regarded their very existence, presence and cultural traditions as offensive noise.

4

'Salvation 'tis a joyful sound': A concluding coda[1]

In the previous chapters of this book, we have dug deep into the colonial origins of British policing *through* the policing of Black/ Afro-diasporic music(s), as a form of political (mis)rule that targeted the creative public expression of the enslaved as discordant noise that would breed disorder, if left unchecked. Indeed, the criminalisation of the various musical styles we have looked at – focusing on Carnival music and calypso/*kaiso* – has hopefully made that fairly clear. Yet the argument, about the political threat that the music(s) of the enslaved or colonially occupied British subjects posed, needs to be explored a little further, lest we delude ourselves by thinking that the enslaved passively submitted to their assigned state of bondage without a murmur. This chapter, therefore, is not intended as a mournful cry against the evils of slavery and colonialism, but as an ode to what Frederick Douglass,[2] who stole his freedom from his captors, described as the 'joyful nois[e]' of the enslaved: as a 'seed of opposition'[3] flowering into freedom struggles. Ringing with cries of resistance and singing of freedom, 'the mere hearing of those songs would do more to impress some minds with the horrible character of slavery, than the readings of whole volumes of philosophy on the subject could do'.[4] This powerful statement flowing from Douglass's sharp pen should be kept alive between our ears, helping us elbow aside any spurious conception of '[t]he docile Negro' as the 'myth' that it is.[5] C.L.R. James has more to say on this in a characteristic passage that deserved to be quoted in full:

> Slaves on slave ships jumped overboard, went on vast hunger strikes, attacked the crews. There are records of slaves overcoming the crew and taking the ship into harbor, a feat of tremendous revolutionary daring. In British Guyana during the eighteenth century the Negro slaves revolted, seized the Dutch colony, and held it for years. They withdrew to the interior, forced the whites to sign a treaty of peace, and have remained free to this day. Every West Indian colony, particularly Jamaica and San Domingo and Cuba, the largest islands, had its settlements of maroons, bold Negroes who had fled into the wilds and organized themselves to defend their freedom. In Jamaica the British government, after vainly trying to suppress them, accepted their existence by treaties of peace, scrupulously observed by both sides over many years, and then broken by British treachery. In America the Negroes made nearly 150 distinct revolts against slavery. The only place where Negroes did not revolt is in the pages of capitalist historians. All this revolutionary history can come as a surprise only to those who, whatever International they belong to, whether Second, Third, or Fourth, have not yet ejected from their systems the pertinacious lies of Anglo-Saxon capitalism. It is not strange that the Negroes revolted. It would have been strange if they had not.[6]

Contrary to dominant representations of the enslaved as hopeless and hapless, non-political actors who were beaten into submission and stoically accepted their fate, the passage quoted reintroduces them as a 'masterless' people[7] who constituted a political force to be reckoned with, vindicating Sylvia Wynter's assertion that '[B]lack slavery in the Caribbean was synonymous with black revolt against [it]'.[8] Such revolutionary activity took various forms: secret meetings, impassioned speeches, anti-slavery pamphlets and of course music and other cultural rituals that circulated like 'common wind'[9] that blew across the Atlantic slave route.[10] Disturbing though the very existence, reality, ideological and architectural design of slave ships certainly is, they should not be seen merely as floating prisons, carrying people who were treated and traded as commodified 'cargoes of human flesh'.[11] They were also cultural and political vessels: a 'living, micro-cultural, micro-political system in motion'.[12] This is not to deny the horrific conditions in which the enslaved were trafficked across the Atlantic. A cursory look at the Liverpool slave ship *Brooks/Brookes* would suffice[13] to make anyone feel physically sick. Rather, it is to acknowledge that the slave ship should also be seen as a 'psycho-physical space capsule'[14] that carries within it aesthetic, expressive, cultural, religious and socio-political traditions that travelled from Africa to the New World, Europe and the Caribbean 'even under the extraordinary conditions of slave trade/slavery'. As Edward Kamau Brathwaite[15] put it, the reality of the Middle Passage was a 'traumatic, destructive experience', but it also became a 'pathway or channel between this tradition and what is being evolved, on new soil'.[16]

In Paul Gilroy's words, such an approach to the slave ship turns our attention to 'the various projects for redemptive return to an African homeland, on the circulation of ideas and activists as well as on the movement of key cultural and political artefacts: tracts, books, gramophone records, and choirs'.[17] Abolitionist tracts and autobiographical 'slave narratives', or freedom narratives as they really should be called are a case in point – featuring a stellar line-up of the Black revolutionary intelligentsia. The names of Olaudah Equiano, Ottobah Cugoano, Ukawsaw Gronniosaw, Ignatius Sancho, Anna Julia Cooper, Frances Ellen Watkins Harper, Mary Prince, Sarah Parker Remond, Sojourner Truth, Harriet Tubman,

David Walker, T. Thomas Fortune, William Wells Brown, Martin Delany, Alexander Crummell, William and Ellen Craft, Henry Highland Garnet and, at the close of the nineteenth century, Ida B. Wells, quickly spring to mind. Equiano in particular should perhaps be singled out here, due to the leading role he played in the British abolitionist movement – alongside other Black and mixed-race figures such as the 'Black Chartist' William Cuffay, William Davidson and Robert Wedderburn, to mention just a few Black anti-slavery advocates who were politically active in London. Indeed, as Peter Linebaugh notes, the formerly enslaved Olaudah Equiano – author of *The Interesting Narrative of the Life of Olaudah Equiano or Gustavus Vassa, the African* – did much to 'pro[d]' and 'assis[t]' the abolitionist movement in England.[18] So much so, that Linebaugh argues that E.P. Thompson's history of *The Making of the English Working Class* should be more accurately renamed: 'the making of the working class in England'; thereby calling attention to the absence of Equiano from the pantheon of working-class radicalism in England.[19]

Such revolutionary fervour, however, did not just take place at sea, or in the imperial-colonial heartlands. It also took shape in the form of free, autonomous guerrilla settlements that sprang up in the sixteenth and seventeenth centuries, like 'the palenques, mocambos, quilombos, and maroon communities that found some-times tenuous, sometimes permanent existences in Mexico, Brazil, and Jamaica'.[20] Most of these were 'nanny-towns, hill-secured free towns, and swamp remote maroon communities'[21] and known by their geographical names: Palmares in Brazil and the Winward and Leeward Maroons in Jamaica, or by the names of leading figures within them – many of whom were women:[22] Nanny of the Maroons and Cudjoe in Jamaica, Zeferina and Zumbi in Brazil and Boukman and Makandal (also known as Makandal or Macandal) in Haiti[23] to mention but a few. In addition to setting up such communities of resistance, marronage also paved the way for full-blown uprisings. The 1739 Stono Rebellion (aka Cato's Conspiracy) in South Carolina is of particular interest here as drumming was banned in its aftermath.[24] But so are Tacky's Revolt in 1760,[25] the Morant Bay Rebellion in 1865[26] and the Haitian Revolution in 1791.[27] Such rebellions whipped colonisers into a state of paranoid frenzy of forceful responses to such political radicalism, which also inspired bizarre ideological fantasies that continued to degrade the humanity and agency of the enslaved, despite evidence to the contrary. An example is to be found in the racist, pseudo-scientific concept of *drapetomania*.[28] Invented by physician Samuel A. Cartright to describe a malady that ostensibly afflicted the enslaved who dared to rebel, *drapetomania* (from the Greek δραπέτης/ *drapétes*: fugitive + μανία/*mania*: madness), served an ideological and political purpose rather that a purely diagnostic or medical one – if 'the medical' and 'the political' can ever be separated.[29] It pathologised the political resistance of the enslaved to deny the reality that they could have human agency, or the ability to conceive of, and carry out, rebellions against the capture, bondage, torture, oppression and 'social death' of slavery.[30] The desire, courage, will and determination to resist, therefore, came to be seen as a hubristic departure from a state of intrinsic obedience that the enslaved were thought to experience by those who forcibly enslaved them. Indeed, such political activity was seen as a sign of disrespect towards the slaveocrats. A characteristic example can be found in the reaction of Scottish scientist, 'explorer' and Mississippi plantation owner[31] William Dunbar, who 'records with astonishment and hurt surprise' a slave rebellion on his plantation: 'Judge my surprise ... Of what avail is kindness & good usage when rewarded by such ingratitude.'[32]

Outrageously irrational though such ways of thinking may seem, they were in fact not irrational at all in the context of colonial slavery and the self-legitimising theories and ideologies it relied on. It was in fact entirely rational and completely in line with the Age of Reason that the Enlightenment (or En-whitenment, as it is referred to here) represented. A characteristic example can be found in the work of John Locke, the English liberal philosopher who we previously met as the author of slave legislation, who is otherwise hailed as a 'founder of the Enlightenment in education as in much else'.[33] In his *Two Treatises of Government*, Locke argued that the enslaved 'are by the right of nature subjected to the absolute dominion and arbitrary power of their masters', claiming that by rebelling they commit 'the crime which consists in violating the law, and varying from the right rule of reason, whereby a man so far becomes degenerate, and declares himself to quit the principles of human nature, and to be a noxious creature' to be 'treated as beasts of prey' and 'noxious brute[s], with whom mankind can have neither society nor security'.[34] Note that Locke was writing all this just as he was revising the Fundamental Constitutions of Carolina[35] as legislation that legalised slavery in the American South. Slavery for Locke was of course 'so vile and miserable an estate of man, and so directly opposite to the generous temper and courage of our nation; that it is hardly to be conceived, that an Englishman, much less a gentleman, should plead for it'.[36] Or so Locke tells us on the very first page of his *Treatises*, reminding us that slavery applies to the enslaved, not to 'Englishmen' or 'gentlemen' – despite the fact that these very Englishmen and gentlemen were the ones responsible for so vile an endeavour. That which is vile is only vile if it is not applied to *us*, Englishmen and gentlemen. When it is imposed on *them*, the enslaved, it is generous and courageous.

Absurd though such asinine delusions may be, there is no logical inconsistency here. Locke's logic is consistent with his ideology, according to which *only* white men, especially Englishmen and gentlemen, can be human. This is what Sylvia Wynter meant when she described '1492' as ushering a 'New World View',[37] which 'ran deep in the bowels of Western culture' in the form of 'racist ideology', 'violent domination' and 'social extraction'.[38] Such a worldview hove into sight as an ideological, moral and political justification for a world *order* "obsessed with domination and the policing of the spirit".[39]

It is in *this* context that the policing of Black/Afro-diasporic music(s) has its roots as an object of scorn, a target of surveillance and a culture of resistance. It would have therefore been impossible as well as irresponsible, unethical, dishonest and factually inaccurate to narrate or make sense of the (hi)story of policing against Black expressive culture(s), without situating it within and discussing it alongside the history of policing, racism, slavery and colonial capitalism. Equally, it would have been impossible to make sense of the ideological, historical and socio-cultural origins of policing, racism, slavery and colonial capitalism without locating and understanding them *within* the history of the racist policing of Black music(s) in the era of colonial capitalist slavery. Black music(s) provide a useful illustration of the nature, historical mission, function and purpose of the ideology of racism, the politics of colonial rule, the economics of capitalist slavery and the existential need for safeguarding all the above with a little help from policing – hence the coining of the word cop-italism (see Glossary), to describe how imperial-colonial ways of seeing and ordering the world come into force through force: the force of the law enforced by the police to serve, protect and defend the interests of the system that gave it a reason to exist. This is the context within which the drum becomes symbolic of the whole imperial-colonial mission: as a sign of dissonance (alien noise), a 'configuration of a closed space' (the slave ship, the plantation) and a source of 'slave resistance, racial solidarity and rhythmic energy' (insurrectionary spirit) that confirmed the colonisers' deepest fears of any 'revolt against the white world'.[40] This is why the mix of music, dance, religious and cultural rituals, or what Cedric Robinson calls the 'cultural syncretisms of the diaspora',[41] was so abhorrent to the coloniser. The history of Haitian Vodou as a radical instrument of insurrection teaches us that. As C.L.R. James points out: 'Voodoo was the medium of the conspiracy [that sparked the Haitian revolution]. In spite of all prohibitions, the slaves travelled miles to sing and dance and practise the rites and talk; and now, since the revolution, to hear the political news and make their plans.'[42] The colonisers knew all this of course and knew it well enough to know the 'song[s]' they tried to 'stamp [out], and the Voodoo cult with which it was linked. In vain. For over two hundred years the slaves sang it at their meetings, as the Jews in Babylon sang of Zion, and the Bantu today sing in secret the national anthem of Africa.'[43] Indeed, the history of policing against Black music(s) may have begun with the birth of cop-italism but it does not end there. Were this so, there would be no more chapters in this book and we have only just put the needle on a historical record that still plays on.

All this part of this book has done so far is draw a picture of the policing against the music(s) of the enslaved, to help us see how the racist politics of law in the colonies and order came to police Black people in the metropole. Without such a historical excursion, how could we hope to understand racism as ideology of biological and cultural hierarchy; policing as technology of social control that is 'endemic to Black life';[44] capitalism as oppression, exploitation and extraction; and colonialism as an intellectual, psychic, socio-cultural and political imaginary that endures even in (nominally) postcolonial nations? Especially when they refuse to give up such a past for a new, different political identity that would not be soaked in so much blood. As you peruse this book in the twenty-sixth year of the twenty-first century, none of these ideologies and practices have lost their bite as intellectual, ideological, cultural and socio-political realities. Which is why it is important to know where they come from and how they came to be, if we have any hope of trying to expose, oppose and elbow them aside to make room for a world that is not complicit in their conceits. Especially when, as we will see in Part II of this book, the post-colonial period is 'post-colonial' in name alone. Imperial-colonial ideology, racism, police racism and the policing of Black music(s) continue unabated, adapting themselves to the life in Britain's metropolises. Not unlike the political activities of the enslaved, however, Black Britons' resistance to police racism and racist politics is nothing short of inspiring. It is to this nominally post-colonial period that we train our eyes upon in turn, leaving behind – but never forgetting – how we got there: ideologically, demographically, socio-culturally and politically too. So let us turn the page to find out more.

PART II

Does it belong here? Policing Black music as 'out of place' in post-war Britain

> We have met before. Four centuries separate our first meeting when Prospero was graced with the role of thief, merchant and man of God. Our hero was 'the right worshipfull and valiant knight sir John Haukins, sometimes treasurer of her Majesties navie Roial'; and its fist Voyage in search of human merchandise.
>
> – George Lamming, *The Pleasures of Exile*[1]

The year is 1948 and *Empire Windrush* docks at Tilbury in Essex, carrying hundreds of West Indian[2] migrants on board. This is how the story of post-war (im)migration in Britain is usually told, omitting many historical truths that official 'mythistories' choose to forget, ignore and deny. Yet, 1948 is *not* 'the' year that signals the start of post-war migration to Britain and *Empire Windrush* was *not* the first or the only ship to make the journey from the Caribbean archipelago to the English Channel. The *Ormonde* arrived in Liverpool on 31 March 1947, over a year before *Windrush*, while the *Almanzora* docked in Southampton on 21 December 1947.[3] Also, and rather ironically perhaps, *Empire Windrush* arrived at Tilbury as a *return* journey, intended to recoup costs by having transported hundreds of ex-service personnel *to* the Caribbean.[4]

The year 1948 was also 'not even the first time that the *Empire Windrush* had brought migrants' to Britain in the post-war years.[5] Indeed, neither 1948, nor *Empire Windrush* initiated the process of large-scale migration to Britain. In fact, 'there were more black people in 1944 than there were in 1948', given the presence of both African American GIs and Black British subjects and citizens, all of whom were stationed as troops in Britain until the end of World War II.[6] Worse still, the passengers on board the *Empire Windrush* were *not* migrants. Their passports described them as British subjects: citizens of the United Kingdom and Colonies, who were allowed to register as British citizens under the British Nationality Act, 1948.[7] The 'four hundred and ninety-two'[8] 'migrants' that came ashore, therefore, cannot exactly be described as migrants – unless they are thought of as such, or unless we would be equally keen to call anyone moving from Leeds to Hastings a migrant. Besides, they were also native speakers of the imperial tongue; English and they were schooled in the same curriculum as their white counterparts in the 'mother country'. As Edward Kamau Brathwaite[9] reminds us:

> [T]he educational system in the Caribbean [...] maintain[ed] the language of the conquistador – the language of the planter, the language of the official, the language of the Anglican preacher. It insisted that not only would English be spoken in the anglophone Caribbean, but that the educational system would carry the contours of an English heritage.

So much so that: 'the people educated in this system came to know more [...] about English kings and queens than they do about our own national heroes, our own slave rebels [...] we are more conscious (in terms of sensibility) of the falling of snow [...] than of the force of the hurricanes which take place every year'.[10]

Brathwaite's razor-sharp analysis, which he unleashed both as an attack on a colonial curriculum and as a defence of Black English as a 'nation language' rather than a 'dialect'[11],[12] is also illustrated by a characteristic memory that Stuart Hall shared from his own journey as a Rhodes scholar from Jamaica to Britain: 'When I first got to England in 1951, I looked out and there were Wordsworth's daffodils. Of course, what else would you expect to find? That's what I knew about. That is what trees and flowers meant. I didn't know the names of the flowers I'd just left behind in Jamaica.'[13]

Finally, Britain was not exactly a nation in 1948. It was an empire and would remain so for another two decades, when most formerly colonised islands in the anglophone Caribbean would achieve their formal independence from the Crown. The British Nationality Act 1948 did of course create the new status of citizen of the United Kingdom and the colonies. Alas, it was not until 1981 that there was 'a legal statute specifying British citizenship as a category distinct from the earlier forms that had created a common citizenship status across the populations of the UK and its colonies'.[14]

In fact, Britain should perhaps be seen as an empire even today – if judged by the fourteen UK Overseas Territories (UKOTs) or British Overseas Territories (BOTs) still held by Britain.[15] Britain's overseas territories may not be enclosed within the UK border and they certainly have their own constitution, government and local legislation. Yet, the King (or Queen) is the Head of State and is represented by a (colonial) governor; given that 'colonials' cannot be completely entrusted with handling their political affairs without the civilising supervision of their colonial overlords. This is not to deny or diminish Britain's status as a democracy, constitutionally speaking. Rather, it is to describe what *kind* of democracy it is: a constitutional *monarchy* whose imperial-colonial symbolism is central to Britain's political and cultural self-portrait. Picking up a box of breakfast cereal means being greeted by a crown and a blurb which explains that our morning snack comes to us by appointment to His Majesty, the King. When the doorbell rings and the post arrives, it is brought to us by Royal Mail. When we visit a park, a museum, a cultural or academic institution, we are reminded that they are all 'Royal' and the very boroughs where we might live are 'Royal' too. If we are unfortunate enough to face arrest or be on trial, and current anti-protest legislation makes this increasingly possible,[16] it will be Crown servants that will detain, prosecute and judge us and it will be an 'R' (meaning: Rex/Regina = King/Queen in Latin), that we are defending ourselves against – hopefully represented by a King's Counsel (KC).

Symbolic though all such imperialist kitsch might be, it is neither superficial nor ornamental. It is essential to Britain's view and sense of itself as an (omni)imperial-colonial nation; ideologically, politically and socio-culturally too. What is symbolic about imperialistic imagery, therefore, does not make it any less true. It reveals *how* and *why* it is true. If such symbolism was unimportant to the cultural and political identity of 'the nation', it would not be symbolic, emblematic or representative of Britain as an omni-imperial/colonial nation. What is symbolic is what is valorised, celebrated, formalised, normalised and institutionalised as the way(s) in which 'this royal throne of kings, this sceptred isle' (Shakespeare, *Richard II*, Act Two, Scene One) sees, defines and projects itself. As such, imperial-colonial symbolism and the history it symbolises cannot be both a source of national pride *and* not exist as a reality. The national (non-alcoholic) drink does not and cannot even grow in Britain. Tea mostly comes from previously colonised territories in or around the Indian Ocean, as does that little sweet spoonful of crystallised grains that sweeten the quintessential British cuppa. Just like the nation they are consumed in, they both have an imperial-colonial history that cannot be wished away. Tea mostly comes from 'the East'. Sugar comes from 'the South'. Both are connected to Britain's colonial imperial capitalism in more ways than one. Both required the expropriation of land and the exploitation of (un)free labour in the form of slavery or indentured servitude. Both were financed, by the 'international drug and slave cartel, or "West India interest[s]"'.[17] Both remain products of the Empire, just like Britain, the nation remains the product of its Empire. Any failure to acknowledge, understand and reckon with Britain's long and ignoble imperial-colonial history, therefore, results in exactly the kind of wilfully produced and collectively suffered amnesia that W.E.B. Du Bois called the 'deliberately educated ignorance of white schools'.[18]

Writing against such jingoistic 'profiteering' that 'panders to national vanity',[19] this part of the book approaches Britain's post-war years as a continuation of imperial-colonial rule 'at home', which treated its own subjects as migrants to be excluded and policed as 'unbelonging' – to borrow a fitting word from the title of a fantastic Joan Riley novel.[20] To do so, we will briefly look at immigration legislation that was drawn up to keep 'coloured Colonials'[21] at bay, followed by a short account of police killings and the uprisings or 'race riots' they inspired – before focusing on the policing of UK soundsystem reggae[22] as a sign of cultural alienness, otherness and 'criminality' too. Central to my argument here is the liminal status that West Indians and Black Britons experienced and resisted, as being 'on the inside but never welcome; present, yet firmly excluded from belonging'[23] – courtesy of the violence of racist border control, policing and law and order politics.[24]

5

'If you brown, they say you can't stick around': Policing and (cr)immigration in post-war Britain[1]

If the docking of *Empire Windrush* at Tilbury became the iconic image of post-war migration to the 'motherland', the British Pathé newsreel that captured the ship's arrival is just as legendary – but no less misleading. The promises of a warm welcome to Britain that the clip's voice-over advertises would soon evaporate, becoming indistinguishable from the first sight of soggy and sooty England. Yet, even such an unpleasant and uninviting panorama was not enough to discourage those aboard *Empire Windrush*, who longed for a new life in the 'mother country'. And there really is no better example of such vibrant optimism, than the mighty Lord Kitchener's legendary *a capella* version of *London is the Place for Me*: a calypso Kitch composed during his passage on the *Windrush* and sung for the Pathé reporter who interviewed him upon arrival.[2] A delight though it always is to hear Kitch sing this classic gem, while mimicking the thumping sound of the double bass, the realities of his arrival – like those of his fellow-passengers – strike a more sombre note. London *may* have been imagined as the place for them, before living there, and the calypsos that were recorded in Britain between the 1940s and the 1960s *do* brim with optimism (e.g. Mighty Terror's *Life in Britain*). Yet, as Paul Gilroy writes in the sleeve notes of the second volume of Honest Jon's Records precious compilation(s) of calypsos recorded in London it is "striking that the dominant tone of these recordings is not angry".[3] The undertones of disillusionment are nevertheless there and they give the whole Windrush story a different spin. How else are we to interpret Lord Kitchener's other tunes like *If You Brown*,[4] *If You're Not White You're Black*[5] and *My Landlady*,[6] other than as a melancholic expression of disillusionment? And what would happen if we were to think more about (Al) Timothy's *Bulldog Don't Bite Me*,[7] as an equally accurate portrayal of how British bulldog ideology greeted their newly arrived neighbours? Lord Kitchener might declare himself 'happy in the mother country,' in *Drink-A-Rum*,[8] but such buoyancy must be seen as the product of wishful thinking and as a commitment to hope against all odds. Calypsos recorded in Britain provide a rich enough archive that teaches us tunefuls of history[9] and attunes us to 'alternative hermeneutics'[10] that 'heal our imperialized eyes'.[11] The same is true however of the work of West Indian writers who also chronicled their own 'journey to an illusion'[12] in print. E.K. Brathwaite's *The Arrivants*, George Lamming's *The Emigrants* and *The Pleasures of Exile*, Beryl Gilroy's *Boy-Sandwich*; *In Praise of Love and Children* and *Black Teacher*, Sam Selvon's *The Lonely Londoners*; *Moses Ascending* and *Moses Migrating* and Andrew Salkey's *Escape to an Autumn Pavement*, to name but a few – all explore white Britain's reaction to the presence of Black people in the post-war years, although 'they' have in fact been here even 'before the English came here'.[13] Sam Selvon's novel *The Lonely Londoners* unearths such sentiments with a refreshing frankness – making his narrator muse despondently about how: 'Under the kiff-kiff laughter, behind the ballad and the episode, the what-happening, the summer-is-hearts, he could see a great aimlessness, a great restless, swaying movement that leaving you standing in the same spot. As if a forlorn shadow of doom fall on all the spades in the country.'[14]

This rather sour note that this work of fiction compels us to listen to and think with, is entirely in harmony with the very legislation, political decision-making and ideological position of the British state, both before and after *Empire Windrush* came (back) to Britain. It is such 'crimmigration' policies that will be explored in turn, to offer some context of just how the state legislated against the presence of African and African Caribbean people in Britain – as unwanted, unwelcome, unbelonging, incomprehensible and inadmissible: culturally and socio-politically 'out of place', just like their music(s).

6

(Don't) ~~Welcome~~ to Britain

Before *Empire Windrush* would sail (back) to Britain, the animus that the state harboured toward (im)migrants was evident in the panic with which it made and unmade promises to its colonial subjects. Faced with Britain's labour shortage in the aftermath of World War II coupled with a widespread economic crisis in the West Indies, the Colonial Office 'dispatched an official to the West Indies to dispel rumours that there were thousands of job vacancies in Britain'.[1] In so doing, it retracted promises made in classified advertisements that did indeed advertise such job opportunities in British newspapers that circulated widely across the anglophone Caribbean. Those reading them would be told that these ads were not 'real openings but "paper vacancies"',[2] the reason being that the Labour government's plans to meet the needs for more workers did not include Black subjects of the British Empire. In fact, such plans were intended to exclude them – intended as such ads were for white foreign Europeans who lived in and fought for Britain during the war. As an official from the Ministry of Labour put it: 'It may become extremely embarrassing if at a time of labour shortage there should be nothing but discouragement for British subjects from the West Indies while we go to great trouble to get foreign workers.'[3]

66

Yet, that's exactly what happened and the clumsy, patronising and racist justification that was concocted was that West Indians would be 'unsuitable for outdoor work in winter owing to their susceptibility to colds and more serious chest and lung ailments'.[4] It is ironic that such concern for the welfare of others, and they really were seen as 'Others', was not voiced when British subjects from the West Indies fought for Britain – exposed to the very same weather conditions. With characteristic BBCesque British impartiality, however, the same statement also claimed that 'they' could not come 'here' to work in the coal mines either – because 'they would find the conditions underground "too hot"'.[5]

Alas, 'they' did arrive 'here' on *Empire Windrush* despite attempts to prevent it from leaving Jamaica, including Clement Attlee's inquiries as to whether it would be possible to divert the ship to East Africa, where West Indian migrants might be offered work as groundnut farmers.[6] Attlee aside, eleven of his own MPs would write to him requesting restrictions on Black immigration to Britain – fearing that; [a]n influx of coloured people domiciled here is likely to impair the harmony, strength and cohesion of our people and social life and cause discord and unhappiness among all concerned'.[7] Such logics could be seen as contradictory to 'the law' – namely, the British Nationality Act of 1948 which, as noted earlier, allowed British subjects to become Commonwealth citizens; armed with the right to enter and settle in Britain. The contradiction ends, however, once we realise that the people that the Act welcomed were those from the 'old' 'white' dominions (Canada, South Africa, Australia, New Zealand) – not Black West Indians.[8] A few years later, Winston Churchill (the British Bulldog personified) would return to No. 10 and form a Conservative government which saw Black people as 'a threat to "the racial character of English people"', as a member of his Cabinet would put it.[9] In an endearing display of coalitionist spirit,

Labour and Conservative MPs soon start gathering information to prove that Black settlers represented a social problem that required new immigration legislation, although no such investigation was carried out for the European Volunteer Workers that were favoured over Black British subjects in the late 1940s.

In 1958, amid such anti-immigration political manoeuvring, 'riots' broke out in Nottingham and Notting Hill following racist attacks against Black Britons who fought back. MPs would exploit these incidents as a pretext to call for more immigration controls, paving the ground for the 1962 Commonwealth Immigrants Act – inaugurating an expanding portfolio of (anti)immigration and race relation Acts, which were designed to respond to the explosive atmosphere that such legislation created in the first place. The 1962 Commonwealth Immigrants Act was the first legislation to restrict the rights of Commonwealth citizens to reside in the UK, which also placed restrictions to the number of Black people to enter the country. Racist hatred was whipped up further and in 1965 the first Race Relations Act was introduced, followed by another in 1968; both of which sought to undo the damage done by the immigration legislation that preceded them.

Lest we read the introduction of such legislation as government-inspired initiatives, we should remind ourselves that the first Race Relations Act of 1965, emerged as a response to the Bristol Bus Boycott.[10] So it is hardly accidental, though it is ironic, that the 1965 Race Relations Act targeted the British Black Power activist Michael X for inciting racial hatred, a charge for which he served one year in prison,[11] just like James Callaghan would ban Stokely Carmichael from (re)entering Britain after a fiery speech he gave on Black power at the Roundhouse in 1967.[12] Enoch Powell's 1968 masterpiece of racist oratory, the infamous Rivers of Blood speech – which opposed legislation that would outlaw discrimination must have not met the criteria for racial hatred I suppose. The Tory MP of the West Midlands' Black Country and former recruiter of migrants for the NHS would be allowed to rail against 'wide-grinning piccaninnies', an 'immigrant-descended population' and their 'dependants' adding that: 'I am filled with foreboding; like the Roman [Virgil in *Aeneid*], I seem to see "the River Tiber foaming with much blood"' and dismayed at 'watching a nation busily engaged in heaping up its own funeral pyre'.[13]

This is a pivotal moment in the history of racism in Britain, as Powell struck a chord in the British imperialist psyche – making him a hero in the eyes of not just the London dock workers who marched in protest at Powell's sacking, but also in the minds of the political establishment who, from now on, had to bow to the nation's racism to secure votes. As Ambalavaner Sivandandan[14] so aptly put it: 'What Powell says today, the Tories say tomorrow and Labour legislates on the day after.' Three years later, the 1971 Commonwealth Immigrants Act would restrict the entry of Kenyan Asians with British passports – removing the rights of entry and residence granted by the Nationality Act 1948. This Act is (in)famous for introducing the openly racist notion of 'patriality' as a criterion for citizenship: a euphemism which favoured migration from the 'white Commonwealth', granting right to live in the UK through the British birth of a parent or grandparent.

Five years later, the 1976 Race Relations Act extended previous acts by identifying direct and indirect discrimination – establishing the Commission for Racial Equality. Not unsurprisingly however, the Race Relations Act 1976 did not include the police or prisons in its scope – leaving state-sanctioned, racist criminalisation intact.[15] Equally unsurprisingly, the prime minister at the time (Labour's James Callaghan), would admit that he 'never wavered from the view that in a small and highly populated country there is a limit to the number of immigrants we can absorb. Therefore, strict control over immigration is necessary.'[16] Labour would also go as far as introducing invasive virginity testing at the UK border, as it was revealed in 1979, to control immigration through a woman's uterus – a practice that would only be made illegal in 2021.[17]

In 1981, the British Nationality Act reclassified citizenship so that British overseas citizens of Asian background could not automatically claim it. Around that time, nationalist groups like the National Front gained prominence and more 'riots' broke out as a result of racist attacks and racist policing. In 1993, the Asylum Immigration (Appeals) Act introduces fingerprinting and removed the rights to public sector housing and three years later another Asylum and Immigration Act penalised those employed without appropriate documentation. During the early part of the twenty-first century almost annual Immigration Acts made it more difficult to enter the UK for migrants (other than highly skilled EU migrants) and in 2013 Operation Vaken (famous for its 'Go Home' vans) was piloted for one month in six London boroughs.

Three years later, the Brexit referendum campaign mobilised hostile and fearful attitudes towards immigration, making it a key issue that was articulated in the language of 'taking back control of *our* borders'.[18] Two years after Britain separated itself ideologically and politically from mainland Europe (aka 'the Continent'), we found ourselves in the middle of the 70th anniversary of the docking of *Empire Windrush* at Tilbury. What better way to greet such a momentous occasion, that was so celebrated in the 2012 Olympics Opening Ceremony in London, than with a scandal that revealed the brutal, cruel deportation of deportations Black Britons who came to 'the motherland' between 1948 and 1971 – nicknamed, 'the Windrush generation'.[19] It is no accident, therefore, and unfortunately quite fitting that the racism that 'the Windrush generation' experienced in 1948 would return with a vengeance seventy years later, in the form of deportation – albeit by plane this time around.[20]

Alas, (cr)immigration policies and border violence do not end in 2018. And they don't get better in the aftermath of the Windrush scandal either. Two contemporary examples should suffice as indication of how (cr)immigration politics rage on. Exhibit no. 1: The UK's most recent general election (4 July 2024) during which the two main contenders in the arena of professional(ised), corporate, electoralist, representative (= representational?) politics wore their anti-immigration stance with pride, promising to 'Stop the Boats' that bring migrants to 'our' shores. Upon winning a landslide victory, the new Labour government created a new UK Border Security Command to 'go after the smuggling gangs facilitating small boat crossings', 'undermining our border security and putting lives at risk'. In faux-humanitarian language the Home Secretary (Yvette Cooper) cried out: 'We can't carry on like this. We need to tackle the root of the problem, going after these dangerous criminals and bringing them to justice.'[21] Working to establish safe routes must obviously be a less humane, compassionate and just response. Exhibit no. 2: Earlier in the spring, an anti-immigration Bill (The Safety of Rwanda (Asylum and Immigration) Bill), devised to transfer people seeking asylum in the UK to Rwanda, became law (and therefore an Act) – despite being unanimously ruled unlawful by the Court of Appeal and the Supreme Court.[22]

What these two recent examples throw into sharp relief is the continuation of the exact racist, anti-immigrant thinking that we traced back to the year *Empire Windrush* came into port. The anti-immigration legislation and politics of the British state, however, are not the source of (xeno)racist discrimination and oppression. The very ideology that blows wind in the sails of institutionalised bigotry has a name and that name is racism. It is racism that turns the movement of people from one place to another into a problem, establishing distinctions about who belongs to 'the nation' and who doesn't – using the language of invasion replete with scary water metaphors, that draw a picture of tidal 'waves' of migrants whose 'influx' threatens to 'swamp' the host country with the unwanted and unwelcome presence of cultural and political 'aliens' (as the 1905 Aliens Act would have it). It is to racism and the damage it causes to its targets that we turn our attention to next, to add a few more details to the record of violence that haunts Britain's post-war years.

7

Racism runs riot

The word 'riot', in a British context, brings the awful spectre of 'urban disturbance' and 'public disorder' to the fore. Usually associated with 1958 and 1981 as key flashpoints of violence, riots are never the sudden, volcanic eruption of anger that they are often thought of. Such misplaced emphasis on shocking incidents (wilfully) ignores the undercurrent of frustration, humiliation and state violence that flows below the surface before it boils over and spills out into the open. Nor does it fit comfortably into the neat timeline that these two dates suggest. To put it crudely, the history of 'riots' in Britain is the history of state and police repression that caused them and they precede 1958 by several decades.

They are also not 'race' riots, as they are often described, but open declarations of the struggle against racism – justifying perhaps Edward Pilkington's characterisation of them as 'white riots'.[1] The first ('race') riot took place on Tyneside in 1860 as an escalation of conflicts between seamen, which was not at all uncommon at the time.[2] The first best-known full-scale ('race') riot, however, took place during the summer of 1919 in Newport, after a Black man was alleged to have made an offensive remark to a white woman[3] – several decades before the brutal murder of Emett Till who was lynched for the same reason in Mississippi.

Not unlike the aftermath of World War II, the origins of lynch mobs and racially driven, violent attacks against Black people coincided with labour shortages after World War I. Black labourers were seen as a threat even though shipping companies chose to sign on only white foreign labourers.[4] Attacks, stabbings and beatings became common as did the wrecking, looting and setting on fire houses where black people resided. And they would continue unabated especially from the 1950s onwards,[5] in an almost predictable pattern reflected in Liverpool in 1948 where racist attacks on Black people and their homes were dubbed 'Liverpool's Racial Disturbances' by *The Times*.[6]

This is the backdrop to the 'riotous' 1950s, 1960s, 1970s and 1980s, although the policies introduced in the 1950s played a major role in setting the conflagration of racism alight. The discriminatory policies known as 'the colour bar' are a characteristic example. Introduced by Labour, the colour bar took the form of discrimination in the workplace and housing but also barred people from entering pubs and dancehalls and staying in hotels too.[7] A landmark case involves the Trinidadian cricketer Learie Constantine, C.L.R. James's friend and biographer,[8] who challenged the colour bar policy in court – after the Imperial Hotel in Russell Square, where the captain of the West Indies cricket team had booked a room, refused to let him stay for more than one night. The reason? 'We are not going to have all these n[*****]s in our hotel.'[9] Although Constantine could not bring charges against the hotel, as there was no law against racist discrimination at the time, he claimed instead that the incident caused him personal injury and was awarded token damages of £5. Constantine won the case and wrote a book about it too.[10]

In so doing, he set a legal precedent against the colour bar. Constantine's challenge, however, did not bring about legislative change. The reason comes in the form of more racist arguments that claimed that racist discrimination need not be tackled this way. It was deemed favourable to educate public opinion instead, although the government made no changes to the curriculum to reflect such a desire to educate people out of their racism. It was also argued that getting 'the law' involved, would discriminate against land-lords and employers by threatening their individual liberties and, finally, it was claimed that such legislation would be unnecessary anyway as racist discrimination didn't exist in Britain.[11]

Alas, it wasn't just (Tory) government ministers that held such views. The unions did too, expecting perhaps that trading in the currency of racism would reward them with the 'public and psy-chological wage' of whiteness[12] as a promise of material advantage, if not moral and cultural superiority too. In 1955, the Transport and General Workers' Union had passed a resolution that recognised 'the grave situation which is revealed by uncontrolled immigration'[13] – resulting in an apology in 2013 when Unite, which had merged with the Transport and General Workers' Union, apologised for supporting the colour bar.[14] Nearly a decade after *Empire Windrush* 'hit' England with a 'hurricane' of (im)migration,[15] the passengers who were described in that iconic 1948 Pathé footage as 'coming to the mother country with good intent',[16] would inspire more sinister reporting that would now describe them as 'our Jamaican problem', though we know that 'they' were always seen this way – even back in the colonies (see Part I of this book). It was *they* who would inspire 'racial troubles in Notting Hill' *not*, say, the supporters or the very presence of the White Defence League who spoke openly against the 'evils of coloured invasion' and feared 'mass interbreed-ing' that would inexorably lead to a 'mulatto Britain' that signals the 'downfall of the civilisation and culture of our country', requiring an immediate stop to immigration and repatriation.[17] Such was the ideological fuel that ignited the Notting Hill and Nottingham uprisings in 1958 against state/police violence and racist 'mob rule' too, to borrow Ida B. Wells's word for it all.[18]

Chronicling the 1958 'Notting Hill white riots', as Pilkington calls them,[19] Paul Gilroy writes that:

> The initial phase of the rioting escalated from a street encounter in which Majbritt Morrison, a young Swedish woman, had taken exception to being called a 'black man's trollop', 'nigger lover' and 'white trash' while walking home from a house party. A murderous mob, chanting 'Keep Britain White!' set fire to the house where Count Suckle, one of London's first Sound System DJs, had been playing Calypsos to an appreciative gathering.[20]

Knowing what we already know about the policing of Black music(s), is it at all surprising that the house party (blues dance or shebeen) where legendary Count Suckle played would be the target of incendiary racist violence?[21] Equally, would it surprise us to note that the first Carnival (the Caribbean Carnival) on British soil was organised as a direct response to the Notting Hill riots of 1958? Indeed, the Caribbean Carnival, organised by Claudia Jones's West India Gazette at St Pancras Town Hall, was intended as a community cohesion initiative and a fundraiser to 'assist the payment of coloured and white youths involved in the Notting Hill events', as the event programme stated.[22]

Such open displays of conviviality and goodwill, however, did not deter those who stabbed Kelso Cochrane a stone's throw away from Notting Hill – prompting protests organised by Amy Ashwood Garvey and Claudia Jones in Whitehall with slogans like: 'Murder in Notting Hill', 'No Little Rock Here'.[23] Little Rock, Notting Hill was not. 'Keep Britain White' and 'Stop the Coloured

Invasion' slogans were nevertheless painted on street walls, also featuring in public demonstrations like a memorable one at Trafalgar Square.

The 1960s, swinging though they certainly were, were also stinging – if judged by the levels of racist police violence, culminating in a report that Joseph A. Hunte published for the West Indian Standing Conference (London region). The report's title, N[*****] Hunting in England, was as shocking as the incidents it described; replete with accounts of how the police would call 'members of the coloured community "black bastards" and "go on the beat claiming that they go out N[*****] hunting"'.[24] In 1969, David Oluwale was hounded to death by cops in Leeds – recording Oluwale's nationality at the Millgarth police station as 'wog'; a widely used racist epithet in the 1960s.[25] Only a few years later, in May 1971, Aseta Sims would die in Stoke Newington police station and Joshua Francis was attacked by four policemen; earning a mention in Linton Kwesi Johnson's Time Come,[26] alongside Oluwale. That same year also witnessed the landmark Mangrove Nine trial against prominent Black Power figures Altheia Jones-LeCointe, Barbara Beese, Frank Crichlow and Darcus Howe among others – because they protested against the frequent police raids on Crichlow's restaurant, The Mangrove.[27] The bittersweet victory for some of the nine defendants, however, would taste more bitter than sweet in 1972 in the Oval Four case[28] – involving Fasimbas[29] member Winston Trew, who wrote an excellent book about it all,[30] and three of his friends who were harassed and arrested by cops in a trial that is discussed to this day as a telling example of miscarriages of justice.[31] Also in 1972, the West Indian Standing Conference would send a memorandum to Parliament, warning of police racism reaching fever pitch: 'a case almost akin to a civil war between the West Indians and the police'.[32]

Police sociologist/criminologist Maureen Cain would describe racism as a key component in cop culture at the time: 'black people were different, separate, incomprehensible. There was, therefore, no good reason for not being violent if the occasion arose.'[33] Such attitudes would be displayed openly again in 1976 in the form of clashes with the police during Carnival, due to the presence of thousands of cops that gathered in Notting Hill to police the event.[34] The far-right groupuscule National Front organised protests (in Fulham) against 'the *existence* of the Notting Hill Carnival'[35] and attracted hundreds of protesters who were met with an anti-racist counter-protest in what is known as The Battle of Lewisham in 1977. A dominant force in the racist politics of 1970s Britain, the National Front would do much to foment anger as evidenced by a provocative meeting they held in Southall Town Hall in 1979, at the heart of a community that saw the murder of Gurdip Singh Chaggar in Southall, in 1976 as well as Kenneth Singh and Altab Ali in the East End in 1978.[36] This was also the year that anti-racist demonstrator Blair Peach was killed by the police during protests against the National Front meeting in Southall. That same year the Institute of Race Relations would submit evidence to the Royal Commission on Criminal Procedure accusing the police of pursuing Black Britons as 'muggers', 'criminals' and 'illegal migrants'.[37]

The 1980s perhaps most popularly associated with the 1981 uprisings in Brixton (London), Toxteth (Liverpool), Moss Side (Manchester), Handsworth (Birmingham) and St Pauls (Bristol) would also see anti-racist struggles blossom, building on the already vibrant activity of the British Black Power Movement.[38] The New Cross Fire (or New Cross Massacre): a suspected racist arson attack on 439 New Cross Road in January 2021 would lead to one of the most historic marches in the history of anti-racist struggle in Britain, rivalled perhaps only by the 2020 Black Lives Matter protests.[39] The Black People's Day of Action, organised by The New Cross Massacre Action Committee, took place later in March 1981 – a month before the notorious 'Brixton Riots'. The 'riots' themselves bubbled up as a result of public indifference to the New Cross Massacre and Operation Swamp: a police operation that lasted ten days 'in which 150 plain clothes officers made 1000 stops and 150 arrests'.[40] The asphyxiating presence of the police resulted in two days of attacks against the police, making the name of the operation as instructive as its consequences. It is tempting, if not obvious, to suggest that the use of the word 'swamped' deliberately echoes, if it doesn't pay tribute to, comments made by Margaret Thatcher in 1978 in a TV interview. Speaking in the characteristic accent of law-and-order authoritarianism that so defined her premiership,[41] Thatcher said:

> [P]eople are really rather afraid that this country might be rather swamped by people with a different culture and, you know, the British character has done so much for democracy, for law and done so much throughout the world that if there is any fear that it might be swamped people are going to react and be rather hostile to those coming in. So, if you want good race relations, you have got to allay peoples' fears on numbers.[42]

Undertaken by the Special Patrol Group (SPG), Operation Swamp – an exercise in saturation policing – ramped up stop and search in the area, using Section 4 of the Vagrancy Act 1824, which was originally intended for the 'Punishment of Idle and Disorderly Persons, and Rogues and Vagabonds'.[43] Nicknamed the 'sus law', or simply 'sus'; the Vagrancy Act was also heavily used in the 1960s and 1970s,[44] but became famous during the uprising in Brixton – leading to the formation of the Brixton Defence Committee to provide guidance and legal support to the community[45] and to the Scarman Report on the 'Brixton Disorders', which rejected the label 'institutional racism' but nevertheless acknowledged the existence of 'racial disadvantage'.[46] Lord Scarman's exact words were: 'Institutional racism' does not exist in Britain: but racial disadvantage and its nasty associate, racial discrimination, have not yet been eliminated.'[47] Where Scarman saw 'clear evidence of the will and the commitment of Parliament and government to the cause of racial equality', however, Black Britons witnessed more police violence.

Those 'swamped', therefore, were Black Britons and they were swamped by the intense policing of their communities, who Liverpool Chief Constable Kenneth Oxford blamed for the 'riots' – arguing that they highlighted 'the problem of half-castes in Liverpool'.[48] And Sir Kenneth Newman, Commissioner of the London Metropolitan Police, would concur stating that: 'In the Jamaicans you have a people who are constitutionally disorderly. It's simply in their make-up.'[49] Read against such public pronouncements by police chiefs Scarman's timid recognition that Black Britons were at a 'racial disadvantage' would do little to end the policing of anti-racist groups that were set up to expose the real magnitude of racism that the Scarman Report did not. It did not take too long before the police killing of Colin Roach in 1983 would cast doubt on Scarman's conclusion, just as it would initiate more police monitoring of radical political activity. In 1983, a Special Branch report on *Political Extremism and the Campaign for Police Accountability Within the Metropolitan Police District* would be published to gather intelligence on campaigns for police accountability. This remarkable piece of police paranoia castigated the Greater London Council's Police Committee, as well as Inquest and the Institute of Race Relations for having the nerve to investigate deaths in police custody and chronicle incidents of police racism. Besides, such campaigns brought together an unwholesome clique of 'Trotskyist sympathisers', 'admitted Marxist[s]', 'extreme left-wing bookshop[s]', 'black militants' and 'penal reform group[s]'.[50]

In 1985, the police shooting of Cherry Groce in Brixton and the police killing of Cynthia Jarrett in Broadwater Farm, Tottenham would spark uprisings in both areas leading to an inquiry into the 'disturbances' by Lord Gifford.[51] Two years later, Clinton McCurbin and Tunay Hassan would die in police custody, as would Vincent Graham two years after that – in a predictable roll call of police violence that Linton Kwesi Johnson so brilliantly captures in *License fi Kill*.[52] More violence would break out in response to the suffocating policing of the 1989 Carnival, nicknamed the 'Police Carnival' by Association for a People's Carnival[53] which, so rightly, described how the Carnival was (and continues to be) treated as 'a public order problem' rather than the 'fantastic cultural and artistic achievement' that it was and is.[54] Indeed, Carnival in Britain has always been seen through the prism of 'criminality', danger and disorder and policed as such to this day.[55] It is no accident that the most memorable confrontations of Black Britons with the police have been during or in the aftermath of Carnival celebrations (especially in 1976 and 1989) – accompanied by increased and aggressive police presence and police powers from the 'sus laws' of the 1970s[56] to facial recognition technology in 2020.[57] In the 1990s it was the racist murder of Stephen Lawrence that 'became a landmark in the politics of "race" in Britain', although Rolan Adams and Rohit Duggal would also be killed 'in comparable circumstances'[58] – to say nothing of Joy Gardner's death in 1993, following an immigration raid at her home where thirteen feet of adhesive tape around her head were used to restrain her. Roy MacFarlane's poetry captures the brutality of the incident in an unforgettably vivid manner:

13ft of tape,
   adhesive sticky tape,
a body belt, chains, handcuffs and tape.
    Bounded her, taped her, tied her up,
       taped her head like a mummy for the hereafter
and right here, after she ceased to breathe they made a mix-tape
    longer than any tape measure could measure.
Police, judiciary and hospital taped together
      a tapestry of events and kept a corpse alive
    until they could taper their stories to a rounded tip.
A mother is bounded by the red tape of officialdom
     until things taper off
      but a mother lights a taper in the darkness until
       my tears will catch them, my tears will catch them.[59]

Before that decade would come to an end, Ahmed el Gammal and Marlon Downes would die in police custody in 1996 and 1997 respectively. But it was the Macpherson Report on the Stephen Lawrence Inquiry[60] that became *the* singular event,[61] finally declaring the London Metropolitan Police institutionally racist – borrowing a term coined by Kwame Ture (Stokely Carmichael) and Charles Hamilton.[62] Hopeful though such an acknowledgement certainly was, the same practices that Macpherson criticised would be in full swing not only as the report was written, but after its publication too, as the police would spy on the Lawrence family's campaign to seek truth and justice.[63]

This is hardly the end of the history of demotic, state or police racism in contemporary Britain. It is not even the beginning, and it is certainly far from exhaustive. It is nevertheless indicative of the asphyxiating atmosphere that the legacy of colonial imperialist violence surrounds an only nominally post-colonial nation. I am writing only three years after the Casey Review found the same force (the Met) to be institutionally racist and in the immediate

aftermath of rent-a-mob racist riots in Britain that are wildly remi-
niscent of 1860 and 1919.[64] As much as I wish I could appear more
optimistic about it all, the fact of the matter is that racism, as both
an ideology and practice that assigns people to different positions in
a hierarchical social order, rages on even as it is denied.[65] Or, rather,
because it is denied. I therefore only stop this dreadful catalogue of
racist violence just before the dawn of the new millennium, because
the noughties will dominate Part III of this book.

We now have enough knowledge of the historical context that
shapes what Britain, the nation, was and did from the 1940s to
the 1990s *because* of what Britain, the Empire was and did in the
heyday of its imperial-colonial rule. The usual refrain, that is really
an excuse and a historical untruth, reassures us that this surplus
of racism can be explained by the hard times of post-war depression, rather than by the symptoms of 'imperialist nostalgia'[66] or
'postcolonial melancholia'.[67] Blaming 'the just war' for ideologies
and practices of injustice that precede it by centuries doesn't quite
cut it. Nor do allusions to competition in the labour market, or
anxieties of sexual and social contact across the colour line – all
of which are interpreted as failings of a beleaguered white British
population, which simply lashed out against the menacing prospect of a 'coffee-coloured Britain'[68] out of 'legitimate' frustration
with job shortages and understandable fears that their 'undesirable
and misplaced'[69] neighbours might have come 'over here' to take
'our' rightful place. Powell and Thatcher's fears of social inter-
mixing are of a piece with Queen Victoria's complaint about 'too
manie of these kinde of people' being *here*,[70] or Samuel Estwick's
earlier plea to Lord Mansfield upon whom he called to introduce
legislation prohibiting the entry of Black people into Britain to
'preferve [preserve] the race of Britons from ftain [stain] and contamination'.[71] As we noted previously, Britain would still be an

empire well into the 1960s, if not the 1980s, if not today and perhaps forever too. As Britain and other Allied forces fought against Nazism and Fascism, it would remain an empire which maintained it stranglehold over its colonies – opposing Nazi doctrines of racial hygiene (*Rassenhygiene*), while feeding on its own racist colonial domination. As Aimé Césaire put it, with reference to all European colonial powers:

> [T]hey tolerated that Nazism before it was inflicted on them, that they absolved it, shut their eyes to it, legitimized it, because, until then, it had been applied only to non-European peoples; that they have cultivated that Nazism, that they are responsible for it, and that before engulfing the whole edifice of Western, Christian civilization in its reddened waters, it oozes, seeps, and trickles from every crack.[72]

And W.E.B. Du Bois would concur, stressing that: 'There was no Nazi atrocity – concentration camps, wholesale maiming and murder, defilement of women or ghastly blasphemy of childhood – which Christian civilization or Europe had not long been practicing against colored folk in all parts of the world in the name of and for the defense of a Superior Race born to rule the world.'[73]

So sacrilegious is this otherwise factual observation that it brought Jamaican novelist Roger Mais[74] a charge of sedition and a six-month stint in prison,[75] for daring to criticise Churchill's obstinate refusal to end Britain's colonial rule, just as he was delivering passionate speeches about democracy and freedom[76] in the wartime years. Indeed, George Padmore said much the same, criticising the fact that 'our hatred of the tyranny of Fascism may cause us to forget the tyranny of Imperialism', adding that 'the truth is four-fifths of the British Empire is as much a dictatorship as the Fascist countries'.[77] Not unlike Mais and Padmore, Du Bois would also express his incredulity at such doublethink after being invited to evaluate proposals for establishing what would later become the United Nations, at the Dunbarton Oaks Conference. Du Bois wrote: 'We have conquered Germany but not [its] ideas. We still believe in white supremacy, keeping negroes in their places and lying about democracy, when we mean imperial control of 750 million human beings in colonies.'[78]

If radical Black thinkers are not to be believed, because – y'know – *they* have a chip on their shoulder, Hannah Arendt[79] and Zygmunt Bauman[80] would make similar arguments, *decades after* Césaire and Du Bois adjusted our eyes to the realities of Western-European politics. Such a realisation maintains its influence even as we attempt more excuses, by alluding to Britain's efforts at equality through the creation of the Keynesian welfare state. Even then, the residual racism that the nation lives by returns with a vengeance. The National Health Service Act 1948, established by the Labour Minister of Health Aneurin Bevan, was championed by the same person who 'arranged for immigration officers to turn back aliens who were coming to this country to secure benefits off the health service'.[81] This unhealthy obsession with racial sovereignty therefore does not go away just because we want it to, or just because we want to tell a different story to soothe the symptoms of World War II-themed nostalgia where plucky Brits *alone* liberated Europe from Hitler's Reich, just like *only* Britain suffered losses during or after the Blitz. Never mind the plight of other countries, like Greece for example, which was *occupied*, suffered mass executions and endured a famine at the hands of the SS and Wehrmacht – to say nothing of Britain's own effort, during the country's 1946–49 civil war, to reinstall monarchy and 'shore up British strategic interests in the Mediterranean'.[82]

Lest we feel seduced by the imagery of the sparkling Aegean sea, now the graveyard of Europe's callous border regime, a return to the industrial viewscape of urban Britain is nevertheless due – so we can explore the policing of UK reggae soundsystems as the sonic embodiment of 'otherness', 'alienness', 'strangeness' and 'out-of-placeness' that the cultural life of Black Britons represented to the dominant racist imaginary of this omni-colonial nation. Not unlike the ideologies of colonial rule, which orchestrated the suppression of Black or Afro-diasporic music, the policing of reggae soundsystems as suspicious and dangerous in twentieth century Britain was an attempt to police cultural belonging by defining Black lives out of it – through tactics that subjugate, monitor, control and curtail the movement and expression of Black Britons. The racist imagery of black 'criminality'[83] takes centre stage here just like Black music becomes the arena where such unequal power relations play out loud.

8

'It gets me 'fraid when Babylon raid'

Not unlike the '(c)rude noise' of African drumming, Black music in twentieth-century Britain would also be derided in very similar ways. The London Dance Institute complained about the twist, insisting that it 'belongs to the African bush'.[1] As an angry letter for *The Times* would have it: 'I need not describe the horrors of American and South American negroid origin.'[2] The *Dancing Times* would also caution readers about how 'a fearsome thing called "Jazz music" has reached us'.[3] Indeed, Revd Canon Drummond of Maidenhead would describe it as 'the dance of low n[*****]s' who endeavour 'with every conceivable crude instrument, not to make music, but to make a noise'.[4] And, finally, a contributor to the *Border Standard* would write repulsed by the 'abominable rhythm and copulative beat [...] imported from Central Africa', additionally likened to an 'engine of Hell to do the Devil's work'.[5] Moral disgust aside, the sonic presence of Black music(s) would also come under police surveillance in Depression era Cardiff against 'bottle parties' that sidestepped licensing laws and were regarded as dens of vice and iniquity.[6] Such policing continued in the form of more police raids of house parties and discriminatory colour bar policies in dancehalls from the late 1950s onwards.[7] The main source of concern and target of police suppression, however, was the reggae soundsystem. But what is 'the soundsystem' and why is it so dangerous?

Starting with the first question, the term 'soundsystem' refers to a music collective, or an ecology of sound, which consists of people (producers, sound engineers, session musicians, selectors, DJs, boxmen, roadies), equipment (speaker boxes, amplifiers, records, microphones, sound effects/dub sirens), as well as distribution networks (record labels, record shops) and events (soundsystem dances). Soundsystems emerged in Jamaica as a countercultural invention to overcome working-class Jamaicans' inability to afford records and personal hi-fis, or even listen to music that was not dictated by radio playlists which largely excluded many forms of Black music, even after Jamaica's independence from the British Crown in 1962. Soundsystems therefore became informal broadcasting networks, as well as hubs of entertainment and community life. Run by entrepreneurial record shop and recording studio owners, soundsystems initially played American rhythm and blues or 'shuffle' records – until Jamaican music started being recorded for and played in soundsystem dances. These dances were organised by soundsystem owners, featuring selectors who played records and DJs who chatted or toasted (= rapped) over the records to represent and 'big up' their soundsystem, as well as energise the crowd by drawing attention to new tunes that were exclusively recorded for, and played at, the soundsystem.[8]

This tradition of Jamaican soundsystem culture grew and spread as Jamaican people and their music migrated to the US and the UK, where Jamaican soundsystem culture was preserved but also evolved as successive generations of soundsystem affiliates took up that tradition, blended it with other styles (e.g. jazz, soul and funk) and created something new. Some of those styles include the birth of American hip-hop, rap[9] and their various offshoots in the US (e.g. trap, Miami bass), the UK (e.g. UK hip-hop, jungle, dub-step, garage, grime) or both (e.g. US and UK drill). Throughout this chapter, UK soundsystem culture is approached as a product of the African diaspora that is rooted in Jamaica but routed through Britain's big cities. It is therefore an 'intercultural' and 'transnational'[10] hybrid that syncretises multiple rhythmic and oral traditions from Africa and its diaspora(s).

If this is what soundsystems are, what about UK soundsystems and UK reggae? UK reggae is also approached from the same Afro-diasporic perspective and refers to music that is produced in Jamaica or Britain but is played by UK soundsystems. 'UK reggae' is therefore understood here as a form of Jamaican or Jamaican-influenced music that is played in UK soundsystems and traverses the whole gamut of styles that precede and succeed it. These include ska (early 1960s), rocksteady (mid-1960s), reggae (late 1960s), roots reggae (early–late 1970s), rub-a-dub (late 1970s) and dancehall (1980s onwards).[11] As this timeline demonstrates, contrary to common (mis)perceptions, reggae is actually a distinct genre of Jamaican music, not a synonym for all Jamaican music. Regrettably however, it will be used generically here to include all variants of Jamaican music from the late 1950s onwards, given that police raids on UK soundsystems did not discriminate between what kind of Black music was being played. They were more preoccupied instead with the very playing of Black music as unwanted and unwelcome noise. UK soundsystem culture therefore encompasses all Black or Afro-diasporic music genres that are tailored to the disco-centric nature of soundsystems, from early Jamaican music to its multiple stylistic variations around the Afro-Atlantic world.

Where is the danger in all this then? Nowhere other than in the mind of the police who saw the gathering of Black Britons as a problem, especially when they took the liberty to express themselves through music, dancing and socialising; be it at a house party, or a night club. If you have listened to enough roots reggae, or simply watched the mighty Jah Shaka drop the heavy dub version of Johnny Clarke's *Babylon* in Franco Rosso's 1980 film of the same name, you probably know enough about the policing of UK (soundsystem) reggae. If not, read on. Starting as police raids that targeted house parties (blues dances/shebeens), youth clubs and other venues where ska, rocksteady and roots reggae were played, from the late 1950s onwards, the policing of soundsystems grew in volume: charging revellers with breaching licensing laws, exceeding permitted noise levels and encouraging drug consumption – with ganja smoking featuring as an arresting symbol of 'danger', 'illegality' and 'trouble'.[12]

Perceived as a form of sonic and social disturbance, reggae dances in the UK were energetically pursued by cops who often violently raided such events, turned down sound systems, damaged sound equipment, attacked partygoers and made arrests for disorderly behaviour.[13] UK reggae would soon become 'police shorthand for dangerous individuals smoking illegal substances'[14] and the hostility that was reserved for soundsystem dances, combined with discriminatory attitudes towards what a famous West Midlands police report (*Shades of Grey*) described as the 'criminal' 'Dreadlock sub-culture'[15] of Rastafarians[16] – creating the impression that the influence of Rastafari[17] on the music (and vice versa) amounted to an 'open commitment to terrorist violence'.[18]

Even sociologists would turn into cops, lending such operations the (assumed) legitimacy of academic rigour. As Horace Campbell and Barry Chevannes note, 'the police have invoked the support of the media and an ideological campaign by sociologists to support their general programme of harassment of black communities throughout Britain'.[19] In fact, violence workers and knowledge workers often become indistinguishable if we remind ourselves how the notorious *Shades of Grey* report[20] was the result of such a synergy. Written by John Brown, a lecturer at the Cranfield Institute of Technology whose politics could not be more different from his nineteenth-century abolitionist revolutionary namesake,[21] this 45-page report became famous for its negative depiction of the Black community in Handsworth, Birmingham. It even made an impression on sociologists, who would channel their inner cop to better understand the militancy of roots reggae and the political radicalism that the Rastafari movement imbued it with. Ernest Cashmore and Barry Troyna detected 'a penchant for violence within the West Indian culture, possibly stemming from the days of slavery when the only method of retaliation was doing physical damage to the overseer, agent or even the slave master'.[22] Cashmore, in particular, is famous for his investment in peddling factually inaccurate myths about Rastafari and roots reggae as sources of 'criminality', writing 'the most dangerous study of the Rastafarian Movement to date'.[23] In what started as a PhD thesis, Cashmore's *Rastaman* obtained its 'first information on the movement [...] from the Inspector of Intelligence Bureau, Metropolitan Police of Toronto',[24] swallowing cops' observations that 'the cult was linked to trafficking in ganja (marijuana), extortion and murder'.[25]

With such an auspicious start, Cashmore's study of the Rastafari movement in England would unfold – piling one factual mistake over another. One of the most telling is his clumsy comparison of Rastafari communities to Charles Manson's Helter Skelter Cult in 1960s California. Writing specifically about Leonard Howell's rural settlement at Pinnacle in the Saint Catherine parish, Cashmore confidently asserted that:

Howell's Commune was subject to periodic raids from police and after one notable incident in 1941, in which Howell's followers had attracted neighbouring dwellers, it was revealed that Howell had insisted that he was Haile Selassie, an interesting acknowledgement of the inherence of God in man; this idea was to be elaborated into the principle of 'I and I', the unity of all people. After two years' imprisonment, Howell decided to rigidify the Pinnacle Commune, installing guards and watch-dogs and exercising his leadership almost tyrannically. The parallels with the family cult which emerged in the 1960s are irresistible. Its despotic leader, Charles Manson, was said to wield a strange mesmeric control over his followers, luring them with his apocalyptic vision of Helter Skelter, the ultimate confrontation between blacks and whites, and commanding them to murder figures representing 'straight society'. Manson's cult used the hallucinogenic drug LSD, Howell's used ganja, a marijuana cultivated on the estate, to which many Rastas were to attach religious significance. Both leaders gained inspiration from reluctant sources: in Howell's case, Garvey, and in Manson's, the Beatles, whom he claimed had sent him messages through their recordings.[26]

It was from this characterisation of the first Rastas as 'murderous' and driven to violence through ganja smoking that Cashmore seeks to explain the growth of the Rasta Movement in the UK, offering an account of British Rastas as a roving gang of thieving 'criminals' insisting that '[g]angs became breeding grounds of Rastafarian themes'.[27] In a characteristic passage, Cashmore informs us that:

[M]embers of the Rastafarian Movement were a threat to the order of the community, that they had scant respect for the law of the land and had no compunction in breaking it. Theft and robbery were their principal methods of gaining income, they preached peace and love yet practised violence and generally constituted a hazard to the community – and one which had to be checked.[28]

Authoritative though such observations might sound, though they really shouldn't, it is worth remembering that the self-appointed

expert on Rastafari in Britain would expose his bottomless ignorance by bafflingly claiming that Natty Dread derives from 'nutty
meaning weird and unstable',[29] rather than referring to the knotted
(natty) look of dreadlocks. Even more laughably, Cashmore would
also translate: 'We are tired of the ism schism game',[30] from Bob
Marley and the Wailers' *Get Up, Stand Up*, as: 'We're tired of your
easing kissing game'. Such irresponsible sophistry would do much
damage by making the 'effect that Rastafari (and reggae)' would
have on 'Afro-Caribbean youth [...] crucial',[31] a link that would
also be made by Ken Pryce, who observed that 'the dread content
of the music, which is no more than the distillation of visceral
images of sex, violence and protest, accompanied by aggressively
menacing and uncompromising drum beats'.[32] By mistaking the
liberation theology and radical political philosophy of Rastafari[33]
and roots reggae with 'criminality', cops that turn into sociologists
and sociologists that turn into cops did not simply 'misrepresent[t]
problems [...] to legitimize the hateful solutions provided for
them'[34] in the form of more policing. They also failed to engage
with the cultural, social, political and spiritual content of Rastafari,
essentially treating the liberatory potential of such forms and sites
of Black expression as a threat. Thankfully, Herbie Miller sets the
record straight, writing that:

Through herbal and spiritual rituals and preaching about the
divinity of Emperor Hail[e] Selassie of Ethiopia, Rastafari aimed
to create a community of peace and love. For that reason, music
comprising drumming and chanting was integral to the communal
activities [...] Music was also important in spreading the Rastafari
faith. By embracing modern jazz musicians, dancers, and singers
together, Rastafari and performers were effective in establishing an
artistic atmosphere through improvisation and self-effacing character. Their artistic collaborations and collective personalities produced an iconography and thematic consciousness that referenced

Africa as source and inspiration. What emerged, therefore, was a cultural consciousness that permeated the embryonic state of Jamaica's popular music.[35]

Leaving the lush green hills of Jamaica to return to the grey rain-soaked streets of England, it is important to pay attention to the ideological fog that such racist, pro-police sociology blows into our face through the interpretive and political work that the imagery of 'criminally inclined Rastafarians' in 'tea cosy hats' does.[36] Such racist fantasies about 'criminal' Rastafarian 'Others', warned 'the nation' about the '"alien" cultures of the blacks [which] are seen either as the cause or else the most visible symptom of the destruction of the "British way of life"'.[37] *This* is what was policed when reggae soundsystems were policed, telling us more about *police violence* than about those who are violently policed as 'violent'. Testimonies of attacks on soundsystems provide an eloquent testimony on it all. As an unnamed blues dance reveller recounts in the documentary *From When You Are Black*: 'One night in 1963 the door just kick down and policeman just step in and you hear funny sound, sound system switch off. Dem just bust up de dance!'[38] And they are far from unreliable recollections of an isolated individual, whose memory may fail them. They echo countless examples of the police mashing up the dance, the most famous perhaps being the story of Dennis Bovell's arrest at a dance, as narrated by Linton Kwesi Johnson – the dub poet and Dennis Bovell's musical collaborator on numerous albums:

A Black youth being pursued by the police ran into a Jah Sufferer's dance in Cricklewood. Dennis Bovill [= Dennis Bovell] was the dee jay and he so happened to be playing Junior Byte's song, 'Beat Down Babylon', when the Police forced their way in. In the ensuing confrontation, he was arrested with eleven others and later charged with inciting the crowd to riot. He was jailed for eighteen months but released after six months on appeal.[39]

In 1975, the legendary Jah Shaka Sound would be similarly shut down in New Cross, an area where Shaka's presence as a soundman, record shop owner and a Fasimba would be so central to its cultural life 'integral to the black history' of New Cross.[40] As *Race Today* would report:

> More than 200 young blacks danced to the sound of the popular Jah Shaka at Malpas Road on Saturday/Sunday 26th–27th. After visiting to demand the sound be turned down, the police reinforced in numbers and violent in attitude ... ordered everyone to leave the building. One of the organisers who stood at the door was dragged out and thrown into the van. The police proceeded to kick, punch and truncheon people indiscriminately. Not content, they went on to wreck £400 of equipment with their truncheons. Sixteen people were charged with crimes ranging from assault to drunk and disorderly behaviour ... one police officer exuding arrogance warned Jah Shaka that the sound was banned from playing in South London.[41]

David Hinds of the reggae group *Steel Pulse* also describes how: 'Things were brewing for trouble – big time. The police was harassing us on the streets and putting many of the brothers behind bars on trumped-up charges. I left school with several O and A levels but couldn't get a job. Our album *Handsworth Revolution* came out in 1978, predicting explosion. In 1981, it happened.'[42]

Footage from broadcasts in the 1980s also document the policing of soundsystem dances as both a *cultural* and *law-breaking* threat. A characteristic example is a TV programme debate from Worcester.[43] Aired in 1987, the programme opens with a clip that drips with the heat of a scorching 80s dancehall, followed by a studio audience segment concentrating on the following question: 'If you had a blues party next to you, what would you do'? Thankfully an audience member immediately replied: 'go'. The enthusiasm was short-lived, however, as another admitted that they 'would move' adding that 'we do have very musical neighbours but it is different music than the sort we have been hearing'. Proceeding with only thinly disguised contempt for 'this sort of music', he stressed how the neighbours' musical diet involved: 'a French horn, a violin, a grand piano and when they play together, they play sweetly and that is not noise as far as I'm concerned. That's very acceptable.'

There goes the argument about noise again, which is never really about volume but about aesthetics and cultural belonging – as we saw in Part I of this book. The audience member simply spoke the language of racism which may sound dispassionate and polite, but actually makes a value judgement about what counts as music and whose cultural presence is perceived as 'noise'. That audience member would probably be delighted to find out that George Steiner, the revered literary critic who loathed rap music as much as he adored Nazi philosopher Martin Heidegger,[44] would not be able to tolerate living next door to Jamaican neighbours 'playing reggae all day'.[45] But there is no racism here, just aesthetic judgement that *is not* and *could not* ever be racist, even when it is. However, one can't help but detect undertones of attitudes that advise Black people that if they should speak at all, they 'ought not to speak in the primitive language of drums. They ought to speak in the civilized language of English [...] or the language of violins and pianos.'[46] As the clip continues, we encounter Superintendent Martin Burton who spoke of an incident where a neighbour 'armed himself with a gun, put it through the window of the blues party and discharged a few bullets into the room which was absolutely packed full of people' and 'unfortunately, someone did die as a result of it'. Officer friendly claims that the neighbour was 'irate', but 'understandably so when they've got pulsating heavy-beat music going on'. The moral of the story surely must be about the murderous rage that Black music inspires in white people but let us turn to our second newsreel on blues dances and the closure of Black clubs in London.[47]

The clip begins with a voice-over that informs us that 'these people are going to a party. The trouble is, every aspect of these parties breaks the law' – namely, the illicit sale of alcohol and smoking weed. In an attempt at tracing the history of Jamaican music from ska to roots reggae, Millie Small's sugary and palatable Top of the Pops sensation (*My Boy Lollipop*) is pitted against the tough angular reggae beat which is obviously unacceptable and dangerous. Indeed, we are told that 'this is really where the problems began, because reggae was bound up with smoking marijuana, or ganja and Rastafarianism', so much so that 'the young blacks by now felt too hostile to white society'. The problem then is the presence of Black Britons and their un-British cultural habits, not the policing logics and tactics that target them. Thankfully, Harvey Weston, manager of the Colombo Club at the heart of London's West End (Carnaby Street), acknowledges that 'we face a mountain of problems here and they all come from the police' like 'harassment and disrupting the dances'. Alas, the tone of the documentary does not apportion blame to the police, even as it lists clubs that closed as a result of such policing: Noreik in Tottenham, Charlie Brown's, also in Tottenham, Nutmeg in Ealing following an SPG raid, Clouds in Brixton and Colombo in Soho.

So omnipresent was the policing of reggae music in the UK that it could go unnoticed, fading into the background but always there. Anyone picking up a Greensleeves 12" single would hold in their hands a record sleeve, designed by Tony McDermot, which features two police officers behind a drummer. Policing makes its presence known, therefore, just by holding a record cover. But the music also speaks loudly about the way it is being silenced. As Max Romeo sings in this classic Lee 'Scratch' Perry Production:

I went to a party
Last Saturday night
When I reached the party
Everything was right

Then Babylon raid, them raid, them raid
It gets me 'fraid, me gets me 'fraid.

(Max Romeo, *Three Blind Mice*)

Cornell Campbell would similarly complain about police harassment in a killer King Tubby mix:

Natty's dreadlocks up in all the streets
Dem babylon, dem cyan not keep dem feet
So dem check I man on Greenwich Farm (yeah)
You could a hear dem a come with dem loud alarm
[...]
What a misery on Greenwich Farm (yeah)
When dem start fi lick mi an' bongo tam
Just because I was preachin' out mi song (yeah)
Babylon grab me an' hold mi in dem arm.

(Cornell Campbell, *Natty Dread Inna Greenwich Farm*)

What Max Romeo and Cornell Campbell document in their lyrics applies as much to the UK as it does to JA, although the cultural threads that connect Jamaica and Britain are difficult to disentangle in a soundsystem context that is shaped by the close contact and intimate diasporic (inter)relationship between the two islands – to say nothing of the continuation of colonial policies even after Jamaica gained its independence in 1962.[48] Besides too many Jamaican artists, Max Romeo and Cornell Campbell among them, would make their careers in Jamaica and England, making it difficult to simply place them 'here' or 'there'.[49] What these two tunes also indicate, however, is the way in which reggae, Rastafari and Blackness come together to paint a picture of 'criminality'.

Noise, ganja-smoking, loc(k)sing and playing reggae music all conspire to create a 'criminal' profile that ostensibly justifies the policing of soundsystems. What hides behind such rationalisations of why the police should police Black cultural life in post-war Britain is the obvious, but perhaps unstated, reality that by policing Black music(s), what is being policed is cultural belonging. What is regarded as excessive noise alongside other minor infractions of the law is merely the pretext to monitor, regulate and control the culture of those who do not, should not and cannot belong. Breaking the law is the excuse to selectively police what is culturally discordant 'noise'. Add to that the fact that roots reggae lyrics castigate, denounce and reject Babylon (= the police and the system/'shitstem' of racist oppression), and the music becomes an enemy of the state and therefore oppositional to 'British values' (= read white British values), like colonial imperialist racist oppression perhaps.

None of this can be tolerated by any self-respecting nation state whose job is to protect the political power it relies on for its existence. Based as nation-state building is on eliminating and neutralising the 'enemy within' and 'intruders from without',[50] none of this should surprise anyone – unless we lose sight of the fact that the maintenance of state power and sovereignty is achieved through coercion: packaged as 'protection' for some (those who belong) against others (who don't). As Judith Shklar reminds us, violence, repression and torture are 'always part of a judicial and political system. To ignore this is to falsify its character and to make any effort to halt or impede it impossible.'[51] What is particularly important to us here, though, is the way in which culture becomes the battleground for what the nation is and who is, can and should (not) be part of it. Racism is the ideology that polices such boundaries and 'the law' and policing are the forces that enforce them. Building on all the examples we have already looked at, it is worth adding a characteristic illustration of how the Thatcher government refused to allocate funding to tackle the social and economic conditions of what management guru Peter Drucker, in characteristic Thatcherite spirit, praised as 'organised abandonment',[52] economic 'dispossession'[53] and (mis)managed decline. Conservative MP Hartley Booth warned Thatcher that setting up a £10m communities programme to tackle inner-city problems would do little more than 'subsidise Rastafarian arts and crafts workshops'. Oliver Letwin, a hero of the Remainers during the Brexit campaign, worked with Booth as a young adviser in Thatcher's Downing Street policy unit and confidently declared that investing in the communities that were reeling from the 1985 Broadwater Farm uprising would be money wasted on the 'disco and drug trade'.[54] Thinking with this example about people who are undeserving of welfare provision because they are culturally unbelonging, invites us to make sense of this entire chapter as a story about the politics of nationhood, 'race' and the policing of Black British culture.[55]

As Paul Gilroy sharply observed, 'racism and nationalism should not be artificially separated' but seen as 'densely interwoven in modern British history' through the 'imagery of black criminality', embodied by the menacing presence of dangerous Rastas and militant reggae.[56] Drawing on exaggerated media representations and authoritarian law and order policies against 'muggings' (robberies) by unruly youths of 'suspicious' ethnic heritage, Stuart Hall and his co-authors carefully point out how the manufacturing of a sense of national unity depends on staging a threat (Black criminality) and policing against it to restore control, during times when the authority and legitimacy of the state is on the wane in the face of a financial turmoil and its political aftershocks.[57] Writing in the context of a deep economic recession which resulted in the devaluation of the pound and a hefty loan from the International Monetary Fund in

1976, Hall showed how essential it was to summon, if not invent, an 'enem[y] of the state' to signal the 'onset of social anarchy' caused by 'the dilution of British stock by alien black elements'.[58] Cast (out) as 'alien Others', 'archetypal deviant[s]' and 'lazy layabout[s]', the 'nigs' that are 'being kept by' and 'live off the Welfare State'[59] were the perfect scapegoat or folk devil for identifying 'crimes and criminals' as a 'racially distinct' threat to the 'homogeneous, white, national "we"', just like the 'law and the ideology of legality' would pose as the solution as crime-fighting institutions that defend 'the nation state and national unity' too.[60]

As Paul Gilroy adds, the law 'embodied in the police erects a barrier not just of respectability but of racial culture or ethnicity' too,[61] making 'race' a 'powerful signifier' of 'criminality' that turns 'black law-breaking' into 'an integral element in black culture' as a whole.[62] Just as the ideologues and practitioners of state-sanctioned racism would reduce 'crime' to 'residual ethnic factors', depicting Black Britons as 'racially distinct' and unrepresentative of the nation.[63] Sir Robert Mark,[64] reflecting on his time as Commissioner of the London Metropolitan Police, thought otherwise – confidently stating that '[s]een objectively against the background of problems of 50 million people, crime is not even among the more serious of our difficulties'.

Sketching out the history of policing against Black Britons and their music as culturally 'out of place' in post-war, and supposedly post-colonial, Britain has hopefully revealed patterns of continuity and (some) change in the way that Black expressive culture(s) have historically been suppressed. It is that very continuum that George Lamming stresses in the opening epigraph of Part II, whose power also resonates throughout the twenty-first century too as we will see in Part III of this book. None of this is to suggest that racist oppression manifests itself in *exactly* the same way at the height of colonial imperialism, in the period of post-colonial, post-war reconstruction, or in the allegedly 'post-racial' present. What is highlighted instead, taking a cue from T. Thomas Fortune, is that racism should be likened to a long chain made up of different links, where the chain is the perennial ideology and practice of racism and the links are the various and shifting ways in which it occurs: 'though today's links are different in form and guise, *the chain is the same*'.[65] The history of immigration control and policing against Black Britons in the post-war year that this chapter provides has hopefully documented how racism becomes legible through the … poli-tricks[66] of (cr)immigration and law and order, or indeed how it becomes audible in the policing of reggae soundsystems. Indeed, much of this febrile atmosphere is also captured on record with Tab Cat Kelly urging *Stop Calling Us Immigrants*; U Brown fighting back with *Tottenham Rock*; Steel Pulse dreaming of a *Handsworth Revolution* and paying a *Tribute to the Martyrs*; Papa Levi speaking of *Riot Inna Birmingham*; Ranking Ann summoning us to *Kill the Police Bill* (i.e. Police and Criminal Evidence Bill, 1983); or Aswad recounting how they *Can't Walk the Streets* and insisting that they are *Not Guilty* of the 'crime' of their existence in the land of 'the Angry-Saxon race'.[67] I therefore hope that we can find solace in such 'rebel music'[68] as we take a deep breath before plunging into the policing and criminalisation of UK rap music in the following pages.

PART III

Isn't it criminal? Black music as 'out of order' in contemporary Britain

Idiots like So Solid Crew [...] are glorifying gun culture and violence ... it has created a culture where killing is almost a fashion accessory. For years I have been very worried about these hateful lyrics that these boasting macho idiot rappers come out with.

— Kim Howells, Labour MP and junior Minister at the Department for Culture, Media and Sport (2001–3)[1]

It would be comforting to believe that the dawning of a new millennium in the year 2000 would usher in a period of euphoria, prosperity, equality and progress. Besides, this is the beginning of the internet era, the introduction of the euro to world financial markets and the ubiquity of portable media players and, later, smartphones that would bring music, and especially world-dominant hip-hop, closer to our ears. Alas, the 'dot-com' bubble which gripped the financial world at the turn of the century burst, the euro brought austerity to Southern Europe and the music that people carry in their pockets continues to be criminalised. If this sounds like a one-step-forward-two-steps-backward situation, that's because it is. Yet, what is forward and what is backward here depends on how people are arranged in rank order by the social hierarchies that shape our world like an 'actuarial chart [which] predicts who would thrive and who would not'.[2] Indeed, the lyrics of Max Romeo's 70s classic *One Step Forward*, another Lee 'Scratch' Perry production, say a lot about the Noughties. There are the 'commercialised' 'conm[e]n' who 'gra[b] at the cash-backs' and there are the 'righteou[s]' for whom 'the road is rough', 'the hill is steep', 'the mountain is high' and 'the valley is deep'. The former are the 'gilded priests of Mammon' sitting in in their 'velvet-cushioned pews'.[3] The latter are the First International's and Frantz Fanon's,[4] 'wretched of the Earth', Both live in a world that doesn't just trade but '*is* trade' and really has 'turned shopkeeper' more than ever before.[5] Much of this is a story of banks too big to fail and people too small to matter and it is certainly a moment of multiple geopolitical crises that eddy around in a whirlpool.

Bubbling below the jubilation that greeted New Labour in the late 1990s, were deep-seated problems that were given a facelift, to fit the curated image of Cool Britannia and multi-ethnic, multi-cultural Britain as a utopia of political inclusion, cultural integration and social equality.[6] Were we to scratch the freshly painted facade, however, we would discover a bleaker reality covered by layers of multicultural gloss to disguise the enduring legacy of a 'multi-racist' Britain instead.[7] Such a 'clinical sanitizing of existing nasties'[8] makes for great PR, but it does not correspond to the reality of state-sanctioned racism – especially as far as policing is concerned. This is not to deny the reality of an 'ordinary',[9] 'banal', 'mundane' and 'unremarkable',[10] 'convivial culture'[11] or 'multiculture'.[12] Rather, it is to stress that this pluralistic and hybrid cosmopolitan mosaic is overshadowed by the cloud of racism as Britain's default climate pattern. To apply Patrick Wolfe's oft-repeated quip about colonisation, racism is understood here as a 'structure rather than an event';[13] a default setting, not a system error.[14] True though it certainly is that social life in postmodern

Britain troubles, complicates, disrupts and challenges preconceived ethnic orderings,[15] the ideological, institutional and political architecture of the dominant social order remains intact. It is therefore possible to witness 'superdiversity' in a single South London street,[16] while also having the spectre of racism hovering just above our heads. The richly stimulating social life of urban multiculture, therefore, walks the streets that racism built as an ideological, sociocultural and political infrastructure centuries ago. Just like post-war Britain cannot be seen as making a clean break from colonial imperialism, post-industrial Britain cannot be seen as having outgrown the racism of the post-war years. Rather than breaking with the past, the present marks 'the culminating point of sweeping processes set in motion centuries ago: industrialization, nationalism, imperialism urbanization, secularization'.[17] This is what Horace Cayton and St Clair Drake wrote about Chicago between the wars, but it applies to Britain too – as a reminder of how the present may bear the mark of its time, but also carries the weight of the past.

This may be the period which saw the publication of the Macpherson Report[18] and the Parekh Report[19] – both offering their recommendations for eliminating institutional racism and countering racial discrimination respectively. But this is also the period where the young Black rapper succeeds 'the pimp of the 1950s', 'the Black power activist of the 1960s', 'the mugger of the 1970s', 'the rioter of the 1980s' and 'the underworld Yardie of the 1990s' as public enemy number one.[20] This is the period where New Labour would celebrate the Macpherson Inquiry into the racist murder of Stephen Lawrence, but this is also the period where the police spied on the Lawrence family's campaign for justice.[21] This is the period where Parekh's Commission on the future of multiethnic Britain aspired to a vibrant multicultural society at ease with its rich diversity. But this is also the period where the threat of 'Islamic terrorism' looms large, prophesying an emergent 'clash of civilisations' – courtesy of Samuel Huntington[22] and other neo-Orientalist ideologues like Bernard Lewis,[23] whose language shaped the geopolitics of the War on Terror[24] and Britain's role in it.[25] Cool Britannia, then, is caught swinging to the tune of imperialist Rule Britannia and multiculturalism confesses to living its political life as a zombie.

On the one hand, cultural diversity is praised fulsomely. On the other it is 'repeatedly declared counterproductive and then pronounced dead, often as part of anxiety-inducing arguments about security, national identity and the menace of Islamic extremism'.[26] Such 'stubbornly undead diversity', therefore, resembles 'zombies' whose presence is 'terrifying to the power and destabilising of the order that pronounced their death', rhetorical or real.[27] At the risk of dampening our spirits, it must nevertheless be stated that this is what thirteen years of New Labour (1997–2010) did to prepare the ground for the wreckage that fourteen years of Tory rule unleashed (2010–24). And seen through the prism of the racist politics of law and order, these twenty-seven years look a lot alike – just like they echo the even more distant past in the ideological voice they speak with. Despite the diverse face of Britain, Albion: the 'white land' (from the Latin *albus*: white) never stopped being ideologically 'white'.[28] It simply sprinkles its whiteness with speckles of 'diversity' that changes how 'the nation' *looks*, but not what it *is* and *does* or how it *thinks*.

Think about this. The same police force that was declared institutionally racist in 1999 continues to be characterised as such in 2023 – unless of course police racism has vanished since the publication of the Casey Review in March 2023.[29] Assuming that it hasn't, much of what follows will focus on some key moments that have characterised the policing against Black people and their music(s) – showing how New Labour's war on 'Black on Black crime', paved the way for the Tories' crackdown on 'gangs', following the 2011 uprisings. Both such crusades seized on 'the myth of black criminality',[30] served as a 'stale dish of inner-city pathology, family breakdown, fatherlessness and chaos'[31] and blamed largely on rap music – specifically, UK grime and UK drill.[32] Focusing on the criminalisation of these two rap subgenres and mostly UK drill as the problem genre of the day, the following chapter will first describe the political atmosphere that made the policing of UK rap possible. This will provide some context before we explore the various ways through which rap is associated with glamorising, glorifying, inciting and even causing violent 'crime' – in the minds of the police, prosecutors and judges, to say nothing of the media that sell violence as news, for profit and titillation too.[33] I am not omitting jungle, pirate radio, dubstep, garage, bashment, or Afrobeats from this story without a heavy heart, or without begging for my readers' forgiveness.[34] My excuse is that I wish to spotlight the two genres that bore the brunt of racist policing in the last decade, hence the emphasis on grime and drill. Starting with a brief exploration of New Labour and the Tories' 'anti-gang' initiatives, we then discuss how such law-and-order agendas succeeded in gradually merging the fearsome image of the 'Black gangster' with its sinister counterpart – the young, Black rapper – by looking at the panoply of legal penal tactics that targeted grime MCs and drill rappers as the archetypal 'criminal' of our time. Diligent readers will hardly be surprised, accustomed as we now are to the ways in which 'criminality' has accompanied Blackness since the era of imperial-colonial slavery (see Parts I and II of this book). They might nevertheless be shocked by the great pains the British state took to give anti-Black racism a fresh lick of paint, so it can continue to shine in the present.

9

To be Black is a crime

You don't get a flattering self-image of a prim and proper, prosperous, successful and ready-for-business nation without concealing how such glamour is achieved. Stock market bubbles and fancy PR are certainly part of the look. But so is the conjuring up a threat which we must unite and fight against to protect 'our' values and way of life too. This is another way of saying that (nation) states need enemies, internal and external, to justify their existence, preserve their integrity, and protect their sense of self from the contaminating influence of 'Others'.[1] Stoking fears and spreading paranoia over criminal intrusion does just that and works marvels as a rhetorical technique that ascribes violence to one group, blames it on their culture and absolves the state of any responsibility – other than going after *them*. According to such (xeno)racist logic(s), 'crime' is no longer the result of law-making that literally creates 'crime' by defining what is legally punishable and what is not. It is a symptom of disorder, caused by those who are culturally violent. As Tony Blair, prime minister at the time, unequivocally stated: 'The black community – the vast majority of whom in these communities are decent, law-abiding people horrified at what is happening – need to be mobilized in denunciation of this gang culture that is killing innocent young black kids. But we won't stop this by pretending it isn't young black kids doing it.'[2]

So begins a protracted battle against 'Black-on-Black crime', and despite calls for being 'tough on crime' *and* on 'the causes of crime' during his time as shadow home secretary,[3] Blair's pendulum in office swung more in the direction of state punishment and personal responsibility rather than towards funding public social infrastructure as a crime prevention philosophy. Were this not so, 'Black-on-Black crime' and 'anti-social behaviour' would not have done so much heavy lifting for New Labour's law and order politics. In response to so-called 'Black-on-Black' gun violence, New Labour introduced a special Operational Command Unit known as Trident, later rebranded: Trident Gang Crime Command and now known as Trident and Area Crime Command. Officially launched in 2000, Operation Trident's publicly stated aim was to tackle 'black-on-black gun and drugs related violence' but soon expanded its remit to focus on 'all firearms murders and shootings within London's black communities'.[4] Trident's target was therefore clear and racially identifiable too. The language that described what Trident was formed to do tells us as much. But so does the imagery it relied on, in the form of posters that warned Black Britons of the consequences of *their* criminal activity.

One depicts the hand of a Black man holding a gun, as the hand of a Black woman is wrapped around his hand in an attempt to stop him. The caption reads: 'Hide his gun and you help commit the crime', followed by: 'Get caught, get 5 years'. Another shows a Black woman with the Trident logo tattooed on her arm, as these words express what she thinks: 'Turn away from guns and drugs.' Yet another reads: 'Don't let gunmen prejudice our children's future', while another shows a Nokia 'brick' phone informing us that 'it can take out a gunman', provided that the person reading the poster calls Crimestoppers. Visual copaganda aside, the words of the then Head of Trident (Mike Fuller) trace the origins and evolution of 'Black criminality' – dutifully informing us that: 'On the street, no one really talks about Yardies anymore [...] That's not what they call themselves. It's all crews and posses. We still have some Jamaicans involved but the vast majority of the shootings we are seeing now are the result of conflicts between rival gangs of British-born blacks.'[5]

Drawing on the menacing figure of the Jamaican Yardie gangster alongside references to crews and posses, in language that takes us back to Part II of this book, the 'race-gang nexus'[6] is now etched into our consciousness – spreading fear and alarm about 'guns, gangsters and drugs' which are blamed on the proto/stereotypical alien, criminal, Black 'Other'.[7] The basic problem here then is not rampant 'criminality' as such, but its racial character. The logic goes a bit like this: since most young Black men are the perpetrators and the victims of such crime, there must be something criminogenic about Blackness either as a biological or a cultural trait. There can be no other explanation for this like, say, involvement in criminal activity because of extreme levels of poverty and disadvantage lived in a social and physical environment that educates and socialises people into violence *by design*. Yet, according to an Equality and Human Rights Commission report[8] Black Britons are disproportionately 'locked into a position of disadvantage for generations': a fact which might serve as a more reliable predictor of violent crime than skin colour or cultural pathology. Such findings were echoed by former UN Special Rapporteur on extreme poverty and human rights, Philip Alston, who exposed Britain's 'systematic immiseration'[9] of 'racial and ethnic minorities' among other groups that were 'the hardest hit' by 'the costs of austerity'.[10] Jess McQuail, Director of *Just Fair* and Olivier De Schutter, UN

Special Rapporteur on extreme poverty and human rights would concur, pointing out that 'UK policies that continue to inflict misery' five years after Alston's report.[11] In fact, De Schutter went as far as arguing that poverty levels in the UK amount to 'violation of international law'.[12]

Against airy-fairy fantasies such as structural disadvantage, however, law and order poli-tricks insist that Blackness is among the causes of crime, much like the evil eye causes natural disasters or fiscal crises. There *must* be something intrinsically 'criminal' about Black people and their deficient 'fatherless' family arrangements and *that* is what the problem is. It couldn't possibly be inequality or social exclusion that lead people to commit desperate and often unjust acts within a violent living environment marred by inequality and social exclusion. The only apparent solution, therefore, must be to police Blackness – not remove the structural barriers that block Black Britons' access to welfare, housing, employment, education and healthcare. Seen this way, 'Black-on-Black crime' comes to be understood as what it really is: the *outcome* of social policy not the *cause* of 'criminality'. And that is exactly how criminalisation operates, as an ideological and political force that turns activities, actions and behaviours into legally punishable offences through 'processes of making laws, of breaking laws, and of reacting toward the breaking of laws'.[13] Or, as Nils Christie puts it: 'Acts are not, they become. So also with crime. Crime does not exist. Crime is created. First there are acts. Then follows a long process of giving meaning to these acts. Social distance is of particular importance. Distance increases the tendency to give certain acts the meaning of being crimes, and the persons the simplified meaning of being criminals.'[14]

In fact, the very notion of 'crime' itself is actually 'the *product*' not the '*object*' of legal penal policy.[15] It is 'a product of perception and political process',[16] which 'deems a certain 'occurrence' or 'situation' as undesirable [and] attributes that undesirable occurrence to an individual'.[17] But that is only half the story. The other half concerns the racialisation of crime as a process that 'impute[s] crime to color',[18] making 'race' an active ingredient of 'crime' in a strange act of transubstantiation where 'crime' is racialised and 'race' is criminalised. The process of criminalisation here is a racialised one, revealing how criminalisation and racialisation work together and occur simultaneously. As Sunita Toor helpfully explains, criminalisation should be understood as 'the act of labelling a community, or indeed its members, as "criminal" due to its perceived associations and engagement with certain illegal and deviant activities', while racialisation 'refers to the processes by which specific understandings of race, ethnicity, culture and faith are used to construct a distinct categorization of [a certain] population.'[19] Just as 'crime' is invoked to avoid talking about state-sanctioned social harm,[20] 'race' stands in for 'crime', in a game of 'hide-and-speak'[21] where 'stupendous iniquity, this giant crime'[22] walks away with impunity, while Black Britons become selectively – that is to say, racially – criminalised. Rather than accepting responsibility for the wilful neglect, organised abandonment and targeted mismanagement of public social infrastructure, the state and its law enforcement institutions blame people instead for their lack of access to a dignified existence in the form of decent and affordable services. Instead of 'improving places' all we get is 'punishing people'.[23]

None of this should come as a surprise as it is entirely consistent with the behaviouralistic, individualistic, entrepreneurial, neoliberal blame-yourself-for-everything and you-can-make-it-if-you-really-try-and-you-must-try-hard-too ethos that New Labour represented. The introduction of Antisocial Behaviour Orders (ASBOs) in the Crime and Disorder Act 1998 exemplifies this by targeting *behaviour*, not social reality that creates, conditions or shapes behaviour that is 'likely to cause harassment, alarm or distress to one or more persons not of the same household'.[24] ASBOs were civil orders that lasted a minimum of two years, but their breach resulted in a criminal offence carrying sanctions that range from fines to a maximum prison sentence of five years. Despite being civil orders, ASBOs were easy to breach and soon became seen for what they really were: another example of criminalisation by the back door, as the logical consequence of New Labour's politics of behaviour and respectability – where concerns about community safety turned Britain into an 'ASBO nation' where the 'criminalisation of nuisance' reigns supreme.[25]

Such politics of 'crime and banishment'[26] was not of course invented by New Labour. A longer history of such 'respectable fears' exists and has its roots in moral panics surrounding the hooligans and garrotters of Edwardian and Victorian Britain respectively.[27] It also has a history before Labour took office in 1997. A cursory look at the party literature unearths publications that promise 'tough action on criminal neighbours' in 1995 and pledges to take crime seriously as 'a challenge to us all' in 1964.[28] It was nevertheless made a priority under Blair's premiership.[29] So much so, that New Labour's youth justice (= youth punishment) policies were nicknamed 'korrectional karaoke'[30] and likened to a form of 'rougher justice'.[31] Alas, the sharp end of such politics of respectability and responsibilisation is not felt by 'us all'. 'Law 'n' order', as Paul Garon[32] playfully calls it, chooses its targets from specific social categories that are marked by hierarchies of 'race' and class. Should it surprise us therefore to hear that the best example of policing through ASBOs comes from the policing of Black music(s), even when the perpetrators are racialised as white? If you are familiar with pirate radio in the grime music era, then you will remember that the first ASBO was allegedly reserved for DJ Slimzee who was forbidden from going above the fifth floor of any building in Tower Hamlets[33] – to stop him from installing transmitters for Rinse FM, when it was still a pirate radio station and a major conduit for grime, alongside Deja Vu, Raw UK, Flex, Mode, Radar, Heat FM and the many mixtapes (grimetapes) and DVDs (e.g. *Conflict, Risky Roadz, Lord of the Mics*) that did so much to spread the music like sonic spray around the city.[34] Never mind that broadcasting music is definitely not *anti*-social, but very *social* indeed. What matters here is the use of the word 'antisocial' to target, monitor and control *what* is being broadcast: that 'criminal' grime music that hurts the ears of respectable Britain.[35] Pirate radio aside, what was and continues to be deemed antisocial may not appeal to everyone, but usually describes public activities like: graffiti, abusive and intimidating language, excessive noise, particularly late at night, littering, drunken behaviour in the streets, drug dealing, hanging around, playing ball games or skateboarding.

This is not to say that all (or any) of these activities are pleasant, though our reaction to them certainly remains subjective. What is stressed instead is that such activities are fundamentally *social*, leaving us very little choice but to approach ASBOs as an attempt to criminalise *some* uses of public space (e.g. graffiti writing) rather than others (e.g. paid advertising) when both could be seen as visually intrusive. What is more important to note, however, is that the word 'antisocial' essentially becomes a euphemism for 'crime' – giving the punitive state sufficient headroom for implementing policies of urban discipline, regulation and social control; using a different name for the same thing. Very few of these behaviours are actually threatening, so clamping down on them must be seen as an attempt to sanitise urban public space to make room for business and shopping at the expense of pleasure and hanging around (which is all that 'loitering' is, by the way). Besides, (neoliberal) belief in unregulated *market* activity requires the regulation of *social* activity. References to antisocial behaviour, therefore, function as a 'politically and economically useful'[36] way of doing the work of criminalisation under a different name. Public life in a 'No Ball Games' society[37] then soon becomes sacrificed for the 'privatization of the architectural public realm' and the 'militarization of city life', where 'public activity is sorted into strictly functional compartments, and circulation is internalized in corridors under the gaze of private police'.[38] Walking on and moving through public spaces becomes trespassing on privatized 'pseudo-public' property[39] – determining who belongs and who does not belong in public and what one can and cannot do in public, with the scales tilting favourably towards those who have the right to be in public because they have the purchasing power to do so.[40] And just like ASBOs chased after pirates on the rooftops of East London, an impromptu grime dance in Shoreditch also provides the perfect setting for the spatial politics of law and order. Journalist, writer and grime music aficionado Dan Hancox recalls:

> It's a mild spring evening, and about a thousand young Londoners have gathered on the uneven gravel and dirt of the Holywell Lane Car Park in Shoreditch, beer cans and spliffs in hand, going completely berserk to grime. This show has no tickets, no VIP, and no permit, just a borrowed sound system set up on the back of a truck parked under a railway overpass. The gates at the entrance have been swung shut, so scores of hyped-up fans are climbing over the 10-foot-high wire fence to get in.[41]

Predictably, the police arrived forty minutes after the event started making this vignette a typical illustration of the 'quality of life', 'broken windows' policing that ASBOs stood for, in all but name.[42] Such zero-tolerance order -maintenance policing philosophies invoke a 'feeling of threat' that 'depends on the acceptance of cultural stereotype[s]',[43] which then feeds into a readily available 'depository of anxieties about mixing' and the sharing of public space.[44] Such disquiet quickly translates into calculations of 'risk', mediated by surveillance technologies and legislation that keep those who are deemed as 'Other(s)' in their place, as outcasts and misfits who ought to be consigned to the margins of civic life. But the policing of Black life in urban space doesn't just take place on the street. It also makes its way into the club too. Here's where the notorious Promotion Event Risk Assessment Form 696 comes into play, as a form of bureaucratic policing against bashment, garage and primarily grime music events.[45]

10

Looking for 'crime' in grime

Form 696 was introduced by the London Metropolitan Police in 2008[1] to 'identify and minimise any risk of most serious violent crime'[2] in planned live music events and club nights, prompted by incidents of fatal shootings in UK garage concerts, by members of So Solid Crew.[3] But it was grime that took the hardest hit,[4] even though there was 'no basis to infer anything but a coincidental link' between crime and grime.[5] The original Form 696 contained leading questions about the 'music style to be played' listing 'Bashment', 'R'n'B' and 'Garage' as the *only* examples – resulting in event cancellations,[6] 'bashment bans'[7]and club closures.[8] A 'key instrument in suppressing the scene's growth in the capital',[9] it was revised in 2009 containing questions about the 'target audience', the 'make up of the patrons' and the nature of the performance: 'DJs or MCs performing to a backing track'.[10] In revising Form 696, the police hoped to disguise the racist assumptions that hid inside it, given that the only music styles that fit the descriptions provided by Form 696 are Black music genres.

A vibrant campaign against it soon emerged, uniting grime artists, venue promoters and fans,[11] who succeeded in having the form removed in November 2017 following an intervention by London

Mayor Sadiq Khan.[12] Salutary though this development was, it came almost a decade after the Form 696 was launched and offered no acknowledgement of its racist nature. The Met's 'nopology' merely expressed regrets that Form 696 was received negatively 'by members of the London music industry, particularly around a perception that events associated with some genres of music were disproportionately affected by this process'. Note how copaganda blames the targets of Form 696 for misperceiving the way grime events were policed, instead of apologising for the way they were policed. Note also that Sadiq Khan's criticism of the form decried the way grime artists and audiences were unfairly targeted but focused on the impact the form had on 'the night-time economy', not on racial justice.[13] What ought to be protected, therefore, is capital rather than those living in the capital – a logic that is eerily consistent with arguments for the abolition of slavery on economic grounds alone, to improve the welfare of non-slaveholding whites in the American South.[14] Such a realisation helps us understand that the scrapping of Form 696 would not herald an era of less punitiveness towards UK grime music.[15]

Two years after Form 696 was abolished, albeit by declaration alone,[16] the association of grime with 'trouble' led Leeds Labour Party Councillor Al Garthwaite to blame grime for the violence that broke out during a brawl at a bar.[17] Worse still, such thinking habits were criticised in a report by the House of Commons Digital, Culture, Media and Sport Committee,[18] which 'welcome[d] the abolition of the Metropolitan Police's 696 Form following concerns that it unfairly targeted certain artists and audiences' – while also acknowledging that 'it is concerning to hear that prejudices against urban acts persist'. Persist they did, as we will see in our discussion of the policing of UK drill later in Chapter 11. But they are also contained in the wording of the committee's report. The use of the word 'urban' speaks volumes here, as a clumsy euphemism for Black music genres,[19] that was deliciously satirised in Wiley's anthemic *Wot Do U Call It* as follows: 'Do you do garage music mate? You got any of that Urban? (Urban, urban, urban) [...] Wot do you call it? Urban? Urban?'

Alas, not even Wiley's humorous lyrics can take our mind off the racist criminalisation of grime that New Labour ushered in, only to be succeeded by the impending Tory blitzkrieg. Fittingly enough, grime provided the soundtrack to 'y' know, the grime' (Dizzee Rascal, *Showtime*), the gritty, grim(e)y reality of life lived in London's council estates in an almost ethnographic fashion,[20] speaking of: 'the have nots and the have less' (Kano, *This is England*), 'bank scams, street robbery, shotters, blotters [= drug-dealers] or HMP' (Dizzee Rascal, *Brand New Day*) and living 'street' while others live 'neat' (Dizzee Rascal, *2 Far*). But grime did more than illustrate how Blair's 'nu-Labour' opened the door for the Tory juggernaut, not unlike Callaghan's Labour oiled the wheels of Thatcherism.[21] It actually espoused the socialist prin-ciples that New Labour abandoned (remember Clause IV of the party's constitution?),[22] with a wave of fresh voices that spoke for an entire generation which grew up with rising student debt, vis-ible and invisible homelessness, custodial sentences, electronic tag-ging, police surveillance, incarceration, austerity, gentrification and displacement, a mental health crisis and 'munpain';[23] the everyday life of mundane pain, loss and trauma,[24] that has so vividly been captured by grime-influenced fiction (e.g. Guy Gunaratne's, *In Our Mad and Furious City*) and poetry too (e.g. D.S. Marriott's, *Duppies*).

Grime's political coming of age, however, is perhaps best exem-plified by the genre's second wave (from the 2010s onwards), as evidenced by grime artists' support for Jeremy Corbyn's Labour leadership campaign (#Grime4Corbyn), as well as by the outcry against the Grenfell Tower fire (#Grime4Grenfell) which engulfed the Grenfell tower block in West London – resulting in the death of 72 people, while hundreds of others were left displaced and traumatised.[25] The political force of grime music was also audible in the student protests against the trebling of tuition fees in 2010, with Lethal Bizzle's *Pow!* becoming their unofficial anthem.[26] But grime also coincided with the 2011 uprisings which showcased the Tories' war against gangs where the fear-inducing image of Blackness was omnipresent. Although such 'riots' were a reaction to the police killing of Mark Duggan in Tottenham, making 2011 look a lot like 1985,[27] the Broadwater Farm uprisings also occurred in a context where 'young people are excluded and marginalized, confined and criminalized' as Paul Gilroy put it in the liner notes of grime producer Eastman's *Red, White and Zero*.[28]

What started as a peaceful assembly to protest Duggan's murder[29] and the Met's failure to inform his family of his death[30] spiralled into violence, which was marked 'not [by] the number of people hurt but the scale of property destruction'.[31] Yet this was an event that was approached as a public order emergency and a legal penal issue, rather than the outcome of yet another incident of racist police violence. Not unlike Blair's jeremiad against 'Black-on-Black crime', David Cameron, who was prime minister at the time, quickly disguised and reduced such fiery opposition to police violence as 'criminality pure and simple'.[32] He was soon joined by racist TV historian David Starkey[33] who lamented over how the 'whites have become black', while old white Marxists like Zygmunt Bauman and David Harvey only saw 'defective and disqualified consumers'[34] and 'mindless rioters' participating in 'feral capitalism'.[35] Let us return to the Beeb's favourite racist talking head, however, as an example of how the ideology that sees 'criminality' in Blackness and

Blackness as a problem is expressed, in openly Powellite language. It is no accident that Enoch Powell is evoked in Starkey's detestable comments, which are worth reading in full:

> There has been a profound cultural change. I have just been rereading Enoch Powell, the Rivers of Blood speech. Its prophecy was absolutely right in one sense. The Tiber didn't foam with blood, but flames lambent, they wrapped around Tottenham and wrapped around Clapham. But it wasn't intercommunal violence. This is where he was completely wrong. What happened is that a substantial section of the chavs that you [= addressing Owen Jones] write about have become black. The whites have become black; a particular sort of violent destructive, nihilistic gangster culture has become the fashion. Black and white, boy and girl operate in this language together. It's language which is wholly false, which is this Jamaican patois that's been intruded in England. And this is why so many of us have this sense of literally a foreign country. Black culture is an enormously important thing. It's not skin colour, it's cultural.[36]

As the camera rolled, Starkey responded to the criticism of his fellow panellists (Dreda Say Mitchell and Owen Jones), asking them: 'You glorify rap?' This prompted the programme's presenter, Emily Maitlis, to ask Starkey: 'Do you equate rap with rioting on the streets?' and the tweedy historian replies: 'It certainly glorifies it.'

In just a few minutes of televised spectacle, we learn that violence and 'criminality' comes from Black culture and rap music, preparing us ideologically for a war against gangs that uses the same arguments, implicitly or explicitly, to racially criminalise Black cultural art forms. Five years before Starkey would embarrass himself on the telly, David Cameron also accused rap, criticising BBC Radio 1 for playing music that 'encourages people to carry guns and knives'.[37] Such ignorant musings were thankfully rebutted by grime MC

Lethal Bizzle,[38] whose music was banned in the heyday of Form 696.[39] Yet, the rap-causes-crime fiction became legal-penal policy when drill music broke into the mainstream in 2018.

What paved the way for the rap-race-crime mythology was Cameron's anti-gang crusade following the 2011 'riots' – in the form of the Ending Gangs and Youth Violence programme. This 'anti-gang' initiative interpreted the 2011 uprisings against racist police violence, as a high point in gang warfare – confidently declaring in a cross-government report that: '[o]ne thing that the riots in August did do was to bring home to the entire country just how serious a problem gang and youth violence has now become'.[40] These are the words of Theresa May who was home secretary at the time. A page later, however, we read that: 'The proportion of rioters known to be gang involved may be low – so too are the numbers of young people involved in gangs.'[41] These are the words of Iain Duncan Smith, who served as the secretary of state for work and pensions back then. The contradiction that is so evident after reading these two sentences together, evaporates once we accept that such 'gang talk'[42] is little more than a political device to divert attention away from the state violence that impoverishes and kills (austerity, police killings), by staging a threat ('gangs') and charging for its elimination with more of the same violence that started it all (more policing). This is rationalised through 'a powerful discourse that stereotypically associates young BAME people with violent, criminal and problematic behaviours'.[43] In so doing, 'the gang' becomes 'specific to, arising from and potentially encompassing, the black community as a whole',[44] making it easy to see why Black people are 'over-represented in police stop and searches, more likely to face prosecution under the country's joint enterprise provisions, and [...] over-represented in the prison system' as well.[45] Thus spoke UN's Special Rapporteur Tendayi Achiume on racism, following her visit to the UK. Expressing how 'shocked' she was 'by the criminalisation of young people from ethnic minorities [and] especially young black men', Achiume's consternation reflects a StopWatch report which asserted that: 'While police narratives about stop and search revolve around knives, gangs, organised crime groups, drug supply, county lines and modern slavery, our analysis tells a different story – one of deprived, minority communities being over-policed and selectively criminalised for minor drug possession offences that are largely ignored in other contexts and for other groups.'[46]

That is the work that the 'gang' label does as a lazy shorthand for young, marginalised Black Britons who are disproportionately criminalised and therefore over-represented in police statistics. How else are we to interpret the fact that '78% of the people on the Met's Gangs Matrix database are Black when the Met's own data shows that only 27% of Black people are accountable for serious youth violence'?[47] Shocking though such figures may be, they should occasion no surprise. They are simply part of Britain's carceral tapestry, as a cursory glance at the latest data of the government's Race Disparity Unit will reveal to the statistically curious.[48] This should be even less surprising, once we realise that the police have admitted that their gang database, the Gangs Violence Matrix, is unlawful, disproportionately targeting young Black people and breaching the right to a private and family life.[49] In a delicious twist of fate, it was a rapper (Awate) who took legal action against the Matrix in an attempt to find out whether he was listed in it. Why would he be? Because rap music was included in the matrix as 'evidence' of involvement in gang activity. By exposing the Matrix for the racist, illiberal and unlawful intelligence-gathering tool that it was, the legal challenge that Awate, Liberty and UNJUST UK won did so much more. Not only was the Met forced to announce that it would stop using the Matrix, but the racist logic behind it was laid bare too – warranting suspicion about what it will be replaced with.[50] As Awate pointed out:

> The Gangs Matrix was a relic of colonialism used by the Met Police to target people it thinks nobody cares about. The secretive nature of the Matrix meant anyone could be on it and not know, and many people like me had their mental health damaged and possibilities limited by thinking they were on it. While I'm glad the Matrix has at last been dismantled, I'm disappointed that it's been replaced by yet another system which looks set to repeat this injustice and continue to discriminate against working-class Black people. Instead, I want to see funding diverted to programmes that improve our lives – not punish us for being poor and neglected by the state.[51]

This may sound far-fetched, especially to those who wish to deny the imperial-colonial roots of police racism in Britain (see Part I of this book). But such denial(ism) doesn't make this fact any less true. As Jasbinder Nijjar[52] reminds us, the ideological roots of gang lore are grounded in Britain's colonial history – where Africans and Indians were depicted as and classified into 'groups', 'bands', 'tribes', 'races' and 'castes' that were 'wild', 'savage', 'plundering' and 'predatory'. What is plundering and predatory, of course, is imperial-colonial statecraft itself. Given that this is too impolite to say, think, or admit, however, we can at least point to how 'certain categories of crime are now identified not merely as those which blacks are most likely to commit, but as crimes which are somehow expressive of the ethnicity of those who carry them out'.[53] *That* is the reason why Black Britons are over-represented in police statistics and gang databases and why Black cultural expression is staged as a public order threat, requiring the tough, heavy-handed, zero-tolerance approach that the 'corporate and electoralist'[54] law and order poli-tricks represent.

There is therefore nothing puzzling about seeing how New Labour's anti-social behaviour agenda and the Tories' anti-gang zeal converge. Law and order rhetoric is always seen as a vote-winner by the Left and the Right alike.[55] It is actually surprising to see that it was David Cameron that enlisted Bill 'broken-windows-policing' Bratton, as an adviser in the aftermath of the 2011 uprisings.[56] Blair's antisocial behaviour agenda was straight out of Bratton's playbook as NYC and LA Police Commissioner, just like Cameron's war-on-gangs has defined the legacy of Bratton's authoritarianism. Bratton was a former military police officer in Vietnam, after all – a fact which should have impressed Blair and Cameron, given their own warmongering in Iraq, Afghanistan and Syria. It is therefore instructive to observe how the 'war on terror' and the 'war on gangs' share the same ideological M.O. – making it difficult to see where militarisation ends and policing begins.[57] States, citizens and their internal and external 'enemies' all operate in a permanently hostile environment. Unwanted groups are construed as something that needs to be 'fought' against and the state must shore up its defence mechanisms: tough measures, punitive and criminalising policies, extensive police powers, closing borders and human rights abuses. All of this becomes a matter of 'self-defence' and 'public safety' that justifies military, police and executive power; allowing the 'exceptional state' to become 'permanently installed'.[58]

This is the legacy of early twenty-first-century British politics. The 'war on Blackness' through the policing of Black music is part of it. And it is not over either. Instead, we find ourselves reliving Britain's racist history in the present. The awful spectre of violent Black music(s), therefore, is very much with us – embodied by the 'crime-stained blackness'[59] of the UK drill rapper of the late 2010s and early 2020s. Given drillers' prominent role as the nation's favourite target of moralising and criminalising, the next chapter is devoted to them – as a corrective to the factually inaccurate, ethically unacceptable and politically dangerous punditry that fills column inches, surfs the airwaves, clogs up the social mediasphere and emboldens legal penal policy; in an unholy alliance that reveals a flagrant disregard for the truth. It is called whitewashing for a reason.

11

Blaming Drill for making people kill

Have you heard of the 'demonic', 'nihilistic', 'knife crime rap'? That scary 'soundtrack to London's murders' which 'spread[s] a message of hatred and violent revenge'? Did you know that this 'music' is 'designed to stir up the most visceral urges of those who listen to it'? This is how *The Times*,[1] *The Sunday Times Magazine*,[2] *The New Yorker*,[3] the *Daily Mail*[4] and *RT*[5] introduced UK drill music to their readers. Bridging the gap between respectable journalism and the gutter press, such hysterical headlines succeeded in striking fear in the hearts of their readers, encouraging them to connote this malign subgenre of rap music with violence and 'criminality'. Cops would soon join the fear-inducing merry-go-round, warning law-abiding Britons about this drill music that serves to 'glamouris[e] violence – murder, stabbings'.[6] Thus spoke the former commissioner of the metropolitan police service, Cressida Dick, whose career is distinguished by conducting the unlawful police killing of Jean Charles De Menezes;[7] denying that institutional racism exists;[8] and leading a force whose racism, sexism and misogyny forced her to resign.[9] Her words were echoed by the actions of Commander Jim Stokley, Met's gang-crime chief at the time, who paired up with the Crown Prosecution Service (CPS) to cobble together existing anti-terrorism legislation against drill music,[10] fulfilling his boss' 'relentless war on gangs'.[11] Such anti-gang efforts include the continuation of Operation Domain, which was launched by the Met in 2015 'to take action against gang related videos encouraging violence',[12] and a Serious Violence Strategy to combat lyrics that 'glamorise gang or drug-selling life, taunt rivals and normalise weapons carrying'.[13]

These measures have resulted in the use of drill music videos as online sources of intelligence gathering, to bring convictions against individuals that are identified in those videos '*without* any proof that the targeted music videos were linked to specific acts of violence'.[14] The former Met Deputy Commissioner, Sir Stephen House, said so during a Police and Crime Committee meeting of the London Assembly – explaining how the police request the removal of drill music videos from YouTube and monitor the playing of UK drill music on air by requesting radio stations (e.g. BBC Radio 1) to pluck drill tracks out of their playlists.[15] The London Metropolitan Police has even formed a Drill Music Translation Cadre, consisting of cops who act as rap expert witnesses; decoding lyrics and translating them into evidence for the prosecution.[16] In fact, the Met boasts an entire operation known as Project Alpha which involves more than thirty staff.[17]

Launched in 2019, Project Alpha was set up by the National Police Chiefs' Council (NPCC), the Home Office and the Metropolitan Police Service (MPS) to scour social media sites in search of 'gang-related music linked to serious violence',[18] prompting serious concerns about racial profiling and potential privacy violations on a large scale by youth violence experts.[19] As a result of this approach, 'anyone identified in the slick videos can be targeted with action including Criminal Behaviour Orders (CBOs) that can prevent suspects from associating with certain people, entering designated areas, wearing hoods, or using social media and unregistered mobile phones'.[20] Drill group 1011, Digga D and Skengdo x AM have all had CBOs made against them,[21] requiring them to inform the police 24 hours in advance of their intention to publish any videos online, while also demanding that they give a 48-hour warning of the date and locations of any planned live performance.[22] Established under Part Two of the Anti-social Behaviour Crime and Policing Act 2014, CBOs are 'ancillary orders' imposed on offenders by the court, in addition to an actual sentence.[23] Although CBOs are court orders that function as a command or an instruction rather than a sentence, breaching a CBO is itself a criminal offence resulting in fines and imprisonment.[24]

Note how easily *antisocial* behaviour becomes *criminal* behaviour and observe how the state's 'action against knife crime'[25] links together knives, gangs and drill music, despite the fact that data from the Mayor's Office for Policing and Crime (MOPAC) on gangs showed no concrete evidence of the link between knife crime and gang membership.[26] Evidence from Stopwatch and Amnesty International on the Metropolitan Police Gang Matrix[27] point to the same conclusion, as does an investigation by the Information Commissioner's Office (ICO) which found the Matrix in breach of data protection laws 'with the potential to cause damage and distress to the disproportionate number of young, black men on the Matrix'.[28] This is eight years before the Matrix was scrapped, laying its racism bare[29] – as 'the basis for surveillance operations against young men and boys who are predominantly black and are listed as potential future violent offenders, sometimes without any basis'.[30] Much the same applies to 'debates around the potential impact of drill music on youth violence [which] are, in the main, a populist distraction from understanding and tackling the real root causes' such as 'childhood trauma, undiagnosed and untreated mental health issues, inadequate state provision, deficient parental support, poverty and social inequality'.[31] So here we have a war against a gang problem that is exaggerated, using policing methods that are declared racist, illiberal and unjust – all in the name of combating an 'epidemic' of knife crime,[32] which the Home Office admits that it has no definition of[33] and only misguided, counterproductive and punitive solutions for.[34] In the absence of a concrete definition for knife crime, therefore, the reported spike in knife crime did not even involve knives necessarily. Any sharply pointed object would do, from broken bottles, glass and screwdrivers to chisels and scissors. Similarly, references to a knife crime 'epidemic' in 2018 ought to be treated with caution. The rise in knife-enabled offences amounted to 5–8 per cent between 1997 and 2017, the majority of which (79%) was committed by adults over the age of 18.[35] So much for all the blustery concern with 'youth violence'.

And that is just the beginning of whipped-up hysteria about knife crime, to say nothing of the sensationalist, racist, state-sanctioned criminalisation of UK drill music. What started as a discovery of a 'crime-ridden' and 'gang-infested' 'knife culture', driven by drillers' beats and rhymes, soon grew into a proper legal penal industry. Police, prosecutors and judges became experts in pursuing, interpreting, legislating against and opining on a music genre that eludes their grasp, but remains in their grip. They therefore saw fit to approach drill as anything other than the music genre that it is, pursuing it instead as 'gang-related music',[36] 'bad character' evidence[37] and proof of 'guilt by association' under joint enterprise law.[38] This being the three-pronged attack that the state, or rather the Crown, reserves for UK drill music, it is these three legal penal contrivances that we discuss in turn – to demonstrate how drill triggered punitive reactions, stirred racist passions and sharpened the critical imagination of those, like me, who research, oppose and campaign against the use of art as evidence in court.[39]

'Gang-related music'

Starting its life as a music genre, drill soon became seen through the prism of law enforcement alone. It is mentioned *by name* in specific legislative guidance drafted for it – namely, the 'Gangs, drill music and social media' section; in order to facilitate decision making in 'gang' related offences.[40] Defined as 'gang-related music' by none other than a Project Alpha operative,[41] drill is analysed, policed and prosecuted as such – without placing the very term 'gang-related music' under critical scrutiny and without questioning the qualifications and credentials of cops who pose as 'experts' on music genres they have little or no demonstrable specialised knowledge of, or rigorously trained professional expertise in.[42] This is important to note, relying as the prosecution of drill does on narratives, intelligence and testimony that are produced by law enforcement professionals who are insufficiently knowledgeable to accurately analyse, interpret, or reliably opine on rap music culture – without being insensitive to, or inadequately aware of, the artistic conventions of the genre.[43] Pointing out how one becomes an 'expert' for the prosecution in the eyes of the law is instructive here. Often enough, all that is required is signing a self-certification form where one certifies *oneself* as an 'expert'. Alternatively, Crown-appointed 'experts' gain their expertise by attending a single five-day course (Expert Evidence: Urban Street Gangs and Slang).[44] Such 'experts' are then instructed as such by the prosecution and taken seriously in the courtroom, although they are laughed out in the auditorium at a sellout play (The UK Drill Project), which ridicules two such cops-turned-'experts' – nicknamed: PC Railings and PC Bars.[45] This should urge us to think (twice!) about just how high standards of evidence actually are in court proceedings, especially as such 'experts' big themselves up by enlisting the authority of another 'expert': a lexicographer specialising in slang, not rap poetry, Black cultural studies or youth culture; who, despite being branded as a 'professor' by our (n)ever-so-diligent cops only holds a bachelor's degree, occupies no university position[46] and is therefore no professor at all – if academic credentials and ranks are to be respected.

Worse still, rap poetry is not 'slang', or 'street slang' set to music. It is a form of lyrical, figurative language which – like other forms of poetry – relies on a full range of literary and dramaturgical devices (e.g. simile, metaphor, alliteration) that 'complicat[e] or even rejec[t] literal interpretation'.[47] But rap lyrics only make sense if they are listened to *as music*, not as a set of lyrics that are separated from it so they can be transcribed, translated and read out in court by (mostly) posh white people in horsehair wigs. Also, rappers write verses in the tradition of Black vernacular traditions and Afro-diasporic orality. They invent new words, invert the meaning of others and lace their lyrics with culturally specific, coded references that defy easy interpretation, especially among listeners unfamiliar with the genre. Furthermore, rappers famously rely on exaggeration and hyperbole as they craft the larger-than-life characters that have entertained fans (and offended critics) for decades.[48] As such, cops with expertise on gangs or linguists with expertise on slang are no experts at all when it comes to rap music. Yet they serve as experts for the prosecution and judges incorrectly assume that no specialised knowledge is required to interpret rap lyrics.[49] 'Everyone can understand what is meant by the defendant's lyrics', goes the familiar refrain that I have heard countless times, in my experience as an expert witness for the defence, in cases that rely on rap music material as 'evidence' of criminal wrongdoing. Alas, these are the standards that operate in turning drill music into evidence of gang affiliation, suggesting that drill is a criminal enterprise (which it is not) rather than an art form (which it actually is).

What makes such 'dangerous associations'[50] between gangs and drill credible, however, are the emotive connotations that the word 'gang' stirs up. Attributing so-called 'gang' membership and involvement in collective offending is one of the ways in which racially minoritised groups become disproportionately criminalised.[51] Not only is there is no accurate or reliable definition of a 'gang',[52] but the ones that are officially used are too broad and selectively applied to particular communities and groups of people that are (racially) criminalised.[53] A fleeting glimpse into the relevant legislation that is weaponised in the state's war against drill tells us as much, so 'the law' takes centre stage in turn; as a racialising and criminalising tool that creates the suspects it seeks to police, prosecute, sentence and incarcerate.[54]

Having already looked at the dubious logic and spurious use of the term 'gang-related music' to describe and criminalise drill music, and having alluded to the alluring mythology of irresponsible 'gang talk',[55] introducing the official definition on gangs that is used when drill takes the defendant's seat in court seems appropriate – to justify and substantiate the scepticism that critical scholars reserve for it. Section 34(5) of the Policing and Crime Act 2009 defines acts as 'gang-related' if the targeted group:

(a) "consists of at least 3 people",
(b) "uses a name, emblem or colour or has any other characteristic that enables its members to be identified by others as a group" and
(c) "is associated with a particular area".

Evidently, such a definition is hopelessly vague to carry any weight – applied, as it could be, on gown-wearing graduands, lanyard-holding conferees, or high-vis vested marathon runners. In the context of drill music, however, things get worse, as anyone who raps on camera with at least two other people, wearing T-shirts with the drill collective's name or logo in their neighbourhood can be identified as a gang member and prosecuted (= persecuted?) as such. The cases of the 'Moss Side 11' and the 'Manchester 10' offer just two disturbing illustrations of such gang lore and deserve a mention here.

Starting with the 'Moss Side 11', it is a story involving eleven teenagers sentenced to a minimum of 168 years collectively, based on a rap video they made as a key piece of evidence to convict them under joint enterprise law.[56] Never mind that the video was organised by a youth worker (Kemoy Walker), part-funded by Greater Manchester Police and shot by a film student at Manchester Metropolitan University. The incriminating factor? The video's title: *Active Only*, a term used by the defendants and other young people in Moss Side, Manchester to describe that they were out and about. According to the CPS, however, these two words – Active Only – signalled gang affiliation and the judge's summing up of the case entertained the possibility of inferring guilt from the 'participation [in] or possession of that video'[57] – making 'possession' of a video sound equivalent to possessing a lethal weapon, doubling perhaps as 'evidence' that the defendants were possessed by a malignant, evil and violent spirit too?

Putting sarcasm to one side, the logic behind, and the implications, of such thinking are clear enough and consistent with the way drill is considered as 'evidence' in British courtrooms. The second case concerns the 'Manchester 10', a group of ten teenagers who were presented as a brutal gang, who listened to drill and plotted revenge. They were all sentenced to a total of 131 years in prison[58] and charged not for *making*, but for merely *downloading* (= possessing?) drill music tracks or watching drill music videos as incriminating evidence of gang conspiracy.[59] Following a long campaign by Kids of Colour, a third-party legal intervention by the law reform and human rights charity JUSTICE and the defendants' criminal defence team, the conviction of Ade Adedeji was quashed by the Court of Appeal in January 2025, while also reducing the sentences of Raymond Savi and Omolade Okoya from eight years to four years and six months each.[60]

Other notable cases include *R v NHF [2022]* EWCA Crim 859, where the defendant's dancing in a drill music video was used at trial to show that he 'was a willing associate' of a gang. The defendant was convicted of being concerned involved in the supply of Class A drugs, as part of a 'county line' drug-dealing operation. He was aged 17 at the time of trial (16 at the time of arrest), autistic and had a history of abuse. He explained that his participation in the video was for fun, and that he had been unaware of the content of the lyrics at the time of filming. The Court of Appeal did not address concerns that the video was wrongly admitted, instead quashing the conviction because the jury had been misdirected on the modern slavery defence. In *R v Sode [2017]* EWCA Crim 705, the Court of Appeal had to determine the admissibility of a music video in which one appellant had allegedly made a gesture and remarks consistent with support for a gang.[61] The video had been made two years *before* the murder at issue, when the appellant was just 14 years old and the only direct evidence of the murder involving the gang was a hearsay statement of questionable reliability. Yet, the Court upheld the use of the music video as 'gang evidence' to help prove motive to participate in the joint enterprise murder. The Court did not consider that, even if the video had been interpreted correctly, references to gangs are common in rap (especially drill), or that non-gang affiliated young people participate in gang-themed music for a variety of reasons. The Court merely stated that the age of the video did not 'reduce its impact or diminish its relevance', with no explanation as to why this is the case. While these cases are hardly coincidental, given the 'vastly expanding' number of cases involving drill as evidence,[62] they nevertheless demonstrate how the law conspires in manufacturing suspects to be criminalised – raising critical questions that question the legitimacy, logic, tactics, purpose and function of an entire legal-penal system, when approached from the perspective of those who are at the receiving end of such carceral machinery.

'Bad character' evidence and joint enterprise

Beyond the largely unfounded accusations of 'gang-banging' culture explored above,[63] drill also finds itself (mis)treated, and certainly (mis)interpreted, as evidence of bad character – or as a justification for securing joint enterprise convictions.[64] Section 98 of the Criminal Justice Act 2003 defines bad character evidence as: 'evidence of, or of a *disposition* towards, misconduct' rather than evidence which 'has to do with the alleged facts of the offence with which the defendant is charged' (emphasis added). Based on such a definition, drill music material is therefore relied on as 'evidence' of the defendants' 'bad character', owing to stereotypical associations between rap and 'criminality' rather than based on incontrovertible evidence of wrongdoing.[65] Similar in logic, but somewhat different in inflection and style, joint enterprise is a legal doctrine that allows the court to show guilt by association between defendants. Given the broad scope of such legislation, it is possible to convict individuals of crimes without committing the criminal act they are charged with, or even being at the scene of the crime. To introduce such 'evidence' in court, prosecutors present such material in conjunction with witness statements that are produced by relevant 'experts' (usually police officers, 'gangs experts' and forensic linguists), who may also be instructed to give evidence in court.

The arguments that such cases are usually based on involve a matter-of-fact presentation of drill-related material – without adequately interrogating the artistic, literary or fictional nature of the 'evidence' that is brought before judges and jurors, even when its nature is acknowledged.[66] Prosecutors, and the 'experts' they appoint, find no contradiction in stating that rap is of course art, only to proceed by treating it as anything but art. Not unlike the garrulous gang discourse peddled by cops and prosecutors, joint enterprise has also sustained considerable critical attack for its disproportionate use to convict young Black people,[67] even after a 2016 Supreme Court ruling found that joint enterprise resulted in over-charging and over-convicting secondary suspects – or 'secondaries' as they are called in the carceral industry.[68] As such, it is hardly surprising to hear that: '[r]ap videos and lyrics are typically being admitted to build group prosecutions against Black children and young men, often tried under "joint enterprise" laws that enable "secondaries" (not suspected of having committed the substantive offence) to be tried for the same crime as the "principal" (the person suspected of the substantive offence).'[69] No case exemplifies such politics of 'penal excess'[70] better than the (ab)use of drill in court – in the well-publicised conviction of the Manchester 10 discussed in this chapter. This case became a cause célèbre, prompting a Manchester MP and former shadow culture secretary (Lucy Powell) to rail against such a verdict.[71]

In a more fictional vein, the folly of guilt by association that joint enterprise is based on is brilliantly captured in a short play by interdisciplinary artist Jay Bernard.[72] Bernard's critique of the racialisation in joint enterprise prosecutions, takes the form of a monologue about a young woman whose teenage friendship ties become 'evidence' of gang association; as an 'accomplice' who is treated as 'parasitic' and 'culturally complicit' to acts of violence she never committed.

Such phenomena are usually and mistakenly associated with the US, where things are supposed to always be worse. Alas, across the Atlantic the Restoring Artistic Protection Act was introduced in the US House of Representatives,[73] seeking to protect artists from the use of their music as legal evidence in criminal and civil cases – following similar legislative moves at the state level in New York and California. On the same day that that a New York Senate State bill became law, promising to get rap lyrics out of courtrooms,[74] in the hallowed turf of British jurisprudence the Manchester 10 appeared in Manchester Crown Court, facing charges that relied heavily on rap lyrics and videos.[75] Such practices continue unabated in Britain's courtrooms, unruffled by the scholarly, legal or public outcry against them.[76] An entire campaign (Art Not Evidence) exists, boasting a Who's Who of UK-based lawyers, academics, music industry professionals, youth workers and human rights organisations – all of whom support the campaign's draft legislation (Criminal Evidence (Creative and Artistic Expression) Bill) that limits the admissibility of evidence of a person's creative and artistic expression in criminal proceedings.[77]

Despite the support of Nadia Whittome MP, who plans to table this new legislation,[78] however, little progress has been made and whether other MPs will vote for it remains uncertain (if not unlikely). Regardless of the fate of this legal challenge, there are existing legal grounds for challenging the criminalisation of drill, but to my knowledge this is almost never done. Objecting to the use of drill-related material in court rests on the argument that the (ab)use of such 'evidence' may have an adverse effect on the fairness of the proceedings (citing Section 78, Police and Criminal Evidence Act 1984), owing to the insubstantial probative value of rap lyrics (citing Section 101, Criminal Justice Act 2003) and concerns about freedom of expression of rappers (citing Article 10 of the Human Rights Act). But such arguments are rarely made and rarely succeed. And so, rap on trial continues to thrive in Britain – as often as it is denied.

The CPS, for example, had no qualms about publicly stating that 'it was not aware of any cases where drill music had been wrongly used as evidence in the past',[79] on the same day that they heard ample evidence to the contrary, in a 'listening exercise' that was aimed at helping the CPS review its guidance on the use of drill as 'evidence'. In addition to representatives of law reform and human rights charities and youth workers, two esteemed academic colleagues and I were invited to contribute to two such listening exercises organised by the CPS on drill music, in January and April 2022. In addition to offering insights and evidence from our extensive research and experience as expert witnesses in cases that rely on drill lyrics and videos as 'evidence', we were also asked to comment on an embargoed version of the CPS' draft legal guidance on gangs, drill and social media, before the April 2022 meeting. As such, the announcement that the CPS is or was 'unaware' of the (mis)use of drill in criminal trials naturally sounds rather alarming. In the light of the above, it is also puzzling to see the same criminalising rhetoric in full force in a CPS article, published in June 2022, which insists on erroneously define drill music as: 'a type of hip-hop often featuring lyrics referring to drug dealing and street crime. A darker side of this genre can see lyrics linked to gang violence and threats to kill, which, if relevant to a case, may form part of the evidence.'[80] Leaving aside the obvious faux pas of conflating rap with hip-hop – when the former refers to rapping over an instrumental track while the latter refers to a broader music genre that can, but doesn't always, feature rap(ping) in it – the same criminalising logic that is criticised in this chapter, is also hard to miss.

Much of this can sound too legalistic or too academic to bear any relation to 'real life'. Yet it is real people whose very real lives are affected by it all, in the name of criminal 'justice'. To humanise what may otherwise seem too technical or too abstract, here's a fictional story that is fictional in form alone. It is otherwise a factual (re)presentation of the racist, state-sanctioned criminalisation of drill music. Imagine that you are a young (teenage) rapper who bears witness to, or is fascinated by, stories of gang feuds, post-code rivalries, 'criminal' lifestyles and violence, driven by a desire to write lyrics, make beats and shoot videos that explore such themes through the medium of rap – with the added bonus of a successful career in music if your creative output attracts enough followers and reaches a critical mass. You create an account on YouTube, upload your video and hope for the best. Meanwhile, dedicated teams of police officers trawl the web in search of 'gang-related music linked to serious violence' and find your video. Hearing you name an incident, a person and a place in hostile and confrontational ways – as is common in most rap music subgenres since 1990s gangsta rap – they add your music track to a gangs database on the grounds that you associate with known gang members – people with whom you might have family or friendship ties. The officers in question are now debating whether they should ask YouTube to remove your track and approach radio stations to forbid them to play your music. They are also toying with the idea of applying for a court order that would force you to inform the police 24 hours in advance of your intention to publish any videos online, while also demanding that you give them a 48-hour warning of the date and locations of any planned live performance. The more they brainstorm the more they like this idea and decide to also prevent you from associating with certain people, entering designated areas, wearing hoods, or using social media and unregistered mobile phones. If they go ahead with this decision and you don't comply, you are committing a serious offence.

Meanwhile, you become better known and more confident in your art and create more tunes reflecting life in your area. As is canonical in your genre, you shoot videos that feature more than three people, who display a logo of your newly created rap collective and do so in a back alley where that video was shot. The feds find that video, see it shared by others via social media and decide that it is enough to bring gang conspiracy charges against you and all the others in that video, given that what you describe fits the facts of a fatal incident they are investigating. The prosecution instructs the officers who collected such material to act as expert witnesses for them, by writing a report where they interpret your lyrics as literal testimony and testify against you in court. You are then charged with an offence and serve time in prison, as the jury has been swayed by the emotive nature of the drill 'evidence' that was presented to them by the Crown.

Needless to say, those who are summoned to the defendant's seat when drill music is on trial are those who don't need to imagine that fictional scenario. This is their reality. And this is what it is made of, should they choose – God forbid – to make beats and rhymes that blindfolded Lady Justice can only see as 'crimes' through the 'two festering sores that once perhaps were eyes', as Langston Hughes's famous poem; *Justice* reveals.[81] I nevertheless suspect that some will maintain that there *must be* something sinister about 'this' music and 'these' people to justify the illiberal and unjust methods by which drill music is racially criminalised. Trawling through pages and pages of legal penal mechanisms that would be regarded as unthinkable, unacceptable and intolerable – were they applied to any other music genre and any other group of people, some find all this entirely appropriate when it comes to rap(pers).

The long and disreputable history of policing against Black or Afro-diasporic music(s) that we have traced in the first three parts of this book should suffice as proof that this story has more to do with criminal injustice than 'Black criminality'. Indeed, it is a story of evidence that is no evidence, experts that are no experts and justice that is no justice. But this too seems too hard a truth to swallow. It is too much for too many. Writing against such barriers of denial(ism), well-intentioned or not, compels us to spend a little more time to pick up a few more controversies that recur like a roll call of frequently asked questions that never seems to end – even when there is more evidence of harm and injustice on this side of the bench, compared to the largely unfounded accusations that fill the prosecutors' table.[82] These stubborn accusations against drill in particular, and rap music in general, usually revolve around violence, misogyny and the gritty realism of the music's graphic imagery. They are taken up in turn – but only briefly – as a synthesis of the relevant scholarship on these questions can be found elsewhere.[83]

12

But isn't Rap violent and misogynistic?

Given the moody, dark and brooding sonic, lyrical and visual qualities of UK drill music, it is hardly surprising to see how charges of violence and misogyny accompany it. The music's haunting deepbass, punchy 808-generated beats[1] certainly sound harsh, raw and menacing and its provocative bars (lyrics) are unabashedly edgy and explicitly violent. Some drill music videos also taunt rivals in vividly shocking terms, describing the harm that awaits them and keeping a tally of stabbings in YouTube 'scoreboards' as a sign of each collective's transgressive capital.[2] This is the seamy underbelly of drill music that doesn't help those, like me, who defend it – without denying or condoning its more unsavoury qualities. Yet drill continued to be a music genre and an art form. And it is definitely not reliable, and I would add, admissible as 'evidence' of wrongdoing – isolated incidents notwithstanding.[3] Nor is this all that drill is, or what *all* drill is. It should therefore worry us that its more positive aspects are so overlooked. Artists like the Hope Dealers see drill music as a medium for expression, spirituality, faith and social change,[4] while journalist and youth worker Ciaran Thapar and journalist Dan Hancox,[5] among others, highlight the genre's potential to function as a culturally and socio-politically conscious youth (sub)culture that voices valid, yet neglected, concerns about the experience of social life in London's ill-mannered manors in the unadorned manner in which life is lived.[6]

No culture vulture or art critic has any trouble with granting poetic licence to artists who vent their anger and channel their aggression through catharsis. Indeed, they would applaud the purification of combustible emotions through creative expression.[7] This was certainly Aristotle's defence of catharsis in his *Poetics* as socially beneficial.[8] And while ancient Greek tragedians may not have populated scoreboards with killings, they could certainly be accused of glamorising or glorifying violence in artistic works that are revered as such to this day – unaccompanied by parental guidance warnings, bans and state suppression. Does anyone remember how Homer's *Iliad* sadistically depicts Achilles dragging Hector's corpse in the dust, having first pierced the tendons of his feet from heel to ankle? Has everyone forgotten Euripides' *Medea* who ruthlessly murders her husband Jason's new lover (Glauce) and her two sons as revenge for Jason's infidelity? These examples are literary and fictional, naysayers will quickly retort – incensed by the comparison that I so sacrilegiously attempt here. But rap is literary and fictional too and one doesn't have to like it to recognise that fact. Nor does anyone have to find it musically or lyrically compelling to defend it against the racist criminalisation that does so much violence *to* the music.

Rap lyrics are first-person narratives but they are not necessarily 'true threats', real-life descriptions or autobiographical confessions of crimes committed. They may be partly or purely performative, fictional, hyperbolic or fabricated even, as is the case with many other music lyrics or literary works. Rappers are not the actual, real-life *persons* that their stage(d) *personas* embody. Indeed, rappers' constructed personas who tell their story in the first person are no different from the narrators of a novel, but we don't conflate, confuse or mistake the author with the narrator. In Bret Easton Ellis's *American Psycho*, for example, Patrick Bateman (the narrator) who tells the story in the first person is not Bret Easton Ellis (the author). Although Ellis (the author) is well known for drawing on certain aspects of his own personal life in his fiction, nobody believes, or suspects, that Ellis actually committed the heinous crimes, the serial killings that take place in the novel. We call that fiction, even if it has elements that correspond to reality. This is where people usually get impatient and point to media coverage of court verdicts to prove that drill rappers do indeed 'live the life they rap about', as the cliché goes, and do indeed commit acts of fatal violence.

But here's the rub. A court verdict is simply evidence of a court procedure that has been successfully concluded. It is not evidence that someone is or isn't guilty, especially when the 'evidence' used against defendants is so rich in prejudicial value and so poor in evidential weight. A court verdict does not tell us how the prosecution's case was made; what evidence it was based on; whether such evidence is relevant, admissible and has sufficient weight to withstand scrutiny; whether such evidence has significant prejudicial impact but little probative/evidential value; what expert witnesses were relied on; what are they experts of/in, what their credentials/qualifications are; whether the success of such evidence depends on making an emotive case to the jury by portraying defendants in a negative light; or whether the law itself, expert witnesses for the defence and relevant academic research on 'rap on trial' challenge simplistic connections between drill music and violence. Irrespective of all this, though, drill rappers also consciously exploit stereotypes of violence, 'gangsterism' and 'ghetto life' as a sought-after commodity to be consumed online by followers whose clicks, views, likes and shares yield material rewards.[9]

Rather than offer a simple 'authentic' voice, rappers are highly attuned to the commercial potential of their work. They deploy themes of violence and crime that they know to be very marketable[10] and many aspiring rappers make drill music to become a successful and therefore escape the clutches of poverty, social isolation and exclusion. The conscious, if not cynical, manipulation of violence, therefore, serves commercial ends. But it is also an essential part of the genre's aesthetic and artistic conventions – not unlike the violence in gangster films, thrillers or zombie movies, to say nothing of martial arts films and Westerns too. It is therefore intriguing to see how easily we mistake what is literary and fictional for what is literal and factual and that we only seem to do so when it comes to a Black music genre.[11] If granting rap and ancient Greek epics the same artistic value is too difficult, if not impossible, let us turn to a scientific experiment that might persuade the recalcitrant in our midst.

In a landmark study, social psychologist Carrie Fried asked participants to read a set of violent lyrics from a 1960s country song (Kingston Trio's *Bad Man's Blunder*). One group was told that these are rap lyrics, while the other was told that these are country music lyrics. The lyrics were the same, but the participants' responses were not. People responded more negatively when the lyrics were represented as rap, demonstrating that the same lyrical passage that was viewed as acceptable in a country song was considered dangerous and offensive when identified as a rap music track. Fried emphasises an important racial dimension; whereas country music is traditionally associated with white performers, rap 'primes the negative culturally held stereotype of urban Blacks'.[12] Fried's experiment was replicated in 2016 and despite the passage of nearly two decades, researchers found the same reactions. Specifically, they reported that 'participants deemed the exact same lyrics to be more offensive, in greater need of regulation, and more literal when characterized as rap compared with country'.[13] Further research has also confirmed that people's views of rap music extend to the people who listen to, or create, it. A 2018 study, for example, considered how people would respond to the author of a piece when they were presented with lyrics they believed were rap, country, or heavy metal (the lyrics were the same for everyone). The results: '[I]t appears that those who write violent "rap" lyrics are more easily associated with crime and violence than those who write identical violent lyrics labeled as different genres'.[14]

Isn't it obvious now that rap pays the price for the hypocritical double standards we use to moralise against it? As Nielson and Dennis remind us '[r]ap is not the only art to trade in outlaw [...] narratives', nor is it 'the only art form to draw from real life for its creations'.[15] But it remains 'the only form of artistic expression to be mischaracterized as pure autobiography [or] real world documentary'.[16] Gone are the nuances that are necessary for understanding and appreciating rap, if we refuse to situate 'gangstas', 'thugs' and 'hustlas' as 'badman' archetypes that have a long pedigree in 'black vernacular folklore',[17] featuring outlaw legends like Stagolee (also Stacker Lee and Stagger Lee), MacDaddy, Smokey Joe, or Bad Lazarus – who fearlessly defy societal norms with casual bravado, like so many country music's sons of a gun.[18] It is also interesting to observe how such accusations disappear when we think of commercially successful rappers who also make references to firearms, drugs and violent gangs, but none of this means that they are actually 'gunmen', 'drug dealers' or 'gang members'. Mack 10 and Lil Uzi Vert routinely employ such language and adopt such personas – as does Stormzy, a leading UK rapper, who calls himself a WickedSkengman (meaning: wicked gunman/ knifeman). On *WickedSkengman 5*, Stormzy raps: 'Wait two secs let me spark this zoot [spliff] / My n*****z they don't talk, they shoot.' This reference to communicating through the gun rather than verbally, is clearly not to be taken literally. Instead, it suggests the slipperiness of rap verse in which rhymes mean the opposite of what they say (inversion).

Indeed, Stormzy has made his career precisely from *talking*, not *shooting*; winning Album of the Year at the 2018 Brit Awards and establishing a successful Cambridge University scholarship programme. He is therefore not the not the WickedSkengman that his rapped first-person narrative describes. He is using poetic licence to adopt a 'badman' persona to excite fans, following long-established genre norms. Such violent themes are commonplace in rap, as they are in other Black music genres too. Bo Diddley's *Who Do You Love*, is exemplary of such explosive hyperbole through imagery that has the song's protagonist walk forty-nine miles of barbwire and wear a cobra snake for a necktie – as evidence of his toughness. The same applies to what Angela Y. Davis calls the 'fearless, unadorned realism of the blues', which 'does not confine us to literal interpretations'.[19] Davis's example here is Bessie Smith's *Mistreatin' Daddy*, where the protagonist sings: 'I'm like a butcher right down the street. I can cut you all to pieces like I would a piece of meat.'[20] Much the same is also true of trickster narratives, of the kind we encountered in Part I of this book. Indeed, William Banfield argues that 'the trickster, the gangsta, the hood-wearing, crotch-grabbing, hustling, jive-talking, double-meaning, self-titled poet, the lover of women/men, the slick, stylish, ego-bearing, macho-minded figure known as the rapper might very well be our old friend Esu-Elegbara in disguise'.[21] Just like violent and aggressive content flows through seventeenth-century English folk music,[22] or opera librettos[23] – it also features in rap. And while it is true that competition has been 'at the heart of hip hop' since the late 1970s and early 1980s, it did much to 'help displace violence and the refuge of destructive drugs like heroin' and 'fostered an attitude of creating from limited materials. Sneakers became high fashion; original music was created from turntables, a mixer and obscure (highly secret) records; entertainment was provided with the kind of showoff street rap that almost any kid was capable of turning on a rival.'[24] Afrika Bambaataa's creation of the Universal Zulu Nation collective testifies to that. Bambaataa was initially the leader of the Black Spades gang but built his hip-hop outfit to dissipate violence. As Erik Nielson and Andrea Dennis point out: 'For Bambaataa and others, hip hop was an alternative to gang culture, one that drew on the inherent territoriality and competitiveness of gang life but offered a creative outlet instead. Hip-hop artists still battled one another, but their battles were metaphorical, fought with turntables, dance moves, and spray paint.'[25]

The same is true in the rap subgenre we know as drill. Besides, as David Toop writes:

> Music whether honky tonk country, hardcore, disco, rock 'n' roll, bubblegum pop or Stravinsky's *Rite of Spring*, has always been a catalyst, one stimulus among many that levers people's wild side over their inhibitions, helps them get crazy, inflames them to riot when they feel like rioting; it goes with getting drunk, having sex, destroying concert halls and driving cars too fast. Without the need for that side of music we would all be in rocking chairs listening to Bing Crosby.[26]

More importantly still, he adds: 'Music may be powerful and influential but no music is strong enough to create this kind of social decay. The raps are fictions, and whether these fictions have their basis in lived reality or overcharged imagination, the world they reflect is moving fast, out of control, too fast to have a mere rap record as a navigator.'[27]

Rather than 'literalise' the violence in rap therefore, we should contextualise it instead – with due regard for how 'each tradition, at least implicitly, contains within it an argument for how it can be read'.[28] We would never dream of taking canonical works of Western literature and art literally. And we would certainly not allow cops to act as arbiters of aesthetic or cultural judgement. Can you imagine a scenario where your favourite music genre, English murder ballads perhaps, becomes the subject of discussion in a Police and Crime Committee Meeting of the London Assembly?[29] Horrible though such a possibility sounds, it is already a reality as far as rap music is concerned. As I type these words into existence, I can almost hear the argument about sexism and misogyny bubble up and I am keen to take the bait. Let us return to that London Assembly meeting I just mentioned for a vivid illustration of the hypocritical double standards by which we judge rap. Referring to drill specifically, the then Met Deputy Commissioner (Sir Stephen House) stated that: 'a lot of it is misogynistic to be honest with you [...] And it may be a matter of opinion. Maybe we're more prudish than Radio 1 listeners, I don't know.' Drill is certainly misogynistic. This I can't deny or defend. But isn't it disturbing to hear a police chief be so selectively prim and proper when it comes to drill – but hardly so, when it comes to not just serving but heading a police force that was declared institutionally misogynistic?[30] I can't think of a more fitting example of the moralistic double-speak and double-think we often hear against rap music. Yet, pointing to and calling out such two-facedness does not deflect the accusation of misogyny in rap. It engages (with) it, by refusing to accept, justify, normalise and excuse it in one cultural tradition but criminalise and condemn it in another.

In pointing at imagery and lyrics that portray women in offensive, objectifying and derogatory ways, accusations of misogyny and sexism in rap come thick and fast. Such chilling representations of male domination over women, littered with nauseating references to 'bitches', 'hoes' (= whores) and 'pussy', obviously disparage women as sexual(ised) male property – in ways that bear all the hallmarks of sexist patriarchal violence. Reducing rap music to 'the violent, brutally sexist reality of a pack of wilding "little Willie Hortons"',[31] however, would be disingenuous, misleading and ill-advised. This echoes the voices of prominent Black feminist scholars like bell hooks,[32] Kimberlé Crenshaw,[33] Tricia Rose[34] and Imani Perry,[35] all of whom argue against prejudicial oversimplifications of the violence in, and complex gender and sexual politics of, rap. Decrying the criminalisation of rap music does not mean denying the existence of offensive and oppressive rap lyrics. Rather, it involves placing such lyrics into the context of a white mainstream culture whose prejudices disproportionately single out rap for its misogynistic content, without adequately interrogating the violence the racial, gender and sexual politics that are excused in more respectable forms of creative expression. As bell hooks notes, the 'sexist, misogynist, patriarchal ways of thinking and behaving that are glorified in gangsta rap are a reflection of the prevailing values in our society, values created and sustained by white supremacist capitalist patriarchy'.[36] References to 'hoes' abound in rap music, but representations of women as 'bad', promiscuous 'whores' who dishonour themselves by violating patriarchal idea(l)s of chastity and marital bondage, are also prevalent in the most revered and sacred repositories of mainstream Western culture.

Couched in variations of the 'Madonna–Whore Dichotomy',[37] the female body in the Western cultural canon is variously viewed as dangerous, unclean and a source of potential contamination in moralistic language that drips with sexualised violence against women. In Chapter 17 of the *Book of Revelation*, Babylon is symbolised as a 'great whore' who will eventually be made 'desolate and naked', her 'flesh' 'devoured' and 'burn[t] up with fire'. Sigmund Freud's[38] classic lectures on psychoanalysis depict women as anatomically inferior, envious and resentful; ostensibly suffering from penis envy. Cesare Lombroso's positivist criminology attributed physical and moral 'anomalies' to female offenders, describing prostitutes as a criminal category that possesses degenerative characteristics.[39] Ovid's *Metamorphoses* is rife with rape scenes, the most famous of which being the Greek myth of Europa's rape by Zeus – which is deemed so central a symbol of European culture as to name an entire continent (Europe) after it. Friedrich Nietzsche's *Thus Spoke Zarathustra* dutifully reminds readers: 'You are going to women? Do not forget the whip!'[40] And many more examples of violent misogyny could be plucked from the pantheon of Western culture. Yet, even when such texts are contextualised or criticised, they are hardly dismissed as sources of cultural pathology or outright misogyny. Instead, they feature as classic works of religious instruction, psychoanalytical scholarship, criminological history, literary appreciation and philosophical meditation.

As Tricia Rose puts it, '[t]he excessive blame levelled at hip hop is astonishing in its refusal to consider the culpability of the larger social and political context'.[41] This does not mean listening to the music by becoming blind to its misogynist narratives. It is to stress that rap should be seen 'as a reflection of dominant values in our culture rather than as an aberrant pathological standpoint'.[42] Indeed, admitting this 'does not mean that a rigorous feminist critique and interrogation of the sexist and misogyny expressed in this music is not needed'.[43] Rather, rethinking misogyny in rap in this way simply advises that it ought to be placed within the social, cultural, political and economic environment that shapes it – namely, 'white supremacist capitalist patriarchy' which 'approves' and 'materially rewards' rappers' tales of misogyny and sexism,[44] by packaging and promoting violence against women as a branded commercial spectacle to be consumed as entertainment. What is objected to, therefore, is the racist demonisation of rap without being sensitive to the 'cultural crossing, mixings, and engagement of black youth culture with the values, attitudes, and concerns of the white majority',[45] or attentive to how similar themes pass unnoticed in other forms of cultural expression that are granted poetic licence, despite the fact that they, too may 'labor in the plantations of misogyny and sexism'.[46] hooks, who features here as the lodestar for thinking about misogyny in rap, illustrates much of the above with reference to Jane Campion's art-house film *The Piano*. According to hooks, *The Piano* is praised as "an incredible film, a truly compelling love story' but '[n]o one speaking about this film mentions misogyny and sexism or white supremacist capitalist patriarchy'.[47]

Set in the 'nineteenth-century world of the white invasion of New Zealand', as hooks puts it,[48] *The Piano* tells the story of Ada who is sold into marriage and expresses herself solely through playing the piano – having not spoken since childhood. After being refused her piano by her husband (Alisdair), owing to lack of space in his patriarchal homestead, a neighbour (Baines) intervenes, trading the piano for some of Alisdair's land; allowing Ada to reunite with her most precious possession, in exchange for molesting Ada while she plays. When Baines realises that it is not sexual assault that Ada visits him for but her chance to play the piano, he returns the piano and forces himself on her; cursing their arrangement for making Ada a 'whore', and him 'wretched'. Ada nevertheless returns to Baines, where she is spied on by Alisdair, who 'unable to win her back [...] expresses his rage, rooted in misogyny and sexism, by physically attacking her and chopping off her finger with an ax'.[49]

Despite ample depictions of '[v]iolence against land, natives, and women', *The Piano's* high-art cinematography 'unlike [...] rap' is 'portrayed uncritically, as though [such imagery] is "natural" – the inevitable climax of conflicting passions'.[50] 'The outcome of this violence is all positive', hooks notes,[51] although the plotline 'betrays feminist visions of female actualization, celebrating and eroticizing male domination'. Such selectivity inevitably begs the question of why it is acceptable for 'folks involved with high culture' to 'celebrate and condone the ideas and values upheld in this film' but decry 'those who celebrate and condone [...] rap'.[52]

Blaming rap for the misogyny and sexism that passes unnoticed in highbrow art, therefore, makes attacks on rap vulnerable to accusations of double standards that falsely accuse rap and do violence to gender and sexual liberation too – in ways that compromise the integrity of critique when it castigates violence against women in *some* forms of creative expression, but not others. Casting rap out as inherently misogynistic, simply exonerates the dominant white, patriarchal, heteronormative social order that creates hierarchies of gender, race, class and sexuality. And in so doing it *racialises* gendered and sexual violence, speaking the language of racism to attack misogyny and sexism. Acknowledging racism as the perspective and the social location from which critiques on rap are mounted, is therefore essential for a sober appraisal of the stigmatisation that rap suffers. Even progressive socio-political movements like feminism (which I celebrate), or rather its 'white', bourgeois variant (which I don't), fail to recognise their complicity in the racist logic(s) that essentialise misogyny by disproportionately blaming it on Black forms of cultural expression. Charging white feminism with racism might sound unfair, but it is impossible to ignore a blind spot that chips away at the movement's integrity as a radical political force.

Just as our appreciation of rap music should not silence concerns about its misogyny, our commitment to feminist politics should not obscure the whiteness that sneaks into its worldview. Pretending that feminism doesn't construct itself by default as normatively and universally 'white', is to ignore and dismiss a rich Black feminist tradition that emerged as a response to feminist politics that assume that 'all the women are white' or that 'all the Blacks are men' as the title of a Black feminist classic has it.[53] As Audre Lorde observes, '[u]nchallenged, racism ultimately will be the death of the women's movement in England, just as it threatens to become the death of any women's movement in those developed countries where it is not addressed'.[54] Exaggerated though such a warning may sound, racism has nevertheless been endemic in white feminism, permeating foundational texts of the movement. Consider Mary Wollstonecraft's[55] *Vindication of the Rights of Woman*, which depicted enslaved Black women as showing an 'immoderate fondness for dress, for pleasure, and for sway', dismissing these as 'the passions of savages; the passions that occupy those uncivilised human beings who have not yet extended the dominion of mind'. Think also about how later modern classics like Shulamith Firestone's *The Dialectic of Sex* 'addres[s] black women's issues in a single chapter, and everywhere else in the book, "woman" – a universal and unmodified noun – does not mean *them*'.[56] Or think about how standard critiques of rape and sexualised male violence, like Susan Brownmiller's *Against our Will*, are 'so intent on pursuing the black-man-as rapist theme that [...] black women's sexual experience, static and reified [...] strike the reader as a rather perverse and exotic exercise'.[57]

These selective passages do not encompass the entire canon of white feminist literature, nor do they pretend to offer an overview of white feminism's racism. Rather, they are mentioned here as a confrontation with white feminist critiques of rap's misogyny that remain oblivious to their own racism. Were this not so, there would not be an entire tradition of Black women's thought that rejects the term 'feminism' to describe its gender politics; opting instead for the word 'womanism', as a word that 'encompasses "feminist" [...] but also means *instinctively* pro-woman' with 'blackness [being] implicit in the term'.[58] 'An advantage of using "womanist", Walker explains,[59] 'is that, because it is from my own culture, I needn't preface it with the word "Black" (an awkward necessity and a problem I have with the word "feminist"), since blackness is implicit in the term; just as for white women there is apparently no felt need to preface "feminist" with the word "white" since the word "feminist" is accepted as coming out of white women's culture'.[60] White feminism's reluctance to interrogate the ways in which its whiteness, as an invisibilised power relation, distorts its agenda for (all) women's liberation, is especially audible in the way it overlooks Black women's agency – including Black women rappers when misogyny in rap is discussed. In so doing, a long history of 'talkin' up to the white woman'[61] is ignored – as is the contribution of hip-hop feminism[62] by Black women rappers who 'wreck'[63] misogynistic representations of Black women within rap. While Black women rappers make room for a progressive feminist 'stage'[64] that openly challenges misogyny, white feminist critique assumes that 'images of Black women as sexually available hoochies'[65] are not sufficiently resisted by their non-white 'sisters'.

Another politics of, and hopefully *with*, rap is therefore possible. But we must refuse to racialise violence and misogyny in rap, as a pretext for criminalising it. Defending Jamaican dancehall culture against similar accusations of 'slackness' (= lewd sexuality),

Carolyn Cooper rightly cautions against dancehall's disparagement as a 'misogynist, homophobic, homicidal discourse', on the grounds that such reactions create a 'dehumanising caricature' that 'reduces both men and women to bare essentials: skeletal remains'.[66] 'Women', Cooper notes, 'are misrepresented as mindless bodies, (un)dressed and on display exclusively for male sexual pleasure' and 'men are stereotyped as dog-hearted predators stalking potential victims'.[67] Cooper celebrates Lady Saw as a performer who 'epitomises the sexual liberation of many African-Jamaican working-class women'.[68] Sometimes, as Jamaican dancehall star Spice says (in *Siddung*): 'mi just siddung and just a bubble and a shake mi batty'. We should perhaps do the same with reference to rappers that queer drill. Shaybo and Ivorian Doll quickly come to mind as popular drill rappers who, like Lady Saw, 'cu[t] loose from the burdens of moral guardianship' and respectability politics.[69] Darkoo, a gender-fluid driller, could also be added to the list for their contribution to opposing and rejecting the heteronormative dictates of rap and patriarchal culture more broadly. Their performance in the chart-topping hit *Body (Remix)* testifies to that, as does the music of Mista Strange whose bars depict life 'on road'[70] but not without celebrating his sexuality as an openly gay rapper.[71]

Racialising misogyny inevitably imposes whiteness as a form of civilising (= colonising) discipline. Racialising violence and 'criminality' does much the same. Both must be abandoned if we are to escape depictions of an entire genre that is (mis)identified as 'the most murderous' element in 'urban civilisations' and imagined as 'the very voice of violence' which leads to the 'brutalisation of the individual' as Cambridge don George Steiner believed.[72] And we must also give up that other bizarre argument I keep on hearing about criminalising other art forms to balance the scales of justice. The point is not to criminalise more art forms, but to protect criminalised music genres from the criminal injustice they endure, resist and transcend. And this cannot be done without calling racism, racism – especially when it is screaming at us. There is nothing calm, sensible, professional, objective, honourable or factual in refusing to mention racism by name or resorting to euphemisms for it: e.g. 'race-related'; 'racially charged'; 'racial'; 'racist' (but only within quotation marks); 'prejudiced'; 'bigoted'; 'controversial'; 'inflammatory' – 'divisive'; 'widely called racist'. Such elaborate hedging gives off the air of nuance and calm, while effectively casting doubt on whether racism exists: prioritising tone over the truth.[73]

Racism aside, however, there is no other explanation for why rap becomes police property. And the fiction that it is violence in rap that justifies how and why it is policed cannot be sustained for much longer, especially if you have read Parts I and II of this book. Nineteenth-century Afro-diasporic musics, calypso, reggae and rap have *all* been policed in very similar ways and what this points to is racist injustice, not 'Black criminality'. Were this not so, we would not be able to compare the suppression of calypso and drill. If it is 'criminality' that is policed when drill is policed, why was calypso policed in strikingly similar ways? What exactly was 'criminal' about calypso in 1930s Trinidad, other than its critique of British colonial rule? If the policing logics and tactics that target joyful and upbeat calypso and drill are essentially the same, then that tells us more about racist *police* violence than it does about violence in Black popular culture(s).

Go back to Part I of this book, read how calypso was banned a century ago and then read how drill is policed today. Spot the difference, or simply compare the following lyrics:

'Imagine our records being banned from entering in our native land.	'They took my videos down, said it's too violent
	I can't do a show, it's getting stopped by Trident
I think they're ungenerous to attempt to take our music from us	It's slowing down my income, they're tryna ban drill'
I think they're ungenerous to attempt to take our music from us'	

You might recognise the lyrics on the left from Chapter 3, as Attila the Hun's *Banning of Records* (recorded in 1938). How different is the reality they describe from Krept & Konan's *Ban Drill* (recorded in 2019)? As you mull over this question, remember that I am essentially asking you to think *about* policing, racism and police racism *with* and *through* Black music(s). And that is exactly what Part IV does too, by (re)introducing Black music(s) both as a *mode* of knowledge (knowing differently, with Black music) and a *source* of knowledge (learning about racist police violence, from Black music).

PART IV

Sounds radical: Black critique(s) of White reason

> If the history of the past is written in the same fashion, it is useless as science and misleading as ethics. It simply shows that with sufficient general agreement and determination among the dominant classes, the truth of history may utterly be distorted and contradicted and changed to any convenient fairy tale that the master of men wish'
> – W.E.B. Du Bois, *Black Reconstruction in America*[1]

To suggest that the musical traditions of the African diaspora sound out a vibrating keynote that radically changes our thinking about thinking risks sounding fanciful to the white scholarly mainstream. To argue that *only* through them and the scholarship they have inspired can we hope to understand how and why they are policed must surely seem hyperbolic. This section nevertheless strings together the fanciful and the hyperbolic to tell a story about how we can know *with* Black music: as an instrument of knowledge production that also educates us about the social world around us in radically transformative ways, through the policing that the state reserves for it. Music is therefore approached here not solely as a purely sonic, but also as an intellectual force that draws sustenance from its cultural roots to blossom into political visions that offer a counterpoint to Eurocentric (onto-epistemic) traditions of being and knowing. Opposing, resisting and rejecting hyper-rational(istic), techno-bureaucratic and corporate Western-liberal mode(l)s of intellectual and political life, Black music attunes us to logics, ethics and politics that un-police our 'racist white imagination'[2] one beat at a time. The reference to *Black* music(s) rather than music(s) in general, therefore, is intentional.

This is not to argue that it is the only music worth listening to or thinking with, but to stress that *only* Black musics have *all* the active ingredients for the intellectual and cultural politics I have in mind here. What sets the musical traditions of the African diaspora apart are the unique and specific aesthetics, ethics and politics of their sound. A sound that Black music practices produce and create through a common, though varied, musical vocabulary. Key characteristics include: an emphasis on rhythm (beats), rhythmic speech (rhymes) and the interaction between musicians and audiences (call and response) – in ways that make the production and consumption of the music feel participatory; an invitation to public, associational life that is rarely offered by Western-European music-making traditions. It should be noted that none of this intends to draw neat boundaries, in order to establish easy distinctions between Afro-diasporic and Western-European habits of music performance or 'soundscape norms'.[3] Rather, the aim here is to identify aesthetic conventions within Black music that are more open, embodied, lived, sensuous and participatory: *heady* rather than (merely) *intellectual* compared to their European counterparts. Such a distinction is also necessary, because references to music otherwise risk universalising Eurocentric canons of music-making.[4]

In contrast to Western criteria of music-making, Afro-diasporic music 'speaks in rhythms that dance'; as a 'collective' and 'communal' art form[5] that 'demand[s] a physical response' through the 'patting of the feet', 'drumming of fingers', 'nodding of the head in time with the beat'[6] – as a 'fleshly endeavor' that makes the 'body articulate'[7] in ways that transcend rational, Cartesian dualisms that mute the body's role in communicating meaning in favour of the mind.[8] Add to that the dimension of 'Afrocentric oral culture' where 'boundaries distinguishing singer from audience, call from response, and thought from action' are 'fluid and permeable'[9] and 'the kinetic orality, emotional physicality, rhythmic syncopation, the protean improvisation, and [...] antiphonal elements'[10] of Black/Afro-diasporic music(s) become audible. This is not to impose essentialist distinctions by arguing that 'emotion is Negro, just like reason is Hellenic' (*L'émotion est nègre, comme la raison est héllène*, author's translation) – as Léopold Senghor so controversially put it.[11] What is argued instead is that the embodied, sensuous and participatory character of Afro-diasporic music is a body of thought, an intellectual tradition and a source of ideas that remains unappreciated as such. Black music is therefore understood here as a unique sonic epistemology that is Black in its 'expressivity, its musicality, its orality, in its rich, deep, and varied attention to speech, in its inflections toward the vernacular and the local, in its rich production of counternarratives, and above all, in its metaphorical use of the musical vocabulary'.[12] It is diasporic, (poly)rhythmic, embodied, non-visual, participatory, radical and de/anti-colonial: aesthetically, intellectually, culturally and politically too. Black/Afro-diasporic music is of course much more than that (i.e. spiritual, metaphysical, life-affirming, healing) and often combines many, if not all, the characteristics listed here.

Limiting our discussion to just those elements of Black/Afro-diasporic music(s), therefore, is evidence of the limitations of this part of the book – not the music itself. Split into two main sections, Part IV argues for a view of Black music(s) as a *mode*, medium, instrument of knowledge and a *source* of knowledge too.

While Chapter 13 makes a case for looking at Black music(s) as a knowledge-making practice, Chapter 14 argues that the policing of Black music(s) furnishes unique and radical insights into racism and criminal injustice that are otherwise unavailable in white, mainstream social science. Chapter 13 therefore focuses on the music itself, while Chapter 14 draws on its policing as a repository of knowledge about the ideologies and politics that make such policing possible. The stage is now set and all that is left for us to do, is listen to how Black sound can change our mind(s) by enriching our scholarly and political ear-magination.

13

Who feels it, knows it: Black radical thought in sound

Approached as (i) diasporic, (ii) (poly)rhythmic, (iii) embodied, (iv) non-visual, (v) participatory, (vi) radical and (vii) de/anti-colonial thought in sound, Black/Afro-diasporic music features here as an intellectual craftscape that encourages us to think differently about thinking itself – as an interlinked, publicly oriented, bodily and critical endeavour that redefines how knowledge can be made and made possible, without, away and against the tutelage of Euro-modern and Euro-postmodern thought. Drawing on the seven aforementioned characteristics that Black/Afro-diasporic music is thought through here, they are explored one by one to explain what each means – while encouraging readers to make connections between them. Instead of parcelling them out into different subsections or listing them separately, they are all brought together and embedded in the narrative so they can speak to each other while we listen carefully to what they mean and have to say.

Not unlike 'Black(ness)', the term diasporic/Afro-diasporic is employed here to denote and describe forms of 'black vernacular culture' that are 'intercultural and transnational'[1] – that is to say ways and 'modes of thinking, being, and seeing' that are neither 'racially particularistic', or 'nationalistic', but 'diasporic or hemispheric, sometime global and occasionally universalist'.[2] Rooted in what Paul Gilroy has termed 'the Black Atlantic',[3] Afrodiasporic culture is approached here as a (pan)African 'diaspora interculture'[4] that is fluid: geographically and culturally. This conception of Afro-diasporic culture focuses not on firmly fixed African cultural origin(s) (or *roots*), but on the flowing movement (or *routes*) of African traditions across and around the world – as a result of the Transatlantic slave trade.[5] References to 'Afro-diasporic' blackness or 'Black' music, culture(s) and politics throughout this chapter are therefore limited to the strict Afrodiasporic sense and meaning of the word 'Black' – to refer to the people and cultures of the African diaspora.[6] This is not to strip the term of its coalitional potential, by including other visible minority ethnic communities who are also oppressed by racism, but to stress the specific usage adopted here. Such usage is nourished by Stuart Hall's powerful thinking about the 'Black' in Black popular culture,[7] but it is also inspired by the work of Sonjah Stanley Niaah on Jamaican dancehall[8] and Hortense Spillers' richly evocative meditations on diaspora, blackness and diasporic blackness.[9] Such thinking invites us to understand Afro-diasporic blackness as a *political culture*, rather than a set of biological, anthropological or demographic traits. As Spillers brilliantly put it, 'blackness' should be likened to 'a *process*, a *strategy*, of culture critique, rather than a condition of physiognomy'.[10] The legendary Kumina Queen (Imogene 'Queenie' Kennedy), who was a contemporary priestess of *kumina* rituals in post-colonial Jamaica, summarises much of the above in this wonderful quote – cited in the opening pages of E.K. Brathwaite's *The Arrivants*:

> Well, muh ol' arrivance ... is from Africa. ... That's muh ol' arrivants family. Muh gran'muddah an' muh gran'fadda. Well, they came out here as slavely ... you unnerstan'?

Well, when them came now, I doan belongs to Africa, I belongs to Jamaica. I born here.

Well, muh gran' parents, she teach me some of the African languages an' the rest I get it at the cotton -tree root ... I take twenty-one days to get all the balance ...'

So I just travel right up to hey, an' gradually come up, an' gradually come up, until I experience all about ... the African set-up...[11]

The 'Blackness' of Black music therefore envisaged here as 'the African set-up' that Kumina Queen refers to, is also what Toni Cade Bambara calls[12] 'a diasporic hookup';[13] a 'relational network' and 'a social ecology of identification'[14] that draws its Blackness from its African-diasporic connections. It is not therefore African *in origin* alone but *in dialogue* with the places where 'Africa is alive and well in the diaspora', as Stuart Hall so brilliantly put it.[15] The plurality of Afro-diasporic Blackness is also echoed in the (poly) rhythmic nature of Black/Afro-diasporic music(s). It is a 'dialectically polyrhythmic',[16] 'percussive culture'[17] where 'rhythms' act as 'vibrating waves of information'[18] that build worldviews whose ideas are communicated through the drum as a 'cultural medi[um] of communication': a 'drum script' that is the 'African equivalent of the alphabetical script'.[19]

We have already highlighted the importance of the drum as both an instrument of rebellion by the colonised and a source of fear by the colonisers in Part I of this book, but its beat goes on as an embodied presence in the music(s) and the culture(s) of the African diaspora. The African (poly)rhythm is lived through the body and the body becomes a thinking organ. It isn't just that the body is 'differently figured in' Black music(s) as the 'life of the organs'.[20] It also encourages a different consciousness, or way of knowing and being in the world: something that we are '*with*'[21] – as the etymology of the word consciousness itself reveals (*con* = with, *scio* = know). Thought therefore becomes 'theorized as [a] bodily phenomen[on]' that is not just embodied but *danced* too, as a form of 'corporeal intelligence',[22] or a 'visualized text' that demands 'a total integration of the mind, body and spirit' – as Halifu Osumare, choreographer and dancer put it in an conversation with Ntozake Shange.[23] Rather than mere expressivity, embodiment through dance becomes understood as a form of thinking *with(in)* the body. As Sylvia Wynter explains: '[t]he dance is central to the epistemology of non-industrial African cultures of origin. The dance communicated above all a mode of social knowledge which could be gained only through praxis, dancing. No one could dance by proxy'.[24] Dancing 'in African life' then, becomes as a practice that 'define[s] reality'.[25] Indeed, Edward Kamau Brathwaite goes as far as describing dance as 'African architecture', that is '*immanent*' and 'carried within the individual/community, not (as in Europe) existentially externalized in building monuments, books, 'the artifacts of civilisation'.[26] This points to ways of making and experiencing thinking and knowledge that come from the body and the senses that are also aural and oral, rather than strictly visual. As Saidiya Hartman argues: 'In Western philosophy, knowledge has been conceived of primarily as an ocular function.[27] To know is to see and to see is the inception of thought. The mind has been described as an inner eye and knowledge as a series of visual perceptions or pictures. Sight is the sense elevated above all others in apprehending the world.'[28]

But writing and reading are not the only 'intellectual technolog[ies]' that exist.[29] Black music(s) offer non-visual alternatives that allow us to 'hear the whole world in a bent note',[30] provided that we learn how to 'look with [our] ears' (Shakespeare, *King Lear*, Act 4, Scene 6). As Edward Kamau Brathwaite notes: 'Reading is an isolated, individualistic expression. The oral tradition on the other hand demands not only the griot[31] but the audience to complete the community: the noise and sounds that the maker makes are responded to by the audience and are returned to him.'[32]

This is what is often referred to as 'orature' which involves not just 'the fusion of all art forms', but also proposes a 'conception of reality' as 'a total view of life'; 'a capsule of feeling, thinking, imagination, taste and hearing. It is the flow of a creative spirit [and] a weapon against the encroaching atomisation of community.'[33] Moving with the body beyond rationalistic and visual conceptions of thinking, knowing and being in the world, also highlights the participatory ethos of Afro-diasporic culture(s) where 'knowledge through participation in experience [...] was central.'[34] This reminds us of 'the meaning of theory in [ancient] Greece' where the word 'theory', according to Wynter who cites Habermas, 'has religious origins'. Indeed, the '*theoros* was the representative sent by Greek cities to public celebrations. Through *theoria*, that is, through looking on, he abandoned himself to the sacred events.'[35] Black musical orature then embodies and is embodied as a diasporic, (poly)rhythmic, non-visual and participatory 'collective art', whose 'spiritual qualities are shared and experienced by all'.[36]

The alternative, empowering and liberatory conceptions of intellectual, cultural and political life that Afro-diasporic music(s) point to, therefore, come to be understood as a radical departure from Euro-modern norms. They 'instigate a great revolution of ideas', as Cuban novelist and musicologist Alejo Carpentier would argue about Afro-Cuban *son*.[37] As a sound that is composed of ideas where the ideas are (in) the music, the music of the African diaspora is not just intellectual – but *radically* so. Instead of approaching Black music as 'intellectual' only when it crosses the threshold of the ivory tower, the printing press, the literary salon or the broadcasting house, what is encouraged here instead is an understanding of Black music as a form of intellectual activity that can and does happen elsewhere.[38] Rather than institutionalising, valorising and taming Black music(s) within the white cultural mainstream, what is suggested here is that we look elsewhere for such activity and in different forms, formats and modes too. Reggae soundsystems, hip-hop ciphers, jazz jam sessions, batucada drumming practice, or playing the irons in a steel band: all involve finding out ways of thinking, making and doing and all of these are sources and instruments of thinking, knowledge and public life too. It's just that the white cultural mainstream lacks the conceptual language and imagination to think of them in this way. What makes Black music a form of radical thought in sound, therefore, is the radical alternative it embodies against the dominant white intellectual imagination. It is rooted in and develops instead from the culture of the African diaspora(s).

This forces us to contend with both meanings of the word 'radical', which combine that which is groundbreaking and that which springs from the ground, the soil, the roots (*radix, radic* = root). Seen this way, Black music doesn't just counter the cultural hegemony of whiteness through its own aesthetic criteria; as a 'counterpoetics'.[39] It also subverts its dominance as a 'sonic critiqu[e] of colonialism, racism, structural inequalities, and other forms of violence'[40] that the politics of whiteness sets loose. The radicalism of the music and its intellect, therefore, are rooted in (the) culture. It is what Rasta intellectuals and roots reggae heads call 'rootikal', to refer to the rootedness of the music in a (pan)African, diasporic worldview. Black/Afro-diasporic music therefore matters as a radical intellectual tradition in ways that blend culture and politics together. What makes Black music *culturally radical* is its dissonant relationship to Eurocentric standards of creative, artistic expression (see Part I of this book). What makes it *politically radical* is its presence as a sonic signifier of 'difference' – a source of unwanted and unwelcome 'noise' that distorts the harmony of the white body politic (see Parts II and III of this book). Even if Black music were entirely devoid of any aesthetic or political message and meaning, the policing it endures automatically renders it political: as a threat to the interests, integrity and homogeneity of the white liberal order.[41] As Eric Hobsbawm wrote about jazz,[42] in his capacity as the *New Stateman's* jazz critic,[43] '[t]he mere fact that it originates among oppressed and unconsidered people, and is looked down upon by orthodox society, can make the simple listening to jazz records into a gesture of social dissent'. This becomes even more true when the music's politics take place in the urban space. As Robin Kelley puts it:

> [T]he movement of young blacks, their music and expressive styles have literally become weapons in a battle over the right to occupy public space. Frequently employing high-decibel car stereos and boom boxes, they 'pump up the volume' not only for their own listening pleasure but also as part of an indirect, ad hoc war of position to take back public space. The 'noise' constitutes a form of cultural resistance that should not be ignored especially when we add those resistive lyrics about destroying the state or retaliating against the police.[44]

As a musical idiom that dares to do so audibly/noisily and visibly/publicly too, Black music becomes a 'living newspaper',[45] or a 'Black [...] CNN'[46] that reports and comments on social life lived under the shadow of racism. Calypsonian/*kaisonian* Mighty Duke describes it as 'an editorial in song of the life we undergo'[47] – conversing with Ice Cube's imagery of rappers as 'underground street reporters',[48] or as the 'young Black griots of the present'.[49] Beyond its capacity to 'convey social realism' as a 'street ethnography of racist institutions',[50] however, Black music's aesthetic and political radicalism also resonates as a powerful medium of de/anti-colonial critique, holding up a mirror to colonially derived racist ideology that sees (idea/*idein* = to see), rationalises (*logos* = reason) and criminalises 'blackness'; as a menacing public presence that connotes danger and inspires fear – as a symbol of cultural 'alienness' that needs to be kept in check, under surveillance, at bay.

Digging deep into its cultural roots to produce radical intellectual political visions for navigating and transforming social life, Black/Afro-diasporic music is de/anti-colonial[51] – for the same reasons that it is radical. It *r*eorients and '*de*-occident[s]'[52] our thinking, by 'allow[ing] the black tradition to speak for itself about its nature and various functions, rather than to read it, or analyze it, in terms of literary theories borrowed whole from other traditions, appropriated from without'.[53] James Baldwin claims that '[t]his is exactly how the music of jazz began, and out of the same necessity: not only to redeem a history unwritten and despised, but to *checkmate the European notion of the world*' (emphasis added).[54] This is also what Patricia Hill Collins described as a process of '[e]mpowerment' which 'involves rejecting the dimensions of knowledge, whether personal, cultural or institutional, that perpetuate objectification and dehumanization'.[55] By training our ears to look where whiteness averts its gaze in disgust, we are Traneing ourselves to step out of the mainstream where liberal En-whitenment thought splashes about. The word 'Traneing' itself comes from a common play on words that John Coltrane devotees indulge in, taking a part of Coltrane's last name (Trane) to pay tribute to the way that his music taught many of to give our imagination free reign.[56] Critical Race Theory stalwart Mari Matsuda, also engages in 'Traneing' by suggesting that: 'Just as John Coltrane could "trane" standard melodies into sounds so unique that no mainstream musician could ever appropriate, radical lawyers hope to transform standard constitutionalism into something [of] their own that no mainstream attorney can exploit.'[57]

Instead of training our minds to conform, nod and go along with the world as it currently is – Traneing teaches us to listen to and think with Black/Afro-diasporic music(s) to resist, oppose and reject the mode(l)s of Western-liberal scholarship and politics we work with(in) – especially in globally dominant, neoliberal Western academia. It is no accident that John Coltrane himself approached music as 'an instrument' that can 'create the initial thought patterns that can change the thinking of the people'.[58] Knowing what we now know about Black/Afro-diasporic music as a sonic epistemology, or 'acoustemology'[59] that helps us know through, think with[60] and even 'live in music',[61] we turn to Black/Afro-diasporic music as a (re)source for thinking (about) the social world around us. In so doing, Black-music-as-knowledge casts a shadow over our socio-cultural and political reality, while also shining a spotlight on the forms of injustice it continues to be met with: intellectually, epistem(olog)ically, socio-culturally and politically alike. In addition to pointing out that such forms and modes of knowing are relegated to the nether ends of academia, I also want to discuss how their policing opens our minds to truths that are otherwise silenced. Frederick Douglass expresses this so movingly, in a passage from his *Narrative* that we encountered in Chapter 4 but feel compelled to revisit here. Douglass writes: 'I have sometimes thought that the mere hearing of those songs would do more to impress some minds with the horrible character of slavery, than the readings of whole volumes of philosophy on the subject could do.'[62]

What may facilely be dismissed as a mere personal observation of little or no scholarly value seems to me to be the exact opposite. Douglass's words are read here as an invitation to make space for Black music, as a counterpoint to habits of thought that refuse to treat it as a source of knowledge that is equivalent to burying our noses in libraries and datasets. Were this not so, a discography would have the same value as a bibliography and sonic resources could replace written sources listed in alphabetical order. Were this not so, we could write a chapter on thinking *with* Black music as radical thought in sound, without the need to cite this or that seminal text. Were this not so, there would be no need to explain why or how Black music can and should be thought of as a source of knowledge and method of knowledge production. Does the need to make a case for such an argument not suggest that we're not quite there yet, if we ever want(ed) to be? Could we seriously claim that instead of writing pages and pages of academic prose we could simply point to a tune that would communicate just as much in just a few minutes? Chapter 15 does that, as an annotated playlist to listen to and think this book with, but we still have unfinished business. Before we attune ourselves to what the music itself can teach us about racism and criminal injustice, academic protocol dictates that more words should be poured on the page to explain what we can learn from the policing of Black music(s) about the ideological, political and cultural forces that turn Black music-making into law-breaking.

14

Who knows it, feels it: Learning about criminal injustice from the policing of Black music(s)

Not unlike Black/Afro-diasporic music(s), the rich reservoir of (folk) wisdom in Afro-diasporic oral culture serves as a reliable guide for making sense of the social world. One saying in particular, strikes me as directly relevant to the issues that this chapter raises – namely, the racial injustice that colonial imperialism and its violent afterlife metes out to its arche/proto/stereo/typical targets: Black people. How does it go? 'Duppy [ghost] know who fi frighten, an' who fi tell good night.' Generally understood to mean that bullies can distinguish between those they can and should intimidate and those who are better left alone, this Jamaican proverb neatly encapsulates how the law means justice, but only for some.[1] Obvious though this is, it is rarely the point of departure for making sense of what the legal penal system is and does. Assuming that the law is by definition fair and neutral to all, when it is seen this way – the injustices it (re)produces are not seen.[2] The remainder of this chapter aims at educating us out of such a mythological conception of 'the law', reintroducing it instead as a form of legal warfare (lawfare) against those who are racially and otherwise criminalised by it. In so doing, this chapter openly challenges legal scholars and criminologists to commit to a radical rethinking of what the state and 'the law' *are* and *do*, who *to* and who *for* – thereby questioning the very legitimacy of 'the law' and liberal state politics too, when democratic states use the rule of law to exercise undemocratic power through law.[3] The law, 'crime', policing and racism are therefore seen here as the blood relatives that they are – instead of the perfect strangers that they are often (mis)taken for. Such idea(l)s are therefore picked up in turn, but only to be swept away as deceitful myths that uphold liberal philosophies of state and law that leave a lot to be desired and struggled for – or rather against.

Starting with the law, it is approached here from the standpoint of those who are victimised by it, as an 'instrument of social control but also a symbolic expression of dominant society',[4] that 'preserve[s] the status quo and only periodically and unpredictably serv[es] as a refuge of oppressed people'.[5] Literary critics, folklorists and Marxist historians often (re)cite such critiques of 'the law' as evidence of class injustice. These range from Anatole France's famous quip about 'the majestic equality of the laws, which forbid rich and poor alike to sleep under the bridges, to beg in the streets, and to steal their bread',[6] to Shakespeare's description of how '[p]oor men's [*sic*] sins are much more noticeable than rich men's', adding that '[c]over[ing] up a crime with gold [...] the arm of justice can't touch it. But dress the crime in rags and it's caught easily' (*King Lear*, Act 4, Scene 6). Such references to legalised injustice also include the anonymous quatrain that reminds us how 'the law locks up the man or woman who steals the goose from the common, but lets the greater villain loose, who steals the common from the goose', mirroring English communist Jerrard (Gerrard) Winstanley's[7] observation that: '[t]he Law is the fox, poore men are the geeffe [geese]; he pulls off their feathers, and feeds upon them'. All this is true. But it is only half the story if class is uncoupled from 'race', or if English law is not traced back to its colonial

origins.[8] Part I of this book has given us a glimpse of that by looking at legislation that criminalised the music(s) of the enslaved. But
it is worth reminding ourselves that imperial-colonial slavery was
perfectly legal.

In addition to slave codes, police regulations and legislation that
administered the social, cultural and political life of Britain's colonial plantocratic system, music-making included, the slave trade
was also governed by Navigation Acts and treaties such as the
Treaty of Utrecht which granted Britain the *asiento* (licence/treaty,
contract) to conduct the trading of human beings as commodified
cargo to be sold, owned and exploited as 'units of labor power'.[9]
This is not to separate class from 'race', but to bring them together,
recognising that 'class relations' also 'function as race relations'
where '[r]ace is [...] also the modality in which class is "lived",
the medium through which class relations are experienced'.[10] Such
an approach also recognises that Black working-class people have
historically been more heavily criminalised than their white counterparts. Besides, the very foundations of capitalism as an economic
and political system, which brought class and 'race' into being
as classifications of humanity, are imperial-colonial in origins –
which is why capitalism should (always) be approached as racial.[11]
Recognising that the ideological and political origins of the law are
to be found in its use(s) as an artefact of imperial-colonial rule alerts
us to the role the law played in institutionalising racial slavery and
class oppression, while also laying the groundwork for racial and
class inequality.

Thinking about the law as a source of injustice also encourages
us to reinterpret democratic rule of law as a fiction that disguises its
function as authoritarian rule through law. In so doing, we begin
to question who and what the law singles out for discipline, regulation, punishment and control: namely 'crime' and 'criminals'.

Previous chapters have already offered a critical discussion of how 'crime' is made in, by and through law as the *result* of law-making rather than its *subject*.[12] We nevertheless return to such a critique to highlight how the fear-inducing effects the word 'crime' stirs in us allow it to function as a fig leaf that apportions blame to people and *their* psychology rather than the social environment people are exposed to and shaped by. Part III also attacked such responsibilising narratives that individualise and pathologise problems that are experienced socially and made politically in, by and through law. We nevertheless raise this question again, to remind ourselves that 'crime' is the outcome of processes of criminalisation that turn activities into legally punishable offences and people, whose very 'existence' is 'apprehended as [a] crime'.[13] Careful readers of this book will remember Aimé Césaire's withering attack in Chapter 4, on the 'the dupe in good faith of a collective hypoc-risy that cleverly misrepresents problems, the better to legitimize the hateful solutions provided for them'.[14] Césaire's wise words, however, bear repetition as they illustrate how effective the state and the law are in hiding the operations that are necessary to their survival behind ideological fictions that cover their tracks. Lest I am suspected of indoctrinating readers in anarchist or abolitionist politics, consider how much of what I say here is *not* true – when approached with the knowledge gained by reading the previous chapters of this book. How else could we make sense of the state or the law, colonial and post-colonial alike, other than through the way it was designed, rationalised and used as a tool that tightens the grip of state power over anything and anyone that poses a threat to its self-identity and self-interests; ideologically, culturally and politically? If this is not true, why would Black/Afro-diasporic musics be policed in the way they have been for centuries? Much of what is sensationalised as 'crime' in the law books, media headlines and mainstream criminology textbooks, are simply the forms of institutionalised state violence that remain hidden – educated and socialised as we are to mistake (superficial visible) symptoms for (deeper, structural) causes. The history of 'crime' on European soil is revealing here. Think about how impossible it is to think of social, cultural and political life without 'crime', as the enemy the state sets up before the eyes of the people to rationalise and legitimise the reasons why we must sacrifice freedom(s) for more security provided by the state and its legal penal institutions.[15] Michel Foucault, who was neither an anarchist nor an abolitionist, argues that:

> At the end of the eighteenth century, people dreamed of a society without crime. And then the dream evaporated. Crime was too useful for them to dream of anything as crazy – or ultimately as dangerous – as a society without crime. No crime means no police. What makes the presence and control of the police tolerable for the population, if not fear of the criminal? This institution of the police, which is so recent and so oppressive, is only justified by that fear. If we accept the presence in our midst of these uniformed men, who have the exclusive right to carry arms, who demand our papers, who come and prowl on our doorsteps, how would any of this be possible if there were no criminals? And if there weren't articles every day in the newspapers telling us how numerous and dangerous our criminals are?[16]

Such a view of 'crime', as a smokescreen that prevents us from seeing the violence it obscures, compels us to recognise and literally rethink (re-*cognise*) how and why we need to focus more on environmental conditions rather than physiological or cultural distinctions in our attempt to locate the roots of violence that 'crime' is used as a shorthand for. In so doing, we move away from blaming systemic injustice on 'race' or other forms of social 'difference'. As Saidiya Hartman writes, it is circumstances of social inequality that create 'rage and despair', 'tumult and upheaval'.[17] People are 'apt to be dangerous' when 'unsatisfied ambition, unrewarded merit, and the dismal prospects positioned them' is the norm. George Jackson, who knew a thing or two about racist injustice having endured and resisted it himself, educated us from his prison cell about the fact that:

> After one concedes that racism if stamped unalterably into the present nature of […] sociopolitical and economic life […] and concedes further that criminals and crime arise from material, economic, sociopolitical causes, we can then burn *all* of the criminology and penology libraries and direct our attention where it will do some good.[18]

Such insights inevitably bring us to a critical conception and discussion of violence, as what the state does to people, rather than the other way around. And it is instructive to observe how willing we are to blame anything, other than the formal political institution(s) we live in, for the violence that shapes the world around us. Thankfully, Dane Archer and Rosemary Gartner's comprehensive, cross-national study demonstrates how states breed violence through their own operations at home (e.g. policing) and abroad (e.g. war-making) – blaming the state for the violence it blames others for.[19] Such a shift in mental gear demands that we begin to think about violence not as an incident but as the *outcome* of the way our social, cultural and political world operates. As June Jordan[20] notes: 'A nation of violence and private property has every reason to dread the violated and the deprived. Its history drives the violated into violence, and one of these days, violence will literally signal the end of violence as a means. We are among those who have been violated into violence.'

Several pages later, she adds: 'Extremity demands, and justifies, extreme response. Violation invites, and teaches, violence. Less than that, less than a scream or a fist, less that the absolute cessation of normal events in the lock of abnormal duress is a lie and, worse than that, is a blasphemous ridicule of the self.'[21]

Hip-hop pioneer Afrika Bambaataa would concur, pointing out that 'America is raised on violence. Only time America really listens is when somebody starts getting violent back.'[22] Such observations depart radically from attempts to look elsewhere when explanations of why violence is inseparable from the mainstream culture that cradles it are right in front of us, and all around us too. George Jackson reminds us of how '[v]iolence is extolled at every exchange: the TV, the motion pictures, the best-seller lists. The newspapers that sell best are those that carry the boldest, bloodiest headlines.'[23] Yet, as we compulsively consume violence for entertainment – *as* entertainment in the form of true crime series or lurid documentaries about the world's toughest prisons, hardest cops and stricter borders – we are quick to condemn the very thing we otherwise greedily gobble up in front of the telly. If you're Quentin Tarantino or Takashi Miike, you can produce ultra-violent films without being accused of glamorising or glorifying violence. If you're a rapper, however, different (double) standards apply. We have already looked at how Black culture is policed as a result of racist hypocrisy in the preceding pages of this book, but what about policing itself as a cultural institution? The former Met Deputy Commissioner Stephen House, speaking at a Police and Crime Committee meeting of the London Assembly,[24] defended the Met's policing of UK drill music by reassuring us that the force he led is 'not the culture police' – even when (Black) culture is *what* they police.

Approached this way, policing comes to be seen as a cultural institution whose order maintenance function has more to do with upholding the dominant social order rather than safeguarding public order, although these two are really one and the same.[25] Other cops are more honest, like the one that playwright David Hare interviewed, who readily pointed out that '[a]ll life goes through a copper's hands'.[26] It should therefore be obvious that policing serves a cultural function that is also as inescapably political as it is ideological. It is not for nothing that this book has painstakingly documented how Black musics have historically been policed as aesthetically *out of tune* (noise), culturally *out of place* (unbelonging) and politically *out of order* (disorderly). The 'job of the police' remains wedded to 'the articulation and administration of techniques of biopower so as to increase the state's control over its inhabitants'.[27] Policing people, however, involves controlling them not merely as 'juridical subjects', but as 'working, trading, living human beings'; as cultural subjects.[28] As Toni Morrison put it with a heavy dose of irony: '[p]olice-heads [are] dirty things with big hats who shoot up out of the ocean to harm loose women and eat disobedient children'.[29] Recognising the cultural dimensions of policing does not overlook the political work that policing does for the state. It simply highlights *how* such political work is undertaken. Disguising itself as a crime-fighting institution that it is *not*, policing stops being seen as the order-maintenance force that it *is*.[30] Even criminologists who produce research for the Police Foundation categorically argue that: 'the claim that the police mission is crime-fighting to be at best partial, more likely wishful fantasy. To call the police crime-fighters is to radically misunderstand the nature of policing.'[31] Such a heretical statement finds its echo in the words of policing studies pioneer David H. Bayley, who also argued that:

> The police do not prevent crime. This is one of the best kept secrets of modern life. Experts know it, the police know it, but the public does not know it. Yet the police pretend that they are society's best

defense against crime and continually argue that if they are given more resources, especially personnel, they will be able to protect communities against crime. This is a myth. ... Governments should either resolve the doubts about the usefulness of the police or face up to the conclusion that preventing crime requires a great deal more than pouring money into law enforcement.[32]

In a more radical vein, Michel Foucault would claim that:

Police consists therefore in the sovereign exercise of royal power over individuals who are subjects. In other words, police is the direct governmentality of the sovereign qua sovereign. Or again, let's say that police is the permanent *coup d'État*. It is the permanent *coup d'État* that is exercised and functions in the name of and in terms of the principles of its own rationality, without having to mould or model itself on the otherwise given rules of justice.[33]

Free from (post)structuralist linguistic somersaults, George Jackson would go even further – linking policing to fascism by defining the latter as 'a police state wherein the political ascendancy is tied into and protects the interest of the upper class – characterized by militarism, *racism* and imperialism' (original emphasis).[34] Taken together, such readings of, and writings on, policing, shine a light on what policing actually *is*, what it *does*, who it does it *to* and who *for*. If it is an order maintenance institution, the order that policing maintains is the dominant social order and the hierarchical social structure that holds it together. If the police are the embodiment of an illegal and unjust force that seizes total control of social and political life as a *coup d'état* or as a tool for fascism, then it has nothing to do with safety or justice – unless the order it defends and the justice it delivers is at the service of 'white supremacist terror'.[35] Were this not true, affluent, white populations would not have such little or no contact with the police. As Martinot and Sexton note, '[f]or those who are not racially profiled or tortured when arrested, who are not tried and sentenced with the presumption of guilt, who are not shot reaching for their identification, all of this is imminently ignorable', unknown and unknowable.[36] Or, as Frank Wilderson sees it, 'white people are not simply "protected" by the police, they are – in their very corporeality – the police'; they embody and are embodied by the police.[37] In a similar vein, James Baldwin writes:

> [I]f one really wishes to know how justice is administered in a country, one does not question the policemen, the lawyers, the judges, or the protected members of the middle class. One goes to the unprotected – those, precisely, who need the law's protection most! – and listens to their testimony. Ask any Mexican, any Puerto Rican, any black man, any poor person – ask the wretched how they fare in the halls of justice, and then you will know, not whether or not the country is just, but whether or not it has any love for justice, or any concept of it. It is certain, in any case, that ignorance, allied with power, is the most ferocious enemy justice can have.[38]

That is why it is impossible to take 'race' out of policing when the history of policing is the history of its racism – as the first three parts of this book have insisted on reminding us, by chronicling the policing against Black music(s) from the era of colonial imperialism to the present day. Understood as a disciplinary tool that serves and protects a racialised socio-cultural and political (world) order, policing becomes seen as the hired gun for maintaining the racial contract that Euromodern states were founded on – when they were still, if they no longer are, imperial-colonial powers. Such a racial contract, Charles Mills contends,[39] is based on the assumption that rights and freedoms in liberal political regimes only apply to those who are racialised as white.[40] White people therefore embody the liberal social order, just like Black people represent disorder 'conceptualized in part as *carrying the state of nature around with them*, incarnating wildness and wilderness in their person'.[41] How can the state not (p)reserve the right to use violence for its protection against such a threat, when staging such a threat provides a great excuse to use violence for self-preservation? This is what the famous Black aphorism suggests when it claims that: 'When white people say justice, they mean just us', a variation of which also argues the reverse to the same effect: white people can appeal to and enjoy justice, but for Black people the only thing that exists is 'just us'.

This version of the saying is perhaps best known by Nas' *Ghetto Reporter*: 'You go down there looking for justice, that's what you find: just us.'[42] 'Black verbal art', be it the 'orally transmitted expressive culture'[43] of folk traditions or rappers' rhymes, speaks loud and clear about racial injustice. So does Black scholarship with whose help racial injustice becomes understood as the product of centuries of imperial-colonial rule and the racist ideology it spawned. W.E.B. Du Bois'[44] emphatic declaration that '[t]he color line belts the world' is illustrative here as a phrase that suggests a double meaning; referring both to the racial boundaries that belt (= tie) the world together through exclusion *and* to belting (= inflicting) violence on some for the benefit of others. In truth, Du Bois' words summarise the history and legacy of imperial Euro-colonial statecraft as a form of racial rule which helps us understand the links between racism, policing and police racism as historical phenomena that do not live in the past but survive in the present – albeit in mutated form. As he so emphatically put it:

This is not Europe gone mad; this is not aberration nor insanity; this *is* Europe; this seeming Terrible is the real soul of white culture – back of all culture, – stripped and visible today. This is where the world has arrived, – these dark and awful depths and not the shining and ineffable heights of which it boasted. Here is whither the might and energy of modern humanity has really gone.[45]

Du Bois' evocative words sound a helpful reminder, lest we continually reproduce the shock that racist police violence and criminal injustice produce when approached and consumed as exceptional, incidental, aberrations that depart from an assumed norm. What such a viewpoint obscures is that the norm is the exclusive preserve of those who are not targeted by police violence or criminal injustice, meaning that what is perceived as the exception is merely what *other* people experience as the norm. Frantz Fanon cautions against such mawkish and hypocritical shock that expresses 'alarm only in connexion with individual cases that are just fit to wrench a tear or to provoke little pangs of conscience' and ignores how the 'social constellation, the cultural whole, are deeply modified by the existence of racism'.[46] Failure to grapple with this insight means refusing to see how social injustice is normal(ised) – so much so that it is rendered invisible to those not affected by or opposed to it. As Walter Benjamin put it in a different, but not unrelated, context, 'the tradition of the oppressed teaches us that the "state of emergency" in which we live is not the exception but the rule', requiring us to attune ourselves to a 'conception of history that is in keeping with this insight'.[47]

The history that is in keeping with such insights, when the topic of discussion is racism or police racism, is the history of colonial imperialism – not as a thing of the past, but as an ongoing process: an omni-colonialism of sorts, that is always 'here' even when it plays hide and seek. This is often referred to as the boomerang effect of colonisation and the racialised logics it has normalised, institutionalised and formalised in formal state institutions – educational, cultural and political. Aimé Césaire first wrote of 'the terrific boomerang effect [...] of colonization'[48] and Hannah Arendt described 'the feared boomerang effect of imperialism upon the homeland'.[49] But it was Michel Foucault who expanded on the motif:

It should never be forgotten that while colonization, with its techniques and its political and juridical weapons, obviously transported
European models to other continents, it also had a considerable boomerang effect on the mechanisms of power in the West, and on the
apparatuses, institutions, and techniques of power. A whole series of
colonial models was brought back to the West, and the result was
that the West could practice something resembling colonization, or
an internal colonialism, on itself.[50]

Helpful though it certainly is to recognise the link between the
colonies and the metropole, the idea and imagery of the boomerang has its limitations – suggesting, as it does, that colonialism as
an ideology and a system of political rule is like a boomerang that
Europe throws in the direction of its colonies which then comes
back and presumably stays put. True though it is that policing
imports the tools, tactics, techniques and forms of colonialism to
rule, regulate and repress domestic populations, the traffic between
colony and metropole is ongoing. This observation urges a rethinking of colonialism as a *continuum* that we move along without clear
dividing points; sometimes smoothly, sometimes back and forth
and sometimes running in place. Rather than a boomerang that
is thrown once and then comes back in its original, unmutated
form, colonialism might be better understood as an ongoing, unfinished project that is subject(ed) to continuity, fluidity, change and
transformation – just like 'race' and racism(s).[51]

If (omni)colonialism is 'still the savage enemy of blackness',[52]
racism remains its ideological weapon – but not as a 'mental quirk',
or 'psychological flaw'[53] that it is often mistaken for by hyper-
individualised, (neo)liberal, psycho-behaviouralistic intellectual
trends. Nor is it 'prejudice' that has 'become unconscious',[54] as
mainstream corporate 'anti-racist' discourse, training sessions and
EDI seminars would have us believe. Racism is not 'an accidental

discovery' or a 'plague of humanity'[55] that violates the principles of white liberal democracy. It is a form of 'systematized oppression' that props up the dominant social, cultural and political order.[56] As Fanon explains, '[i]f in England, in Belgium, or in France, despite the democratic principles affirmed by these respective nations, there are still racists, it is these racists who, in their opposition to the country as a whole, are logically consistent',[57] adding that '[t]he racist in a culture with racism is therefore normal'. Rather than an anomaly, racism should be understood as an essential element, a foundational doctrine of Western civilisation that brings with it a 'raciological ordering of the world' that feeds on 'the manifold structures of a racial nomos – a legal, governmental, and spatial order'.[58] As a 'state-sanctioned or extralegal production and exploitation of group-differentiated vulnerability to premature death', racism provides 'the ordinary means through which [...] the practice of dehumanizing people produces racial categories' that enable and justify inequality, exclusion, policing and mass incarceration.[59] Singer, actor and activist Paul Robeson sums it all up quite nicely in his attempt to depersonalise racism as prejudice, writing that:

> I say that it is utterly false to maintain, as so many do, that the crux of the issue is personal prejudice. In a baseball game, an umpire's decision may be based upon some prejudice *in his mind*, but a state law that makes it a crime for Negroes to play baseball with whites is a statute *on the books*. The Jim Crow laws and practices which deny equal rights to millions of Negroes in the South – and not only in the South – are not private emotions and personal sentiments: they are a system of legal and extralegal *force* which violates and nullifies the Constitution of the United States.[60]

Rather than violating or nullifying the Constitution of the US or any other country, however, racism infuses the logic of such foundational political documents. As we have seen throughout this book racism writes the laws that police Blackness through the policing of Black music culture(s). Aimé Césaire sets the record straight yet again, situating the racial violence of colonial statecraft at the very heart of the most cherished principles of Western liberal thought. He writes, or rather asks: 'Security? Culture? The rule of law? [...] I look around and wherever there are colonisers and colonized face to face I see force, barbarity, cruelty, sadism, conflict, and in a parody of education, the hasty manufacture of a few thousand subordinate functionaries [...] necessary for the smooth operation of business.'[61]

Indeed, it is racist ideology that holds together an entire civilisation's conception of its racialised subjects as: '[S]avage inferior beast[s], invested with an insatiable and uncontrolled sexuality, and a blind and merciless capacity for violence, to which is added an animal grace, a primitive sense of rhythm, and all the vitality and the capacity for emotion which are prohibited by the Protestant, the capitalist ethic'.[62]

Racism is what gives omni-colonial nations their repertoire of physical and cultural distinctions, stereotypes and excuses for the continuation of oppression in the name of democracy, equality and justice before the law. It is the law that racially criminalises people as quintessentially violent 'criminals' that ought to be surveilled, policed, prosecuted and jailed in the disproportionate manner that Black people are – anywhere and everywhere colonial imperialism took root as a form of racial rule. It should therefore be clear by now that omni/perma-colonialism, or what other scholars call coloniality,[63] holds the key to understanding how patterns of racial oppression, exploitation and authoritarian rule by law came to be historically and how they continue to come together in our time. This should be all too obvious. Alas, white, liberal (mis)education approaches colonialism as 'a pageant full of large ships sailing on blue water'[64] so some reconceptualisation is necessary to show how the law, 'crime', policing and racism are the ideological, cultural and political tools of domination, in colonial and, only nominally, post-colonial times alike. This would, and perhaps will be, dismissed offhandedly as sheer millennial 'wokery' by those who seriously believe and want the rest of us to believe that racism as a colonising logic has already been abolished by the very systems of thought and political rule, whose ideological and historical origins lie in the era of racist colonial governance – which also happens to be the era of Enlightenment/En*whitenment* and modernity; that birthed Europe and the West as an ideological and political 'project', rather than a geographical 'place'.[65] Frantz Fanon exposes the deliberate self-deception with which the West denies its own history, just as it profits from it by creating self-serving mythologies that 'take refuge in ignorance of the facts and claim to be innocent of the colonization'.[66] W.E.B. Du Bois adds even more heat in the bubbling cauldron of anti-colonial critique, noting that:

> The methods by which this continent [Africa] has been stolen have been contemptible and dishonest beyond expression. Lying treaties, rivers of rum, murder, assassination, mutilation, rape, and torture have marked the progress of Englishman, German, Frenchman, and Belgian on the dark continent. The only way in which the world has been able to endure the horrible tale is by deliberately stopping its ears and changing the subject of conversation while the devilry went on.[67]

Much of this will sound too historical, too theoretical, too ideologically or politically charged to accurately describe contemporary empirical reality. Yet, the reverse is true. History, theory and anti-colonial ideology and politics are simply enlisted here as guides to understand how the present came to be and how ideologies and histories of racist oppression go on, just as they are hidden in and denied by formal educational, cultural and political institutions – whose origins are indebted to that history and can only be understood through anti-colonial theory and Black critique. White mainstream thought only accepts polite, palatable versions of such truths that must be calm in tone – as evidence of scientific objectivity and neutrality that covers up the wounds created by centuries of omni-colonial, racist violence. Entire generations of scholars are trained to prioritise a cold, rational and dispassionate *tone* over historical *truth* – sealing off the possibility of engaging with the world we study in the way it is actually experienced: from specific political ideologies; from specific social and cultural locations; and in emotive, affective and embodied ways. Every social scientist is reminded, in undergraduate social research methods courses, that there are no bird's-eye views from nowhere or from anywhere and everywhere.[68] Alas, the methods and analyses of mainstream social science proceed as if there is such a non-place from which the world can be viewed, thought about and understood. Thankfully, we have W.E.B. Du Bois'[69] acknowledgement that 'one could not be a calm, cool, and detached scientist while Negroes were lynched, murdered and starved'.

Lynched, murdered and starved they were, not only in Jim Crow America but in racial states around the world too – especially in those that don't just *have* an imperial-colonial past but *are* or have *become* their past in the present. This is what Saidiya Hartman meant when she wrote that 'I, TOO, LIVE in the time of slavery, by which I mean I am living in the future created by it.'[70] And this is what W.E.B. Du Bois' idea of abolition democracy educates our political consciousness to do – namely, recognise the fact that slavery may have officially, formally ended but the logics, ideologies, cultural and political traditions that made it possible are still with us.[71] They are the stuff we are educated and socialised into, which is why Hartman is famous for writing about 'the afterlife of slavery', to refer to 'skewed life chances, limited access to health and education, premature death, incarceration, and impoverishment';[72] all of which are the product of ideologies, culture(s) and politics of colonisation and the racial (b)ordering of the world.

I don't know how to conclude this chapter, or this book, other than by directing readers to the preceding pages for detailed evidence of how the legacy of imperial-colonial rule shapes everything that post-colonial nations, in name alone, are and do. That is why we traced the history of policing against Black/Afro-diasporic music(s) to the era of colonial slavery, to show how the colonial past has evolved into the racialised (= racist) world we live in today – unless and until we struggle against it by thinking about, rehearsing for and working towards ending the 'shamescape' and 'crapcrashchaos' that defines the planet that racism built.[73] In truth, I am not sure I want this book or the silent conversation I have with you to end. But it must for now, until we meet again. I therefore thought I'd bring it to a close by weaving the main threads that hold this book together in a single stitch. What this book has argued is simply that the foundational logic, mission and function of policing is to be found in its racist history. Which is the product of imperial-colonial politics. Which created the laws, the science(s), the economy and the cultural and political institutions that ... instituted the world we live in, as we know it. It is racism as the governing ideology of colonial imperialism that saw, or rather heard, Black or Afro-diasporic as aesthetically out of tune (= noise), culturally out of place (= unbelonging) and politically out of order (= disorderly). It is colonialism that made laws to normalise, formalise and institutionalise the subjugation of the enslaved. It is racist colonial worldviews that created policing as an instrument of social control to enforce the laws that regulated and suppressed the life of the enslaved. And it is the same worldviews that racialise 'crime' and therefore (re)produce criminal injustice today. This is the story this book has told and narrated it through the policing of Black or Afro-diasporic music(s) to attune us to the fact that just because today's racialised 'criminal' is embodied by the UK drill rapper does not mean that this is where the story begins or ends. All I can hope is that we listen. And it is to listening that the next and final section of this book is devoted, inviting readers to listen to this book through an annotated playlist that does more that words could ever do to bring this issue alive and do it justice too.

15
Listen to this book:
An annotated playlist

Having spent so much time reading, I hope you will welcome my invitation to *listen* to this book through the annotated playlist that I have lovingly assembled here. It is envisaged as an accompaniment to the book, whose aim is to convey the sonic atmosphere of each section of the book. The music I have handpicked for our consideration, therefore, is not a complete discography. Nor is it a deep dive into ethnomusicological waters, or a chronological index of recordings that catalogues the historical context that each section is steeped in. It is a selection of tunes that express what words cannot. Being a playlist, it offers a guide to the music I had in mind when writing this book, in the hope that it communicates a sense of how and why music has been so important in the making of this book. Indeed, my education into the themes of this book came from music first so I have no choice but to give music the last word. But I have also added some comments, that explain what I hear when I listen to the music. Imagine that you are in a record shop and that you are trying to situate the contents of this book into the stacks of wax around you. What follows is the product of such a record digging expedition. Tune in and enjoy!

Part I

The music that features here primarily attempts to convey what I mean by 'Afro-diasporic music(s)', in sound rather than in words. As such, I am not curating a historical archive of (field) recordings. Besides, the music(s) that the enslaved made were not captured on record. They nevertheless left their trace in other musical forms that developed out of the turbulent waters of the Black Atlantic. I am therefore limiting myself to examples of African traditions of music-making evolved, mutated and changed – just as they retain elements that connect them to Africa and its diaspora(s). The music featured below is recorded decades and sometimes centuries after the era of colonial slavery. It nevertheless tries to capture the sonic atmosphere created by Black music(s) that travelled, mingled, blended and nourished the diaspora(s) where Africa is audibly present in every beat.

LPs

- **Orquestra Afro Brasileira, *Obaluayê***: Originally recorded in 1957, this record was almost impossible to find (especially at an affordable price). Thankfully, it was reissued in 2021 by the Night Dreamer label. It is a rare gem that fuses jazz improvisation with Afro-Brazilian rhythms and Yoruba spirituality. The title of the album refers to Obaluayê, who is the orisha (deity) of infectious diseases and healing in Afro-Brazilian candomblé. A must!
- **J.B. De Carvalho, *J.B. De Carvalho E Seu Terreiro***: Deep and rare, this record is pure dynamite. Hard percussive work by J.B. de Carvalho (aka O Batuqueiro Famoso, o Feiticeiro do Ritmo, o Rei da Macumba), who takes Afro-Brazilian umbanda spirituality to the party. Drums, chants, hand-clapping and

earthy basslines. Listen to *Luanda* and *Fui À Umbanda* and you'll understand.

- **Count Ossie & The Mystic Revelation of Rastafari,** *Groun-ation*: I often think of this landmark album as the Jamaican equivalent of *Obaluayê* (see above). The heartbeat of this record, and Count Ossie's music in general, pulses with Nyabinghi drumming traditions where three drums in particular – the bass drum, the funde and the repeater – provide the rhythmic structure for chants and melodic improvisations. The Mystic Revelation of Rastafari formed in 1970s Kingston, uniting Count Ossie's Rastafarian nyabinghi drummers (also known as his African Drums, Wareikas or his Afro-Combo) and the saxophonist Cedric Im Brooks's horns ensemble, The Mystics. A true intellectual and spiritual experience with narrations that are really examples of anticolonial thought ... in sound. The music here is as 'traditional' as it is avant-garde. Essential and sublime stuff!

- **Ginger Johnson and His African Messengers,** *African Party*: Recorded in Britain in 1967, this breathtaking record – also a rarity until it was reissued in 2015 by Freestyle Records – really is a party on wax. Originally from Nigeria, Ginger Johnson came to the UK after World War II as a sailor and made a name for himself as someone who fused West African highlife with jazz. Johnson's Club Iroko in Haverstock Hill, North London hosted groups like Osibisa, Fela Kuti, Funkadelic and Sun Ra. Ginger Johnson was a popular session musician recording with London jazz stalwarts Ronnie Scott and Pete King, but he is also known for his collaboration with The Rolling Stones on *Sympathy For the Devil*, his appearance in the Hammer Films cult classic *She* and his musical contribution to the James Bond film *Live & Let Die*. But listen to what he and his African Messengers do in this stunning album, that is a precious piece of Black London's musical history. Expect thunderous drumming, soulful chanting and some wicked horn licks too.

- **Olatunji, *Drums of Passion*:** Flaming rhythms by a drummer who has become a legend as a solo artist and a session musician for jazz icons like Max Roach and Clark Terry, even featuring as a guest in Robert Farris Thompson's lectures at Yale – with his drum kit of course! Thompson even wrote the liner notes for (Babatunde) Olatunji's album, *Zungo!* that is also a killer – a stellar line-up. The title track *Jin-Go-Lo Ba* (Drums of Passion), is the original version of *Jingo*, as covered by Santana and Candido. Heavy, heavy, heavy!

- **Tito Puente, *Top Percussion*:** The title says it all! Deep Afro-Latin percussion, replete with chants to the orishas and featuring a wicked line-up that includes Mongo Santamaria.

- **Guy Warren, *Africa Speaks America Answers*:** One of the first serious attempts to fuse jazz with traditional West African music, this is a precious gift by a brilliant musician. Born in Accra, Guy Warren fell in love with jazz as a young schoolboy and became a versatile musician who has played highlife, calypso, mambo and jazz – working with Duke Ellington, Lionel Hampton, Dizzy Gillespie and Thelonious Monk. An astonishingly rich record.

- **Salah Ragab and The Cairo Jazz Band, *Egyptian Jazz*:** An incredible record which sounds like the Egyptian equivalent to Guy Warren's album above. Blending jazz with Arabic music, this album travels from the Mediterranean to the Atlantic and back – with a big band ensemble that is groovy as it is cinematic in the imagery that its sound produces. Ragab's band consists of five saxophones, four trumpets, four trombones, piano, bass, drums and other percussive instruments. Compulsory listening!

Given the focus of Part I on calypso/*kaiso*, here's a list of albums that I love and hope that you will love too:

- The Duke of Iron, *Calypso Carnival*
- The Mighty Sparrow, *The Mighty Sparrow Sings True Life Stories of Passion, People & Politics*
- Lord Melody, *Calypso Through the Looking Glass*
- Lord Flea and His Calypsonians, *Swingin' Calypsos*
- The Fabulous McClevertys, *Calypso!* The leader/singer is The Charmer, better known as Nation of Islam's Louis Farakhan

7"/45 singles

- **Roland Downer & Count Ossie with His Band, *Ethiopian Kingdom* and *A Ju Ju Wah*:** More mystical nyabinghi drumming with jazz experimentation. Africa meets Jamaica once again!
- **Joe Bataan, *Jumping with Symphony Sid*:** An Afro-Latin 'take' on Lester Young's (aka Pres) tune of the same name, which has also been recorded by Dizzy Gillespie. Both pay tribute to the famous jazz radio DJ 'Symphony Sid' Torin, who became a big supporter of Latin music in the early 1960s – alongside his DJ rivals, Dick 'Ricardo' Sugar and Geronimo Mendez Rojas. Joe Bataan's version brings together Afro-Latin traditions, soul and jazz, making it impossible to separate one from the other. A true Nu-Yorican gem!
- **James Waynes, *Junco Partner*:** A junkie jailbird anthem covered by Professor Longhair, James Booker, Dr John and The Clash. It condenses rhythm and blues, Caribbean rhumba and mambo rhythms with some impossibly break-heavy rhythms – especially towards the end of the track. Didn't you know that Nola is actually the northernmost part of the Caribbean?

- **Dave Bartholomew, *Shrimp & Gumbo*:** A gumbo mix of New Orleans music, bringing together African polyrhythms, the music of Nola's Mardi Gras Indian parading traditions and mambo in one. A party tune that nevertheless covers *so* much musical history in less than three minutes!
- **Cachao y su Orquestra, *Siboney*:** Legendary double bassist Israel 'Cachao' López with a *conjunto* that is pure fire and stitches together Afro-Cuban rhythms and jazz improvisation. Famous for his jam sessions or *descargas*, Cachao leads a combo that switches musical styles with such ease that will either inspire you to play like them or make you sell your instrument right away. ¡A gozaaar!
- **Mulatu Astatke, feat. Frank Holder & Niaaza Alsherif, *Asiyo Bellema*:** A stunning piece of Afro-diasporic musicianship that moves to the beat of steel pan and solos on the vibraphone and congas, topped with the distinct sonics of Ethio-jazz singing too. Jaw-dropping stuff that brings Addis Ababa, Trinidad, London and NYC together. An irresistible dancefloor filler!

Part II

This part of the playlist covers Britain's post-war years, with an emphasis on UK soundsystem reggae – which is the main Black music genre discussed in Part II of this book.

LPs

- **Volumes 1–8 of Honest Jon's Records' *London is the Place for Me*:** compilation series are an indispensable archive of calypsos, as well as kwela, jazz and highlife that shook the streets of young, Black London.

- **Louisa Markswoman Mark,** *Breakout*: A lovers' rock classic, featuring a Who's Who of reggae musicians like The Heptones, Rico and Vin Gordon, The In Crowd, Dave Barker, Owen Gray and more. Louisa Markswoman Mark made her name with a Dennis Bovell produced version of Robert Parker's *Caught You in A Lie*, but this album brims with even more beautiful music.

- **Johnny Osbourne,** *Never Stop Fighting*: Classic 1982 Johnny Osbourne, produced by Henry 'Junjo' Lawes, featuring the Roots Radics at Channel One and mixed by Scientist at King Tubby's. This was the winning formula in the 1980s that Greensleeves records capitalised on, and this record is a characteristic example.

- **Ranking Ann,** *A Slice of English Toast*: A 1982 classic produced and mixed by Mad Professor, showcasing Ranking Ann as a top-ranking DJ indeed. The title of the album is a clever play on words, denoting both a slice of toast and toasting (= rhyming/DJing/MCing).

- **The Simeons,** *Dub Conference in London*: The sound of London dub in 1978 on the Freedom Sounds label. Alongside Dennis Bovell's (as Blackbeard) own Dub Conference album (with Winston Edwards), this the UK's answer to the Dub Conference record that King Tubby made for Harry Mudie. Check out *16 Track Rock*, *L.T. Time*, *More Time* and *Jah Rastafari*. The latter was also reissued as a 7" by the Roots Traders label with a killer dub version!

- **Zulu Warriors,** *Warrior Dub*: One of the best UK steppers albums, without a shadow of a doubt. Produced by Steve 'Jah Warrior' Mosco, with a little help from Blacker Dread (if I am not mistaken), featuring Keety Roots and Naphtali. Originally released in 1989, but recently reissued by Partial Records. Check out *Dub in the Year 2000*.

12" and 7" 45 singles

- **Derrick Harriott and The Crystallites, *The Tickler***: This was Duke Vin's signature tune – one of Britain's original soundsystem selectors alongside Count Suckle. He adopted the nickname 'The Tickler' for a reason!
- **Steel An' Skin, *Afro Punk Reggae Dub***: Straight from late 1970s Ladbroke Grove, an infectious mix of disco and dub-inflected steel pan music. The sound of London in a 12" by the Ladbroke Grove-based label Honest Jon's.
- **Still Cool, *To Be Poor is a Crime***: A group of 12 Tribes of Israel devotees, who were mostly active in the 1970s and recorded this beautiful tune that Jah Shaka loved so much that he reissued it on his own label. The title is also a lesson for mainstream criminologists and legal penal functionaries. It's all about redistribution, not retribution!
- **Sharon Little, *Don't Mash Up Creation***: A classic proto-digital roots anthem, originally out in 1981 and regularly played by Jah Shaka.
- **Johnny Clarke, *Blood Dunza***: A Shaka do-over of Johnny Clarke's 1970s roots classic. The original was mixed by King Tubby and is a heavy as can be, but the Shaka version is pure dynamite too – a tried and tested soundsystem banger.
- **Sis Nya, *Jah Jah Way***: Another Shaka killer from the 1986, dripping with conscious lyrics.
- **Abakush, *Batta Dem***: A flawless 1984 tune from the all-women British group. Abacush/Abakush can still be heard today with a band that plays tough roots and sweet rocksteady too!
- **Fabian, *Prophecy***: A roots classic, recorded sometime around 1976–77. Produced by Jack Ruby in Jamaica, it was originally released in the UK as a 12" on Lloydie Coxsone's Tribes Man

label alongside Jimmy Lindsay's *Easy*. The song is written and sung by Fabienne Miranda: a Californian poet who moved to Jamaica, inspired by the vision of Ras Daniel Heartman (as Pedro) in the movie *The Harder They Come*. She cut two songs, *Prophecy* and *Destiny* – an alternative version of which is sung in French (as *La Destinèe* [*sic*]). Just listen to the rumbling bassline on *Prophecy* and you'll understand where dubstep came from …

- **Pablo Gad, *Hard Times***: A 1980s UK roots anthem that would make Dickens blush with its portrayal of, well, hard times! Every soundsystem DJ has this in their bag and inspired countless jungle and dubstep remixes.
- **Lion Youth, *Rat Cut a Bottle***: Essential 1980s soundsystem fare! The label suggest that it was recorded in 1978, but it's probably more like 1980–81 when this wicked stepper by UK-based Lion Youth first hit Thatcher's Britain.
- **Aswad, *Dub Charge*** (Radikal Roots Re-Edit, straight from Brixton): Dub version of the iconic Aswad instrumental: *Warrior Charge*, featuring Vin Gordon (aka Trommie/Don D. Jr.) on the trombone. *Warrior Charge* first appeared in the soundtrack of the cult classic film *Babylon*, as the Lion sound's signature tune that ends the film – after the legendary scene that features a young Shaka pounding on the Synare 3 dub siren.
- **The Cimarons, *Rooting For a Cause***: A beautiful roots tune by UK reggae band, The Cimarons on the Talent label, whose head honcho was Tommy Cowan of The Jamaicans. From the heart of Harlesden to our ears!
- **Misty In Roots, *Live At The Counter Eurovision 79***: Non-stop stepping roots beauty that talks back at Eurovision! I am grateful to Luke Martell who gifted me a copy during my PhD years.
- **Steel Pulse, *Ku Klux Klan***: An anti-lynching anthem by Birmingham's Steel Pulse.

- **Dennis Brown,** *Promised Land*: Crucial Dennis Brown, backed by Aswad with three dub cuts that are all killers. You might recognise it as sampled by Damian Marley and Nas, whose version (*Land of Promise*) is also an absolute banger.
- **Twinkle Brothers,** *Jahovia*: Epic roots classic that was a Shaka favourite, check it!
- **Shandi I & the Shanti Ites,** *Inna Sanctuary*: A steppers rarity and a classic in Abba-Shanti-I's dances. Tough!
- **Tippa Irie,** *All The Time The Lyric A Rhyme* **and** *It's Good to Have the Feeling You're the Best*: Tippa gives Willi Williams's Studio One hit *Armagideon Time*, a dancehall twist that is a bomb of a tune. *It's Good to Have the Feeling You're the Best* is based on The Uniques' *My Conversation* and showcases Tippa's lyrical talent on the mic, just like *All The Time The Lyric A Rhyme*, of course!
- **Papa Levi,** *Mi God Mi King*: Another legendary tune by a Saxon Sound DJ. Lyrical skills and a tough riddim too.
- **Asher Senator,** *Fast Style Origination*: One of the greatest British DJs/MCs and a fast-chat pioneer alongside Tippa Irie, Papa Levi and Smiley Culture.
- **Smiley Culture,** *Cockney Translation, Police Officer* **and** *Slam Bam*: All classics, showcasing Smiley Culture's lyrical dexterity and humour too. Cockney translation *has to be* the definition of what Paul Gilroy calls convivial, urban multiculture which explains why he writes about this tune so often and rightly so.
- **Top Cat,** *Love Mi Ses*: A ganja anthem and a party tune. An absolute killer to play out loud! Watch how the people are dancing …
- **Pato Banton,** *Nice Up the Session*: More quality British DJing here by Pato, which gets listeners ready for the dance.

Part III

Not unlike the previous sections of this playlist, the selections featured here try to reflect the sonic context of UK rap music by identifying a few examples of it from different hip/hop/rap subgenres, from boom bap sounding hip-hop that retains its debt to reggae to contemporary drill music tracks. This list is not, and could by no means be, exhaustive. The selections here are just that: selections. My choice was guided by what *I* personally think captures the flavour of the music and the (urban) geographies that nourished it. You will also notice that I am not referring strictly to vinyl records here, as a lot of the more contemporary releases tend to be almost exclusively digital.

Albums/LPs

- **The Ragga Twins, *Rinsin' Lyrics*:** Ragga meets hip-hop in a collaboration between The Ragga Twins and Us3 that fuses Latin boogaloo samples (Willie Bobo's *Guajira* and Ray Baretto's *The Teacher of Love*) and atmospheric tunes like *One Thing* which, for some reason, always makes me think of London.
- **Black Twang, *Dettwork SouthEast*:** I nearly included *Kik Off*, but opted for this 1996 gem primarily for US listeners who often regard UK hip-hop as a less worthy relative. Featuring Jehst, Rodney P & Samson, aka Black The Ripper.
- **Dizzee Rascal, *Boy in Da Corner*:** A quirky debut album that launched Dizzee's career and exposed many of us to grime music. I still find it hard to tune out of this one, sonically at least.
- **Kano, *Made in the Manor*:** A really rich and thoughtful album which celebrates Black music(s), past and present, while staking its claims as a grime classic that is a politically conscious 'concept

album' – but refreshingly free from the pretensions that accompany such a term. In many ways, I see it as a precursor to Kano's equally impressive *Hoodies All Summer*.

- **Skepta, *Konnichiwa*:** If the sonics of Dizzee's music were unique, this rings true of *Konnichiwa*. The title track is pure genius!

Singles

The following four tracks all come from Keith Lawrence's Muzik-Ed label, which beautifully and flawlessly blends reggae samples with hip-hop beats, with rhyming/MCing that owes just as much to Jamaican soundsystem culture as it does to US hip-hop, while being both at the same time and identifiably British too. No naff tunes here …

- **Keith Lawrence and Mystro**, *Step By Step*
- **Keith Lawrence and Seanie T**, *Shonoluv* and *Muzik-Ed Special*
- **Serocee & Seanie T**, *Sero & Seanie*
- **Pesci**, *Heavyweight MC*
- **Serocee, *You'll Never Find*:** A reggae hip-hop take on John Holt's *You'll Never Find*, which pays tribute to soundsystem clashes in a very playful manner. Jambrum representing!
- **A-Tola, *Soundbwoy*:** Rude boy tales from A-Tola, heavily based on the instrumental of Fabian's *Prophecy*. Tough!
- **Blind Alphabetz, *Hammer*:** A feelgood gem by UK Muslim hip-hop duo, Iron Braydz and Mohammed Yahya – sampling Bob Marley and The Wailers' *Hammer*. Infectiously good and the send-off track to my students at the very last lectures they have with me before they graduate.

- **Rodney P, *The Nice Up* and *Riddim Killa***: Stone cold UK rap classics that never date. *The Nice Up* samples and 'references' Michigan and Smiley's DJ version of the *Real Rock* riddim. Studio One meets heavy hip-hop beats!
- **Kelly G, *Never Going to Let You Go***: UK garage remix of Tina Moore's American R&B single *Never Going to Let You Go* from 1995.
- **Roots Manuva, *Again and Again***: A stalwart of the UK hip-hop scene, Roots Manuva is known to all and many would take offence for not including an entire LP of his here. I have simply opted for my personal choice of what I regard as my favourite tune of his and this has to be *Again and Again*, alongside his duo with Ty (see below!).
- **Ty (feat. Roots Manuva) *Oh U Want More?***: Mercury prize-nominated Ty, who so suddenly and so sadly died due to complications from coronavirus, certainly did not get his dues. Yet. he is universally admired and so key to bridging grime with older UK hip-hop styles. *Oh U Want More?* is an infectious smash hit of a tune and this version feat. Roots Manuva to me showcases the unique sonics of UK rap.
- **Wiley, *Wot Do U Call It?***: Irresistible proto-grime, before grime had a name. It's funny, nervy and forced me to pay attention to grime as it was emerging as the sound of the day.
- **Stylo G, *Call Me a Yardie***: This dancehall hit was heard everywhere in the 2010s and is indicative of modern dancehall.
- **Jago ft. Ghost Writers, Jnr Dangerous & Serocee, *The Wicked Try***: A dubby, hip-hop flavoured tune that is rootsy, but also dancefloor-friendly. This is Jago's first release, I think, who might be best known for in the form of the production duo Hylu & Jago. He is joined by Serocee, Ghost Writerz & Junior Dangerous, featuring a remix by DJ Vadim.

The following tunes chart the journey from late grime to drill music and give a sense of what cops, prosecutors, judges and the legal penal friendly commentariat are so irate about when it comes to rap. It is interesting to see that the critiques of policing and social inequality that these tunes offer, go unnoticed ...

- **67**, *Lambeth Maps*
- **Big Narstie**, *Pain Therapy*
- **G Smarko (Kuku) × MizOrMac**, *War*
- **Harlem Spartans (Blanco × MizOrMac × Bis)**, *Kent Nizzy*
- **JME**, *96 Fuckries*
- **Krept and Konan feat. Skepta**, *F.W.T.S/Active*
- **Lethal Bizzle feat. Stormzy**, *Dude*
- **Mostack and Mist**, *On My Ones*
- **New Gen feat. 67**, *Jackets*
- **Stormzy and Chip**, *Hear Dis*
- **Tinie Tempah feat. G Frsh and Wretch 32**, *All You*
- **Wretch 32 and Avelino**, *Fire in the Booth*
- **Yungen and Sneakbo**, *Don't Waste My Time Remix*
- **Headie One**, *Martin's Sofa*
- **K Trap**, *A to B*
- **Frosty**, *County Lines*
- **Digga D**, *Woi*
- **Mɪllionz**, *Lagga*
- **The Mitchell Brothers ft. Kano & The Streets**, *Routine Check*
- **OFB BandoKay & Double Lz Featuring Abra Cadabra**, *BLM*

Part IV

What does Black music have to teach us about thinking away from Euromodern conceptions of what thinking is? Part IV attempts an answer in words, but this is what the music itself has to say. I am listing them as tunes, regardless of format – to strike a balance between those who play records and those who play digital music files. However you choose to listen to these, I hope you listen carefully!

- **Nina Simone, *Four Women***: A story about slavery, not just as stolen labour but as negated life and violated flesh that also introduced notions of racial capitalism that explain how capitalism was propelled in the era of colonial slavery as a system of racial, gendered and sexual violence. So much is packed in a few minutes here and it is a remarkable tune, lyrically and musically too.
- **The Heptones, *Equal Rights***: The musical equivalent of John Rawls's First Principle as articulated in his *Theory of Justice*. Rawls writes that 'each person is to have an equal right to the most extensive total system of equal basic liberties compatible with a similar system of liberty for all'. But I play this to my students to ask why Rawls's words is a better source of that message that the lyrics of this track: not to forget the nyabinghi drums that make this a gem of a tune, although the whole album (*On Top*) is essential Studio One niceness.
- **Cutty Ranks in Skateland**: OK, I am cheating a bit here as this is actually a video that can easily be found on YouTube. It is also released in a compilation album by VP Records that features Cutty's music. Cutty Ranks is chatting over the Sleng Teng riddim here: one of the first digital riddims produced by Prince Jammy in the 1980s that incorporated the Casio keyboard into the bass-heavy soundsystem sonics. Watch the interaction between DJ and selector and audience participation. A perfect example of how to occupy and create public space and public

life, where people assemble to encounter each other as active members of their political community – by engaging in dialogue or communicating via dance to perform citizenship in open public spaces.

- **I Roy, *Sound Education*:** Self-explanatory really but a tongue-in-cheek commentary of what Part IV of this book aspires to. A ... sound education in and with Black music(s). Wicked rhymes on a Jimmy Radway production on the Fe Me Time label.

- **Leadbelly, *Go Down, Old Hannah*:** Mournful and hopeful in equal measure, this prison work song pleads 'Old Hannah'; a nickname for the sun to go down as it meant that the prisoners' work day at state penitentiaries would soon be over. Yet it also sends out a message of deliverance: 'If you rise in the morning, well, well, well, bring judgement sure', which summons hope as a resource against resignation and despair. What is also impressive about this song is the way in which it allows us to connect slavery to incarceration as a continuum of oppression and subjugation, as an aural contender to classic prison writings from George Jackson's prison letters to Malcolm X, Angela Y. Davis, Assata Shakur, Safiya Bukhari and Mumia Abu-Jamal's reflections on their imprisonment in their respective writings.

- **Max Roach and Abbey Lincoln, *Driva' Man*:** Mixing blues with modern jazz, this tune – plucked from Max Roach's *We Insist! Freedom Now Suite* – describes the violence of the slave driver and the overseer in the starkest terms, but both Abbey Lincoln's powerful vocals and Coleman Hawkins', (aka Bean) screeching tenor saxophone solo communicate defiance, not subjugation.

- **The 24-Carat Black, *Poverty's Paradise*:** This snippet from The 24-Carat Black's classic soul concept album offers a haunting portrayal of urban poverty, as does the entire album which focuses on the idea of 'the ghetto' as 'misfortune's wealth'. To be heard alongside Joe Cuba's, *Do You Feel It*?

- **Johnny Clarke, *Crazy Baldheads*:** Originally written by Bob Marley and also sung by Bunny Wailer, nothing compares to *this* version mixed by dub master King Tubby for producer Bunny 'Striker' Lee. Apart from its sonic richness however, Crazy Baldheads emerges as an anti-racist anthem which calls for 'chasing crazy baldheads (non-Rastafarians) out of town'. The term 'baldhead', however, should be understood as a synonym for oppressors, rather than as a culturally nationalist term which describes non-believers in the philosophy and theology of Rastafari. This assumes even greater significance if it is interpreted as a critique of the violence perpetrated not just by colonial overseers or metropolitan police officers, to echo KRS-One's genealogy of policing in both sides of the Atlantic, but by the beneficiaries of and affiliates to racism as an ideology and a form of structural inequality.

- **Brand Nubian, *Concerto in X Minor*:** A seductively upbeat and witty commentary on structural racism and a study in Black Power, which impressively brings together critiques of policing and state violence, racial injustice and militancy in less than four minutes! This is what hip-hop can and does sound like, if and when it is not reduced to its hyper-commercialised siblings.

- **A Tribe Called Quest, *We the People*:** Another exemplary 'conscious', progressive hip-hop classic of our times which attacks the punitive, authoritarian politics of (racial) capitalism and the hatred that produces, and is produced by, it. I can't help but think of it as the soundtrack of Trump's America although it clearly resonates further afield, if not close to home.

- **Abbey Lincoln,** *Blue Monk*: Black womanist intellectual, jazz singer and actress Abbey Lincoln adds her own lyrics to a Thelonious Monk classic that invents a new word: 'monkery' to invite self-searching and deep thinking. This is the equivalent of Traneing that Part IV discusses, so there is no better way to end this section of the book. Keep monkering!

Postscript: Of skinfolk and kinfolk: A rap on 'Whiteness'

These are my ancestors, these are my people. They are yours too, if you want them.

– C.L.R. James, *Spheres of Existence*[1]

You are holding a book about, or rather against, the policing of Black music(s) that is written by someone who is racialised as white. I therefore need to introduce myself to you by acknowledging my racial(ised) status and accounting for it too, through a critical appraisal of my personal, ethical, political and socio-cultural relationship to 'whiteness'. As Peter Fryer notes, acknowledging his own social position as a white Yorkshireman who wrote books about Black history: 'A white person who ventures to speak or write on any aspect of black history must first answer the question: "What has black history got to do with white people?" If I don't ask this question myself and try to answer it, right at the beginning, someone is inevitably going to ask it from the floor. And rightly so.'[2]

Now it is my turn to do the same, approaching whiteness – not as skin colour, but as an ideology that emerged in an imperial-colonial context to justify relationships of domination and uphold structures of power. Rather than a natural or neutral physiological trait, whiteness has a political history as an 'organizing grammar' of oppression which designates colour-coded hierarchies of superiority and inferiority that 'reproduce the unequal relationships into which Europeans coerced the populations concerned'.[3] It should therefore be understood as a way of being (ontology), a way of seeing (ideology) and a way of acting (a power relation) that valorises, normalises, formalises and institutionalises the moral and legal right to exercise authority over those who are racially inferiorised as non-white. Although it may elude us by making itself invisible, whiteness writes itself into existence as a background script that assumes the quality of a universal norm against which everyone else is judged. This compels us to approach it 'not a biological status but a political color that distinguished the free from the unfree, the equal from inferior, the citizen from the slave'.[4] Walter Rodney expands:

> [T]he white world defines who is white and who is black. In the US, if one is not white, then one is black; in Britain, if one is not white then one is coloured; in South Africa, one can be white, coloured or black depending upon how white people classify you [...] The definition which is most widely used the world over is that once you are not obviously white, then you are black and are excluded from power – Power is kept pure milky white.[5]

Were this not so 'what on earth' could whiteness be 'that one should so desire it?', W.E.B. Du Bois[6] asked, only to conclude that it 'the ownership of the earth forever and ever, Amen!' But what has any of that got to do with me? In asking that question, I do not mean: 'Do not blame *me*, I was not there. I did not do it.'[7] I am situating myself instead as a beneficiary of the structures of privilege and social advantage that 'whiteness' confers to me as someone who is racialised as 'white'. Alas, I am 'white' in social status alone – not in 'complacency', to borrow Alice Walker's phrase.[8] This means that although whiteness claims me as its own, I am unfaithful, disloyal and opposed to it ideologically, ethically and politically too. While I still profit from being seen and treated as 'white', apart from when I am identified as a dirty foreigner in public and at the UK border too, this is not who I am, how I think, or how I relate to the world around me. As James Baldwin observes, whiteness is 'a moral choice'[9] and I have chosen to stand against it, to oppose it and to reject it. Whiteness is not the 'colour of [my] politics'.[10] Anti-racism is, as a critique of the social, cultural and political violence that white, Euromodern intellectual traditions bequeathed, a 'dominant scientific knowledge system' that 'was and is often articulated as a reason for colonialism'.[11]

Odd though this may sound to many, I do not know what I know through the knowledge systems that the Enwhitenment created on the backs of the enslaved – whose (un)free labour filled the bank vaults of the racial capitalist economy. I was certainly *taught* the canon of 'great' Western-European thought, or what Baldwin calls 'the pantheon of the relentlessly mediocre'.[12] But I was never really *educated* in it, having fallen in love with Black music(s) first – not as a thrill-seeking tourist jaunt into Black exotica, but as a life-altering and consciousness-raising journey. All I learned through my schooling was how to educate myself *out* of whiteness by refusing to play along, when the people whose music(s) shaped my life, my thinking and my very being were either absent – or reduced to demeaning and dehumanising caricatures I could not accept as the truth. Because it was never the truth. It was, and is, the fiction that the 'civilised', Enwhitened West dreamt up – to avoid reckoning with the devastation that made it rich, powerful, arrogant and ignorant of its own guilty conscience.

This is a long way of saying that my 'skin-folks' are not my 'kinfolks', to echo Zora Neal Hurston's impossibly sharp phrase.[13]

And it is another way of paying tribute to Black creative expression, without claiming it as my own – as C.L.R. James might encourage someone like me to, in the passage that opens this postscript. With such insights and with Black music(s) as our guide, I hope we can listen attentively and learn how to build politics that dismantle the house that racism built together; beat by beat.

Glossary

Black

The term 'Black' is used here to refer to the people and cultures of the African diaspora. Although the term 'Black' has come to include 'African, African-Caribbean, Asian and other visible minority ethnic communities who are oppressed by racism',[1] it is used here to exclusively refer to 'African Diasporic Blackness'.[2] This is not meant to deny the term its coalitional meaning or potential in global anti-racist movements, but to apply it more narrowly to the specific Afro-diasporic cultures that are discussed here. Rather than biological, anthropological or demographic, Blackness is understood here as both cultural and political, as a conscious and empowering form of identification, borne out of struggles against structural racism – not as a form of racial classification. For a more expansive reading of Afro-diasporic Blackness, see Part IV of this book.

Cistem

The term cistem is adopted here to point to the gendered nature of both colonial imperialism and capitalism, as political systems that are created, invented, maintained and policed in an unequal social order that is marked by divisions of gender, 'race'/ethnicity, class, sexuality, (dis)ability, age, or migration status. In using this word, therefore, I want to draw our attention to such interconnectedness – between 'interlocking' forms of oppression that require an understanding and 'the destruction of the political-economic systems of capitalism and imperialism as well as patriarchy', as the authors of the Combahee River Collective Statement[3] would have it.[4] In the memorable words of Ronald Hyam,'[t]he expansion of Europe was not just a matter of "Christianity and commerce", it was also a matter of copulation and concubinage'.[5] In fact, the dismantling of imperial-colonial capitalism as a system of concubinage, gendered and sexual violence was at the heart of abolitionist critiques of slavery – using 'the figure of the lascivious and immoral slave-owner' as 'one of the rallying cries for the abolition of slavery', thereby pointing to how '[g]ender and race structured the organization of property and power in slave society'.[6] For excellent book-length arguments on the gendered and sexual nature of imperial-colonial capitalism, see Balani and Hall.[7]

Cop-italism

A new word (= neologism), introduced for the purposes of this book and Part I in particular, to reflect the intimate relationship between policing and the political ideology and economic system of capitalism. Cop-italism essentially refers to how policing acts at the behest of capital (money), capitalism (economy), the state and its policing, economic and political institutions. Its historical, ideological and political foundations, mission and purpose tell us this much, however difficult this might be to accept, educated and socialised as we have been into copaganda (= police propaganda), which reassures but misleads us into thinking that policing is a neutral, apolitical crime-fighting institution rather than an order maintenance one. The word 'cop-italism', therefore, serves to remind us of the historical, ideological and political role of the police, as a professional or informal force that was set up to protect the interests of wealth and private property under capitalism.

Legal penal system

The term 'legal penal system' – not unlike the abolitionist catchphrase 'criminal legal system' – is coined here to problematise and refuse the term 'criminal justice system'; insisting that the latter is a system of laws that (literally) *creates* 'crime' – both as a concept and a reality – through turning certain activities into punishable offences. This is not to deny that violence and harm exist, or that there are people who commit violent acts that cause harm. Rather, it is to stress that 'crime' is a political category that condemns, stigmatises, marginalises and racialises violence as the inherent trait, individual anomaly, cultural pathology and personal responsibility of 'deviant' individuals and groups. Notions like 'law' and 'justice', therefore, are not understood here as interchangeable or synonymous. As William Quigley argues, '[w]e must never confuse law and justice. What is legal is often not just. And what is just is often not at all legal'.[8] Legal practitioners, therefore, do not (necessarily) observe principles and ideas of 'justice', but enforce 'the law'; the technical and legal(istic) restrictions on the behaviour, actions and activities of 'the public'. While 'justice' denotes and embodies notions and ethical standards of fairness, 'the law' is 'the technical embodiment of attempts to order society'.[9] What we refer to or think as 'the law', therefore, simply refers to 'written law, codes, [and] systems of obedience',[10] *not* that higher, 'just' ethical plane that we think that the law signifies, or stands for. For that reason, the term 'legal penal system' is used throughout this book to stress that the state's juridical infrastructure delivers punishments not justice – using 'the law' as an instrument of political (mis)rule.

Liberalism

Liberalism is splintered into multiple and conflicting definitions that stress different aspects of it as dominant, depending on how it is approached. It is understood here as an ideology and political philosophy that emerged during the Enlightenment and forms the basis of Western liberal democracies, whose main tenets include support of individual rights, a free-market economy and the rule of law. Unlike mainstream interpretations of it, however, liberalism is also seen here as an ideology at the service of enslavement and bondage rather than a freedom gospel – especially as it only included those who were/are deemed worthy of liberty/freedom, thereby excluding the enslaved.[11] Part I offers a discussion of this, with reference to the liberal philosophy of John Locke. Liberalism is therefore approached here as what Caroline Elkins calls 'liberal imperialism'[12] to refer to liberalism as an ideology that 'integrated Britain's sovereign claims to empire with a massive undertaking to reform imperial subjects and shepherd them into the modern world'. As such, liberalism is seen here as an imperialist dogma that 'found further expression in scientific racism's evolutionary model' by preaching '[d]evelopmentalism', as a doctrine that 'cleaved to racial hierarchies that likened colonial subjects to children who needed paternalistic guidance to reach full maturity'.[13] The 'liberty' in liberalism therefore is likened here to Bertrand Russell's satirical definition of it as 'the right to obey the police'.[14]

Racial capitalism

The term 'racial capitalism' was first used by Legassick and Hemson in the context of anti-apartheid struggles in South Africa,[15] but became popularised by, and synonymous with, the work of Cedric Robinson.[16] To fully grasp what the 'racial' in racial capitalism refers to, capitalism has to be rethought and understood not just as a system of trade and industry, a mode of production or a phase of European economic development from the sixteenth century onwards. Rather, it should be understood as a process of accumulating wealth (= capital) through the expropriation of land and the exploitation of labour, not just on European soil but in the Old Continent's colonised territories too. (Racial) capitalism should best be thought of as an economic system with a specific (geo)political history whose very nature is imperial-colonial. What makes capitalism 'racial', therefore, is the historical moment in which capitalism developed as the economic system of colonial imperialism. This imperial-colonial capitalist system of trade and industry depended on the transatlantic slave trade for buying and selling goods, which kept industries in the imperial centre going full steam ahead. To justify this profit-making trade network, a supporting ideology was necessary to rationalise the plunder of conquered lands, the extermination of indigenous people and the forced importation of slaves to plant, tend, cut and process crops.

This imperial(ist) ideology was racism in its original form, before it became embedded and absorbed into contemporary social, political, economic, cultural and educational institutions – all of which have their origins in, and owe their development to, the establishment of colonial slavery at the heyday of capitalism. This is not to claim that racial classifications suddenly emerged with the expansion of imperial-colonial capitalism, but to stress that they were turbocharged during the period of European colonial conquest and unprecedented in the way such classifications determined the very humanity of the enslaved. As Robin Kelley put it, '[c]apitalism and racism ... did not break from the old [feudal] order but rather evolved from it to produce a modern world system of 'racial capitalism' dependent on slavery, violence, imperialism, and genocide.[17] Capitalism was 'racial' not because of some conspiracy to divide workers or justify slavery and dispossession, but because racialism had already permeated Western feudal society'. The difference between the 'racialism' of feudal times and the 'White racism'[18] of capitalism, therefore, is one of scale and degree. The racial 'Others' of feudal Europe wore white skins yet were still racialised as 'inferior' and subordinate human categories.[19] However, it is the advent of colonial-imperial capitalism that made racial classification its official ideology of political (mis)rule. As St Clair Drake notes: '[a]lthough some negative attitudes and emotions about blackness and black people existed in Mediterranean and European cultures, these concepts did not create the system of racial slavery or the ideology that sanctioned it, White racism. That was accomplished by the capitalist system's need for a plentiful supply of low-cost labour.'[20] For a short introduction to racial capitalism, see my introduction to the term at *The Sage Handbook of Decolonial Theory*.[21]

A note on language

You will have noticed that throughout this book some words are capitalised and others are not. Similarly, and relatedly, some words are placed within single quotation marks. This is to draw attention to the political nature and use of language, given that the words we use to describe and discuss certain terms, phenomena, realities and people carry with them specific histories, ideologies and contexts that give meaning to the words we use. And that meaning is never neutral. It is always political.

'Race'

'Race' is bookended by single quotation marks, to remind readers that it is an ideologically tinged, historically invented and socially constructed word that describes, assigns, assumes and (re)produces hierarchies of visible or cultural human 'difference'. 'Race' is the outcome of racialisation and racism which are processes that draw on physiological/physical/biological or cultural characteristics/traits that place people in specific categories that classify and order us in a hierarchical fashion. 'Race', therefore, is a word that involves the practice of differentiating between groups of people – based on biology (what people look like) or culture (what they do). The danger with using the word 'race' uncritically without drawing attention to its constructed nature, is that it imposes itself on people as a label or 'badge'[22] that comes to describe them against their will, allowing us to make harmful generalisations about each other. Given its bloody history, it should therefore be used with extreme caution. 'Race' is the by-product of racism, as the driving ideology of imperial-colonial slavery which encouraged the ordering humanity in rank order – to assign people an inferior or superior status and justify the violence meted out to those who were racially inferiorised. As W.E.B. Du Bois puts it in his classic essay *The Conservation of Races*, attempting to explain and account for 'the grosser physical differences of color, hair and bone', 'race' also serves to explain 'the different roles which groups of men have played in human progress' and therefore 'separat[e] men into groups' and different racial categories that come to define who they are, what they are capable of and where/whether they belong.[23]

'Crime'

As Part III shows, 'crime' – like 'race' – is the product of ideological and political processes of criminalisation. It is the turning of actions, activities and behaviours into legally punishable offences: 'crimes' that make 'crime' a 'crime'. Rather than being an observable phenomenon, 'crime' does not objectively exist. It is *made*. It is not an inherent *quality* of anything or anyone, but the *outcome* of processes of description in, by and through law and the formal institutions that enforce it.

Black and white

The word 'Black' is capitalised to reflect a shared sense of identity and community, culturally and politically too. The word 'white' is not, as it carries (within it) a different set of meanings and history too. Given the long history of racial/racist violence that has been reserved for people who are racialised as Black and the long history of struggles against such violence, Black/Blackness are capitalised to reflect and communicate a sense of empowerment; ideologically, culturally and politically too. The history of 'whiteness' is tied to the history of white supremacist racism that created 'Black' and 'white' as racial designations applied to human beings. Since 'whiteness' created itself as a category or racial superiority to justify the violence or imperial-colonial slavery and institutionalised racism thereafter, capitalising it reinforces and legitimises the meanings (and practices) of superiority that are attached to that word: whiteness therefore denotes racial domination. Like Blackness, it is not a skin colour but unlike Blackness, whiteness is used to prop up structures of power and relationships of domination over people who are racialised as non-white.

British policing

Throughout this book the term 'British policing' is used to refer to the police forces of the British state, in the British mainland *and* its colonial outposts. The focus may be on the London Metropolitan

Police and the colonial police forces it was modelled after, as Part I of this book demonstrates, but the adjective 'British' in this book denotes the national and colonial government and formal institutions of Britain. This is not to suggest that there is a single, unified, national British police institution, to deny the operational independence of Britain's police forces, or to assume any equivalence or sameness among them. Rather, 'British policing' is used here as a shorthand to refer to police forces and policing practices throughout Britain and its colonial overseas territories. This is consistent with a view of Britain as 'an *imperial* state, not a national one'.[24] Instead of consenting to a (frankly, ahistorical) view of Britain as an 'island nation', 'intire of it selfe'[25] (entire of itself), it is conceived, throughout this book and especially in Part II, as inescapably tied up with the geopolitics of its imperial-colonial history.

Abbreviations

ASBO	Anti-social Behaviour Order
CBO	Criminal Behaviour Order
CJA	Criminal Justice Act
CPS	Crown Prosecution Service
EDI	Equality, Diversity and Inclusion (DEI in the US, Australia and elsewhere)
EHRC	Equality and Human Rights Commission
HASC	Home Affairs Select Committee
ICO	Information Commissioner's Office
MOPAC	Mayor's Office for Policing and Crime
Met	London Metropolitan Police
MPS	Metropolitan Police Service
NPCC	National Police Chiefs' Council
OHCHR	Office of the United Nations High Commissioner for Human Rights
UN	United Nations

Acknowledgements

Nothing anyone ever does is the product of their own individual labour alone, flattering though it may be to think otherwise. This book is no exception. It nevertheless feels impossible to acknowledge others' contributions, unless I render my thanks and confer my indebtedness to the entire universe. Perhaps I just did. I can therefore return to the earthbound plane of human existence and selectively acknowledge (only) those who did something to make this book possible: by encouraging me, listening to me, working with me and making space for me to keep writing – without begrudging the necessary time it took me to add the final full stop to the typescript.

This book would not exist, in the way it was imagined, without Tam Joseph's *The Spirit of The Carnival*. This painting has provided the visual backdrop that dramatises the themes that animate this book. Granting me permission to use this image as the cover of this book is a true honour. I am therefore grateful to Cameron Amiri, the Director of Felix & Spear Gallery, without whose help I would not have been able to get hold of the artist. I cannot thank either of you enough and I hope that my work has done justice to your generosity.

I owe Paul Gilroy my warmest and most sincere gratitude for taking the time to write the Foreword for this book. Without it, this book would not be the same and without his scholarship I doubt that I would be able to write it.

My Brighton crew: Raph Schlembach, Roxana Pessoa Cavalcanti and Deanna Dadusc are kindred spirits, whose intellectual companionship and friendship are a precious gift.

A special shout-out goes to those who have offered a listening ear, sound advice and encouragement to think how I think and do what I do. Thank you Gabriella Beckles-Raymond, Angela Francis, Anthony Gunter, Kenny Monrose and Joy White for getting, feeling and knowing 'it'.

My Prosecuting Rap and Art Not Evidence co-conspirators are living proof that unity is strength. Regardless of whether we will succeed in decriminalising rap or not, the truth is on our side.

I am grateful to my soundsystem fraternity, which has nurtured and emboldened me to put in words what we all already know from the music. Anna Mystic, you are a role model and a teacher. Playing with and being around you is an honour. Ras Styler, Champian, MC Trooper, MC Ishu and Serocee, you are examples of what I mean when I drone on about MCs as public intellectuals. I am lucky to know you and to have shared the stage with you. Three cheers to my radiobubble comrades, who so lovingly embraced my two-hour, all-vinyl radio show for five years. Jon Jones, Richie Phoe and DJ Cut La Vis, my life would be empty without your earth-shattering beats, good vibes and real friendship too. Babylon will fall!

I owe a debt of gratitude to Free University Brighton, The Feminist Bookshop and Brighton Copwatch for proudly demonstrating that community is where transformative change is imagined and made. You continue to be an inspiration.

Massive props to my beloved friend Julia, whose copyediting *skillz* saved me from losing my mind. Danke schön and χίλια ευχαριστώ! Let's not do this ever again though ...

I am incredibly fortunate to meet, know, listen and talk to hundreds of students every year. Our bond is special and I cherish it more than you can imagine. You give me hope and I hope that sharing what I know has sharpened your political consciousness and ethical conscience too, just like it sharpened mine.

Many colleagues have given me reasons to be hopeful about humanity's place, even within the confines of neoliberal academia. You know who you are, so I won't expose you – to protect you from being tainted by association. Being together means building meaningful relationships, beautiful visions and freedom dreams that will help us survive, resist, oppose, reject and bypass the oppressive world we are forced to inhabit.

I have no choice but to acknowledge the geopolitical context that this book has been written against. There are no thanks to be given here. Alas, this book would not have been written were it not for the white supremacist, heteropatriarchal, (trans)misogynist, ecocidal capitalist cistem we live in. Much of what assumed the form of words on a page is a direct response to ideologies of superiority, relationships of domination and structures of power that continue to make excuses for the violence, slaughter and terror that legal penal systems, social injustice policies and (settler) colonial regimes unleash on those who are perceived, policed and persecuted as disposable human waste.

Thankfully, Black music(s) offer a counterpoint to the ideological, historical, socio-cultural and political forces that made both the policing of Black music(s) and the writing of a book about such policing possible. The intellectual, cultural, spiritual and political traditions that Black music(s) educated me into, taught me how to best defend them against the machinations of the state and the law.

Vasiliki (Βασιλική) and Neféli (Νεφέλη), your presence in my life is music to my ears.

Text acknowledgements and permissions

I should wish to extend my gratitude to the following publishers, who have granted me the right to (re)use some material that has previously appeared elsewhere. These include:

Fatsis, L. and Lamb, M. (2022) *Policing the Pandemic: How Public Health Becomes Public Order*. Reproduced by permission of Bristol University Press.

Fatsis, L. (2023) 'Arresting Sounds What UK Soundsystem Culture Teaches Us about Police Racism and Public Life', in M. Charles and M.W. Gani (eds), *Black Music in Britain in the 21st Century*. Reproduced by permission of Liverpool University Press.

'When Art Becomes Evidence', *Proof* Magazine, No. 6 (May 2024). Reproduced by permission of *Proof* Magazine.

Fatsis, L. (2023) 'Decriminalising Rap Beat by Beat: Two Questions in Search of Answers', in E. Peters (ed.), *Music in Crime, Resistance, and Identity*. Reproduced by permission of Taylor & Francis Group.

Fatsis, L. (2023) 'From Overseer to Officer: A Brief History of British Policing Through Afro-Diasporic Music Culture', in R.P. Cavalcanti, P. Squires and Z. Waseem (eds), *Southern Perspectives on Policing, Security and Social Order*. Reproduced by permission of Bristol University Press.

Notes

Foreword

1 The copyright of this Foreword is retained by Paul Gilroy. Quotation from it is permitted, provided that full acknowledgement is made. This Foreword may not be reproduced without the prior written consent of its author.

2 James Baldwin, *The Cross of Redemption: Uncollected Writings* (New York: Pantheon Books, 2010), p. 124.

3 This is Pumla Gobodo Madikizela's phrase. See her 'Empathic Repair after Mass Trauma: When Vengeance is Arrested', *European Journal of Social Theory*, 1:1 (2008), p. 331.

Introduction

1 A digital version of this gem of a political calypso recorded in the 1930s can be found at Sedition Law, *King Radio – Topic* (2019), www.youtube.com/watch?v=yBKrVLortGQ (accessed 16 June 2025).

2 The story survives in the form of a newspaper clipping that is exhibited at the Backstreet Cultural Museum in the Tremé neighbourhood of New Orleans, where I was fortunate enough to see it in 2016 – thanks to curator Sylvester Francis, who so faithfully documents the brass band and Mardis Gras parading traditions of the city. For more info on the policing of brass band jazz in the Crescent City, see: John Swenson, *New Atlantis: Musicians Battle for the Survival of New Orleans* (Oxford: Oxford University Press, 2011), pp. 41, 111, 187–8, and Jason Berry, Jonathan Foose and Tad Jones, *Up from the Cradle of Jazz: New Orleans Music since World War II* (Lafayette: University of Louisiana at Lafayette Press, 2009), pp. 311–14.

3 Langston Hughes and Arna Bontemps, *The Book of Negro Folklore* (New York: Dodd and Mead, 1958), pp. 608–9.

4 Robin D.G. Kelley, *Thelonious Monk: The Life and Times of an American Original* (New York: The Free Press, 2009), p. 89; Scott DeVeaux, *The Birth of Bebop: A Social and Musical History* (London: University of California Press, 1997), pp. 20–1.

5 Barbara Browning, *Samba: Resistance in Motion* (Bloomington: Indiana University Press, 1995), p. 97.

6 Caroline Elkins, *Legacy of Violence: A History of the British Empire* (London: The Bodley Head, 2022), pp. 24, 47–8.

7 John Collins, 'One Hundred Years of Censorship in Ghanaian Popular Performance', in Michael Drewett and Martin Cloonan (eds), *Popular Music Censorship in Africa* (Farnham: Ashgate, 2006), pp. 171–86.

8 Marc A. Hertzman, *Making Samba: A New History of Race and Music in Brazil* (Durham, NC: Duke University Press, 2013), pp. 31–65.

9 Robin D. Moore, *Nationalizing Blackness: Afrocubanismo and Artistic Revolution in Havana, 1920–1940* (Pittsburgh: University of Pittsburgh Press, 1997), pp. 71–2, 75; Isabelle Leymarie, *Cuban Fire: The Saga of Salsa and Latin Jazz* (London: Continuum, 2002), pp. 44–5, 54–6.

10 Anne Schumann, 'The Beat that Beat Apartheid: The Role of Music in the Resistance Against Apartheid in South Africa', *Stichproben: Wiener Zeitschrift für kritische Afrikastudien*, 8:14 (2008), 17–39.

11 Bryan Wagner, *Disturbing the Peace: Black Culture and the Police Power after Slavery* (Cambridge, MA: Harvard University Press, 2009), pp. 5, 60–1.

12 Paul Gilroy, *The Black Atlantic: Modernity and Double Consciousness* (London: Verso, 1999), pp. 72, 1–40.

13 Julius S. Scott, *The Common Wind: Afro-American Currents in the Age of the Haitian Revolution* (London: Verso, 2018); Peter Linebaugh and Marcus Rediker, *The Many-Headed Hydra: Sailors, Slaves, Commoners, and the Hidden History of the Revolutionary Atlantic* (Boston: Beacon Press, 2000).

14 E.g. Adèle Oliver, *Deeping It: Colonialism, Culture and Criminalisation of UK Drill* (Edinburgh: Ink 404 Press, 2023).

15 Saidiya Hartman, *Wayward Lives, Beautiful Experiments* (London: Serpent's Tail, 2021), p. 220.

16 David Theo Goldberg, *Are We All Postracial Yet?* (London: Polity, 2015).

17 Fred Moten, *In the Break: The Aesthetics of the Black Radical Tradition* (London: University of Minnesota Press, 2003), p. 68.

18   Jennifer Nash, *Black Feminism Reimagined: After Intersectionality* (Durham, NC: Duke University Press, 2019), p. 57.

19   Zoé Samudzi and William C. Anderson, *As Black as Resistance: Finding the Conditions for Liberation* (Edinburgh: AK Press, 2018), pp. 69–70; Butch Lee and Red Rover, *Night-Vision: Illuminating War and Class on the Neo-Colonial Terrain* (Montreal: Kersplebedeb, 2017); Marquis Bey, *Anarcho-Blackness: Notes Toward a Black Anarchism* (Edinburgh: AK Press, 2020).

Part I: Is it even music? Policing Black music as 'out of tune' under British colonial rule

1   Joseph Conrad, *The Heart of Darkness and Other Tales* (Oxford: Oxford University Press, 2008), p. 107. For a neat riposte to Conrad, see Chinua Achebe, *An Image of Africa* (London: Penguin Press, 2010).

2   Both Britain and its policing institutions are situated in their imperial-colonial context throughout the book. A more detailed explanation on this point is offered in the Glossary entry for 'British policing' at the end of this book.

3   For a detailed explanation of how the words 'Black' and 'Afro-diasporic' are thought about and employed here, and throughout the whole book, see: Glossary (for 'Black') and Part IV.

4   Lambros Fatsis, 'Sounds Dangerous: Black Music Subcultures as Victims of State Regulation and Social Control', in N. Peršak and A. Di Ronco (eds), *Harm and Disorder in the Urban Space: Social Control, Sense and Sensibility* (London: Routledge, 2021), pp. 35–7; Lambros Fatsis, 'From Overseer to Officer: A Brief History of British Policing Through Afro-Diasporic Music Culture', in R.P. Cavalcanti, P. Squires and Z. Waseem (eds), *Southern Perspectives on Policing, Security and Social Order* (Bristol: Bristol University Press, 2023), pp. 45–61.

5   Lambros Fatsis and Melayna Lamb, *Policing the Pandemic: How Public Health Becomes Public Order* (Bristol: Policy Press, 2022), pp. 23–8; Lambros Fatsis, 'Policing the Union's Black: The Racial Politics of Law and Order in Contemporary Britain', in Flora Gordon and Daniel Newman (eds), *Leading Works in Law and Social Justice* (London: Routledge, 2021), pp. 137–50.

6   Lambros Fatsis, 'When Police Racism is Denied, Does it Go Away?', *The British Society of Criminology Blog* (2019), https://thebscblog.wordpress.com/2019/08/28/denying-institutional-racism (accessed 25 July 2024).

7   Toni Morrison, *Beloved* (New York: Alfred A. Knopf, 1987), p. 191.

8 Carolyn Cooper, *Noises in the Blood: Orality, Gender, and the "Vulgar" Body of Jamaican Popular Culture* (Durham: Duke University Press, 1995), p. 103. Toni Morrison uses the word *'rememory'* both as a noun and a verb (see Morrison, *Beloved*, pp. 36, 99, 189 for its use as a noun; pp. 191, 201, 215 for its use as a verb). The play on words borrowed here from Cooper, *Noises in the Blood*, p. 103, has been changed from the original ('restor(i)ed') to avoid the overuse of square brackets that would otherwise indicate how the adopted use here differs from Cooper's formulation.

9 Micol Seigel, *Violence Work: State Power and the Limits of Police* (Durham, NC: Duke University Press, 2018).

1 Cop-italism and slavery: Excavating the colonial origins of British policing

1 Mark Neocleous, *The Fabrication of Social Order: A Critical Theory of Police Power* (London: Pluto Press, 2000).

2 David Taylor, *The New Police in Nineteenth-Century England: Crime, Conflict and Control* (Manchester: Manchester University Press, 1997); Robert Reiner, *The Politics of the Police* (Oxford: Oxford University Press, 2010).

3 Phil Cohen, 'Policing the Working-Class City', in *Capitalism and the Rule of Law*, ed. National Deviancy Conference (London: Hutchinson & Co., 1979), pp. 118–36; Robert Storch, 'The Policeman as Domestic Missionary: Urban Discipline and Popular Culture in Northern England, 1850–80', in R. Morris and R. Rodger (eds), *The Victorian City: A Reader in British Urban History, 1820–1914* (London: Longman, 1993), pp. 281–306.

4 Robert Storch, 'The Problem of Working-Class Leisure: Some Roots of Middle-Class Moral Reform in the Industrial North: 1825–50', in A.P. Donajgrodzki (ed.), *Social Control in Nineteenth Century Britain* (London: Croom Helm, 1977), pp. 138–62.

5 Alex S. Vitale, *The End of Policing* (London: Verso, 2017).

6 Vitale, *The End of Policing*, p. 38.

7 David Arnold, *Police Power and Colonial Rule, Madras, 1859–1947* (New York: Oxford University Press, 1986); Mike Brogden, 'The Emergence of the Police – The Colonial Dimension', *British Journal of Criminology*, 27:1 (1987), 4–14; Dilip K. Das and Arvind Verma, 'The Armed Police in the British Colonial Tradition', *Policing: An International Journal of Police Strategies & Management*, 21:2 (1998), 354–67; Mark Brown, 'The Politics of Penal Excess and the Echo of Colonial Penality',

Punishment and Society, 4:4 (2002), 403–23; Randall Williams, 'A State of Permanent Exception: The Birth of Modern Policing in Colonial Capitalism', *Interventions*, 5:3 (2003), 322–44; Emma Bell, 'Normalising the Exceptional: British Colonial Policing Cultures Come Home', *Mémoire(s), identité(s), marginalité(s) dans le monde occidental contemporain, Cahiers du MIMMOC* (2013), https://journals.openedition. org/mimmoc/1286 (accessed 25 July 2024); Clive Emsley, 'Policing the Empire / Policing the Metropole: Some Thoughts on Models and Types', *Crime, Histoire & Sociétés / Crime, History & Societies*, 8:2 (2014), 5–25; Nicole Jackson, 'Imperial Suspect: Policing Colonies within "Post"-Imperial England', *Callaloo*, 39:1 (2016), 203–15; Georgina Sinclair, '"Get into a Crack Force and Earn £20 a Month and All Found …": The Influence of the Palestine Police upon Colonial Policing 1922–1948', *European Review of History: Revue Européenne d'histoire*, 13:1 (2006), 49–65; Georgina Sinclair, *At the End of the Line: Colonial Policing and the Imperial Endgame 1945–80* (Manchester: Manchester University Press, 2010); Georgina Sinclair and Chris A. Williams, '"Home and Away": The Cross-Fertilisation between "Colonial" and "British" Policing, 1921–85', *Journal of Imperial and Commonwealth History*, 35:2 (2007), 221–38; Gargi Bhattacharyya, Adam Elliott-Cooper, Sita Balani, Kerem Nişancıoğlu, Kojo Koram, Dalia Gebrial, Nadine El-Enany and Luke de Noronha, *Empire's Endgame: Racism and the British State* (London: Pluto Press, 2021); Julian Go, *Policing Empires: Militarization, Race and the Imperial Boomerang in Britain and the US* (Oxford: Oxford University Press, 2024).

8   Storch, 'The Policeman as Domestic Missionary'.

9   Peter Fryer, *Aspects of British Black History* (Surrey: Index Books, 1993), p. 15.

10 Fryer, *Aspects of British Black History*, p. 16; see also Eric Williams, *Capitalism and Slavery* (New York: Capricorn Books, 1996); Ian Baucom, *Specters of the Atlantic: Finance Capital, Slavery and the Philosophy of History* (Durham, NC: Duke University Press, 2005); Timothy Thomas Fortune, *Black and White: Land, Labor, and Politics in the South* (New York: Fords, Howard, & Hulbert, 1884); Peter Linebaugh, *The London Hanged: Crime and Civil Society in the Eighteenth Century* (London: Verso, 2006), pp. 146–53.

11 Karl Marx, *The Poverty of Philosophy* (Moscow: Foreign Languages Publishing House, 1892), p. 108, nauseatingly explains that: 'Slavery is an economic category like any other. Thus it also has its two sides. Let us leave alone the bad side and talk about the good side of slavery', adding

that: '[w]ithout slavery North America, the most progressive of countries, would be transformed into a patriarchal country. Wipe North America off the map of the world, and you will have anarchy – the complete decay of modern commerce and civilization.' Contrary to hagiographies of Marx, he also spoke the language of colonialism as a civilising mission – sounding a bit like J.S. Mill when writing that 'England has to fulfil a double mission in India: one destructive, the other regenerating – the annihilation of old Asiatic Society, and the laying of the material foundations of Western society in Asia.' Karl Marx, *Political Writings Volume II: Surveys from Exile* (New York: Vintage Books, 1974), p. 320. This should be hardly surprising to those who may (want to) be sensitive to Marx's equally troublingly patronising view of the proletariat – adopting colonial language to describe their place in the body politic: 'They cannot represent one another, they must themselves be represented. Their representative must at the same time appear as their master, as an authority over them.' Karl Marx, *The Eighteenth Brumaire of Louis Bonaparte* (Chicago: Charles H. Kerr & Company, 1907), p. 71.

12   Marx, *The Poverty of Philosophy*, p. 108.

13   In David Dabydeen, John Gilmore and Cecily Jones (eds), *The Oxford Companion to Black British History* (Oxford: Oxford University Press, 2007), p. 37.

14   Somerville in Dabydeen et al. (eds), *The Oxford Companion to Black British History*, p. 37.

15   Dabydeen et al. (eds), *The Oxford Companion to Black British History*, p. 534, see also James Walvin, *The Zong: A Massacre, the Law and the End of Slavery* (New Haven, CT: Yale University Press, 2011). For a more literary account of the Zong's trials and 'trouble(s) at sea', see Michelle Cliff's *Free Enterprise* (San Francisco: City Lights, 2004). The story of the Zong and other slave-holding vessels is also memorialised by English Romantic painter Joseph Mallord William Turner, *Slave Ship (Slavers Throwing Overboard the Dead and Dying, Typhoon Coming On)*, 1840. Tate, www.tate.org.uk/tate-etc/issue-50-autumn-2020/winsome-pinnock-jmw-turner-slave-ship (accessed 16 June 2025).

16   This approach to capitalism and policing as intimate bedfellows owes much intellectual debt to the opening passage of the Introduction to Peter Linebaugh, *The London Hanged*, p. xvii.: 'In criminology as in economics there is scarcely a more powerful word than "capital". In the former discipline it denotes death; in the latter it has designated the "substance" or the "stock" of life: apparently opposite meanings. Just why the same

word, "capital", has come to mean both crimes punishable by death and the accumulation of wealth founded on the produce of previous (or dead) labour might be left to etymologists were not the association so striking, so contradictory and so exact in expressing the theme of this book. For this book explores the relationship between the organized death of living labour (capital punishment) and the oppression of the living by dead labour (the punishment of capital).' See, also, Glossary entry for 'cop-italism'.

17 Fryer, *Aspects of British Black History*, p. 17.
18 Karl Marx, *Capital: A Critique of Political Economy, Volume 1* (Chicago: Charles H. Kerr & Company, 1906), p. 834.
19 See Glossary for a more detailed explanation of what is meant by 'racial capitalism' and 'cistem'.
20 See John Gilmore in Dabydeen et al. (eds), *The Oxford Companion to Black British History*, p. 2.
21 James Walvin in Dabydeen et al. (eds), *The Oxford Companion to Black British History*, p. 154.
22 See e.g. Lambros Fatsis, 'Grime: Criminal Subculture or Public Counterculture? A Critical Investigation into the Criminalization of Black Musical Subcultures in the UK', *Crime Media Culture*, 15:3 (2019), 447–61, or Part III of this book.
23 Storch, 'The Policeman as Domestic Missionary', p. 282.
24 Fryer, *Aspects of British Black History*, p. 9.
25 Elsa V. Goveia, 'The West Indian Slave Laws of the Eighteenth Century', *Revista de Ciencias Sociales*, IV (1960), 75–105 at p. 82.
26 W.E.B. Du Bois, *Black Reconstruction in America* (New York: Harcourt, Brace and Company, 1935), p. 12.
27 Linebaugh, *The London Hanged*, p. 409.
28 Linebaugh, *The London Hanged*, pp. 409–10.
29 Linebaugh, *The London Hanged*, p. 433.
30 Linebaugh, *The London Hanged*, p. 410.
31 Linebaugh, *The London Hanged*, p. 426.
32 Brown, 'The Politics of Penal Excess'.
33 Adam Elliott-Cooper, *Black Resistance to British Policing* (Manchester: Manchester University Press, 2021), p. 148.
34 Saidiya Hartman, *Lose Your Mother: A Journey Along the Atlantic Slave Route* (New York: Farrar, Straus and Giroux, 2007), p. 6.
35 Louise Casey, *An Independent Review into the Standards of Behaviour and Internal Culture of the Metropolitan Police Service* (London: Metropolitan

Police, 2023), www.met.police.uk/SysSiteAssets/media/downloads/met/about-us/baroness-casey-review/update-march-2023/baroness-casey-review-march-2023a.pdf (accessed 17 June 2024).

36 Angelo Herndon, *Let Me Live* (Ann Arbor: The University of Michigan Press, 2007), p. 156.

37 Linebaugh, *The London Hanged*, p. 68.

38 Sylvia Wynter, *Black Metamorphosis: New Natives in a New World* (unpublished manuscript, n.d.), p. 372.

39 June Jordan, *Civil Wars* (New York: Simon & Schuster, 1995), p. 47.

40 Paul Gilroy, *After Empire: Melancholia or Convivial Culture?* (London: Routledge, 2004), p. 46.

41 Frantz Fanon, *The Wretched of the Earth* (New York: Grove Press, 1963), p. 40.

42 Cedric J. Robinson, *Black Movements in America* (New York: Routledge, 1997), p. 134.

43 Robinson, *Black Movements in America*, p. 134. Cedric J. Robinson, 'An Inventory of Contemporary Black Politics', *Emergency*, 2:21–8 (1984), p. 21, further cautioned against reductive, economic determinist analyses showing how: '[i]n this fashion, human history was reduced to labour and the relations of production, human life to abstracted, aggregated labour, and historical cultures to mirrors of production'.

44 Wynter, *Black Metamorphosis*, p. 168 (emphasis added).

45 Aimé Césaire, *Return to My Native Land*, trans. John Berger and Anna Bostock (Baltimore: Penguin Books, 1969), p. 67.

46 George Padmore, *How Britain Rules Africa* (New York: Negro Universities Press, 1969); Walter Rodney, *How Europe Underdeveloped Africa* (London: Verso, 2018).

47 Wynter, *Black Metamorphosis*, p. 599.

48 Fatsis, 'Sounds Dangerous', pp. 30–51.

49 Edward W. Said, *Orientalism* (New York: Vintage Books, 1979), p. 254.

50 Carl Schmitt, *The Concept of the Political* (Chicago: University of Chicago Press, 1996), p. 54.

2 Crude noise of a 'vile race': The danger of Black music(s)

1 The expression 'vile race' is taken from Shakespeare's *The Tempest* (Act One, Scene Two). It is also interesting to note, for context, that: 'Like many of his patrons and benefactors, such as the Earl of Southampton, Shakespeare himself invested in the Virginia Company, the spearhead of

English colonization' (Linebaugh and Rediker, *The Many-Headed Hydra*, p. 14). Shakespeare also 'participated in enclosure. He owned a half share in a lease of tithes at Welcombe, whose open fields William Combe proposed to enclose in 1614' (Linebaugh and Rediker, *The Many-Headed Hydra*, p. 18).

2 Grégoire Chamayou, *Manhunts: A Philosophical History* (Princeton: Princeton University Press, 2012), p. 5 and esp. pp. 43–56.

3 Cedric J. Robinson, "The First Attack Is an Attack on Culture," in H.L.T. Quan (ed.), *Cedric J. Robinson: On Racial Capitalism, Black Internationalism, and Cultures of Resistance* (London: Pluto Press, 2019), pp. 69–74.

4 As Ngũgĩ Wa Thiong'o, *Decolonising the Mind: The Politics of Language in African Literature* (London: James Currey, 1986), p. 3, put it: 'the biggest weapon wielded and actually daily unleashed by imperialism […] is the cultural bomb. The effect of a cultural bomb is to annihilate a people's belief in their names, in their languages, in their environment, in their heritage of struggle, in their unity, in their capacities and ultimately in themselves. It makes them see their past as one wasteland of non-achievement and it makes them want to distance themselves from that wasteland.'

5 Calypso is also often referred to as 'kaiso', a word whose origins are unclear. As such the word's etymology is thought to derive from the Hausa language of West Africa (*kaico*), or creolised versions of the French word 'carrousseaux' (*cariso*) and the Spanish word 'caliso'. It eventually became established as 'calypso' owing to the growing dominance of the English language in Trinidad (Errol Hill, 'On the Origin of the Term Calypso', *Ethnomusicology* 11:3 (1967), 359–67; Raymond Quevedo, *Atilla's Kaiso: A Short History of Trinidad Calypso* (St Augustine, Trinidad & Tobago: University of West Indies Press, 1983), p. 4.

6 Georg W.F. Hegel, *Aesthetics: Lectures on Fine Art*, vol. 1 (Oxford: Clarendon Press, 1988), pp. 44–5.

7 Maria Nugent, *Lady Nugent's Journal of Her Residence in Jamaica from 1801 to 1805* (Mona, Jamaica: University of West Indies Press, 2002), p. 138.

8 Simon Gikandi, *Slavery and the Culture of Taste* (Princeton: Princeton University Press, 2011), pp. 263–4.

9 Edmund Davis, 'The History of Theological Education in Jamaica' (PhD thesis, University of Utrecht, 1998), https://dspace.library.uu.nl/bitstream/handle/1874/594/full.pdf?sequence=19 (accessed 10 July 2024), p. 60.

10 Kofi Agawu, 'Representing African Music', *Critical Inquiry* 18:2 (1992), 245–66, at p. 248.
11 Kofi Agawu, *Audible Empire: Music, Global Politics, Critique* (Durham, NC: Duke University Press, 2016), pp. 334–55.
12 Francis Bebey, *African Music: A People's Art* (Chicago: Lawrence Hill Books, 1975), p. 115.
13 Max Horkheimer and Theodor W. Adorno, *Dialectic of Enlightenment* (New York: Continuum, 1990), p. 21.
14 Jacob Ross, *Song for Simone and Other Stories* (London: Karia Press, 1986), pp. 71, 95.
15 Peter Manuel, *Caribbean Currents: Caribbean Music from Rumba to Reggae* (Philadelphia: Temple University Press, 1995), p. 6.
16 Howard S. Becker, *What About Mozart? What About Murder? Reasoning from Cases* (Chicago: University of Chicago Press, 2014), p. 125.
17 Mary Douglas, *Purity and Danger: An Analysis of the Concepts of Pollution and Taboo* (London: Routledge, 1966), pp. 41, 161.
18 Earl Lovelace, *Salt* (London: Faber & Faber, 1996), p. 230.
19 Albert Murray, *The Omni-Americans: Some Alternatives to the Folklore of White Supremacy* (New York: Library of America, 2020), p. 10.
20 W.E.B. Du Bois, *The World and Africa* (Millwood, New York: Kraus-Thomson Organization, 1976), pp. 23, 149.
21 Georg W.F. Hegel, *The Philosophy of History* (New York: The Colonial Press, 1899), pp. 204, 218, 91.
22 Hegel, *The Philosophy of History*, p. 93.
23 Hegel, *The Philosophy of History*, p. 99.
24 Sepulveda in Sylvia Wynter, *We Must Learn to Sit Down Together and Talk About a Little Culture: Decolonising Essays 1967–1984* (Leeds: Peepal Tree Press, 2022), p. 241.
25 Thomas Jefferson, *Notes on the State of Virginia* (Richmond, VA: J.W. Randolph, 1853), p. 151.
26 Jefferson, *Notes on the State of Virginia*, p. 155. Abraham Lincoln, *Complete Works of Abraham Lincoln* (New York: Francis D. Tandy Company, 1905), pp. 142–3, who is otherwise fêted for issuing the Emancipation Proclamation that declared forever free those who were enslaved within the Confederacy, nevertheless expressed similar sentiments to those of his predecessor: 'There is a physical difference between the two which, in my judgment, will probably forever forbid their living together upon the footing of perfect equality, and inasmuch as it becomes a necessity that there must be a difference, I, as well as Judge Douglas, am in favor of the

race to which I belong having a superior position.' In fact, Honest Abe's intentions behind his support of the Emancipation Proclamation have to be seen as a commitment to saving the union of North and South. T. Thomas Fortune, *Black and White*, pp. 22–4, insists on that point and quotes Lincoln who admitted that: 'My paramount object in this struggle is to *save the Union, and is not either to save or to destroy slavery*. If I could save the Union *without* freeing *any* slave *I would do it*; and if I could save it by freeing *all* the slaves I would do it; and if I could save it by freeing some and leaving others alone I would also do that. *What I do about slavery and the colored race, I do because I believe it helps to save the Union*' (Fortune, *Black and White*, p. 23).

27   Wynter, *Black Metamorphosis*, p. 10.

28   Charles Darwin, *The Descent of Man* (New York: Appleton and Company, 1871), p. 203. For anyone shocked to see how the language of natural selection played a leading role in the ideology of racism, and scientific racism in particular, reading the title of Darwin's most famous oeuvre in full might prove even more revealing and much less puzzling: *On the Origin of Species by Means of Natural Selection, or the Preservation of Favoured Races in the Struggle for Life*. For a classic and readable critique of scientific racism(s), see: Stephen J. Gould, *The Mismeasure of Man* (New York: Norton, 1981), alongside Richard C. Lewontin, Steven P. Rose and Leon J. Kamin, *Not In Our Genes: Biology, Ideology, and Human Nature* (New York: Pantheon Books, 1984) as a take-down of biological determinism.

29   Sartre in Fanon, *The Wretched of the Earth*, p. 26.

30   André Breton et al., 'Murderous Humanitarianism', *Race Traitor*, No. 9 (Summer 1998), pp. 67–9.

31   Immanuel Kant, *Observations on the Feeling of the Beautiful and Sublime* (Berkeley: University of California Press, 1960), p. 113, is famous for these unwise words: 'this fellow was quite black from head to foot, a clear proof that what he said was stupid', as he is perhaps for his emphatic declaration that 'The Negroes of Africa have by nature no feeling that rises above the trifling. Mr Hume challenges anyone to cite a single example in which a Negro has shown talents [...] not a single one was ever found who presented anything great in art or science or any other praise-worthy quality' (Kant, *Observations on the Feeling of the Beautiful and Sublime*, pp. 110–11). David Hume, 'Of National Characters', in K. Haakonssen (ed.), *Hume: Political Essays* (Cambridge: Cambridge University Press, 1994), pp. 78–92, 86, to whom Kant referred above and elsewhere (Kant, *Observations on the Feeling of the Beautiful and Sublime*,

p. 123), admitted that: 'I am apt to suspect the negroes and in general all other species of men (for there are four or five different kinds) to be naturally inferior to the whites. There never was a civilized nation of any other complexion than white, nor even any individual eminent either in action or speculation. No ingenious manufactures amongst them, no arts, no science.'

32 Vijay Prashad, *The Darker Nations: A People's History of the Third World* (New York: The New Press, 2008). Such hypocrisy will be exposed at the concluding section of this section, especially with reference to Locke. Suffice to say that when such thinkers criticised slavery, it wasn't meant as a 'protest against the enslavement of black Africans on New World plantations, least of all in colonies that were British. Rather, slavery was a metaphor for legal tyranny, as it was used generally in British parliamentary debates on constitutional theory.' Susan Buck-Morss, 'Hegel and Haiti', *Critical Inquiry* 26:4 (2000), 821–65, at p. 826.

33 Robinson, *Black Movements in America*, p. 134.

34 Toni Cade Bambara, *Deep Sightings and Rescue Missions* (London: The Women's Press, 1996), p. 163.

35 Daniel A. Offiong, 'The Cheerful School and the Myth of the Civilizing Mission of Colonial Imperialism', *Pan-African Journal* 9:1 (1976), 35–54.

36 Edward Kamau Brathwaite, *Folk Culture of the Slaves in Jamaica* (London: New Beacon Books, 1981), p. 17.

37 Aimé Césaire, *Discourse on Colonialism*, trans. Joan Pinkham (New York: Monthly Review Press, 2000), p. 42.

38 Beryl Gilroy, 'Black Old Age … the Diaspora of the Senses?', in Kwesi Owusu (ed.), *Black British Culture and Society: A Text Reader* (London: Routledge, 2000), pp. 129–34, at p. 129.

39 Sylvia Wynter, 'The Ceremony Found: Towards the Autopoetic Turn/ Overturn, its Autonomy of Human Agency and Extraterritoriality of (Self-)Cognition', in J.R. Ambroise and S. Broeck (eds), *Black Knowledges/ Black Struggles: Essays in Critical Epistemology* (Liverpool: Liverpool University Press, 2015), pp. 184–245, 199.

40 Camara Laye, *The Radiance of the King* (New York: The New York Review of Books, 2001), p. 19.

3 Policing 'dangerous noise' one beat at a time

1 David J. McCord, *Statutes at Large of South Carolina*, vol. 9, part 2 (Columbia, SC: A.S. Johnston, 1841), p. 640.

2   Michael Drewett and Martin Cloonan (eds), *Popular Music Censorship in Africa* (Farnham: Ashgate, 2006); John Cowley, *Carnival, Canboulay and Calypso: Traditions in the Making* (New York: Cambridge University Press, 1996); Peter Fryer, *Rhythms of Resistance: African Musical Heritage in Brazil* (London: Pluto Press, 2000).

3   Wagner, *Disturbing the Peace*, p. 5.

4   Cowley, *Carnival, Canboulay and Calypso*, p. 84.

5   Moore, *Nationalizing Blackness*, p. 69.

6   Collins, 'One Hundred Years of Censorship'.

7   Hartman, *Wayward Lives, Beautiful Experiments*, p. 248.

8   Hartman, *Wayward Lives, Beautiful Experiments*, pp. 437–8.

9   Edward B. Rugemer, 'The Development of Mastery and Race in the Comprehensive Slave Codes of the Greater Caribbean during the Seventeenth Century', *The William and Mary Quarterly* 70:3 (2013), 429–58, at p. 443.

10 George Lamming, *The Pleasures of Exile* (London: Pluto Press, 2005), p. 35.

11 Go, *Policing Empires*, p. 57.

12 Fryer, *Aspects of British Black History*, p. 29; Linebaugh, *The London Hanged*, pp. 52–3.

13 Buck-Morss, 'Hegel and Haiti', pp. 826–7.

14 See e.g. David B. Davis, *The Problem of Slavery in Western Culture* (Ithaca, NY: Cornell University Press, 1966); Louis Sala-Molins, *Le Code noir, ou, Le calvaire de Canaan* (Paris: Presses Universitaires de France, 1987).

15 Goveia, 'The West Indian Slave Laws of the Eighteenth Century', p. 84.

16 Goveia, 'The West Indian Slave Laws of the Eighteenth Century', p. 84.

17 This Act legislated for the governance, treatment and punishment of the enslaved people in Jamaica.

18 Wynter, *Black Metamorphosis*, p. 84.

19 Wynter, *Black Metamorphosis*, p. 84.

20 Wynter, *We Must Learn to Sit Down Together and Talk About a Little Culture*, p. 264.

21 Brathwaite, *Folk Culture of the Slaves in Jamaica*, p. 34; Horace Campbell, *Rasta and Resistance: From Marcus Garvey to Walter Rodney* (London: Hansib, 2007), pp. 25, 34.

22 John Storm Roberts, *Black Music of Two Worlds* (New York: Original Music, 1972), p. 37.

23 Roberts, *Black Music of Two Worlds*; Katherine Dunham, *Island Possessed* (Chicago: The University of Chicago Press, 1969), p. 26; Emily

Z. Marshall, *American Trickster: Trauma, Tradition, and Brer Rabbit* (New York: Rowman & Littlefield International, 2019), p. 22.

24 Lamming, *The Pleasures of Exile*, p. 9.

25 Errol Hill is referring here to the offer of capitulation that British invaders successfully made to Spanish governors, who ruled over Trinidad before Britain took over.

26 Errol Hill, *The Trinidad Carnival* (London: New Beacon Books, 1997), p. 33.

27 In Wynter, *Black Metamorphosis*, p. 87; see also: Richard C. Rath, 'African Music in Seventeenth-Century Jamaica: Cultural Transit and Transition', *The William and Mary Quarterly* 50:4 (1993), 700–26, at p. 177.

28 Hill, *The Trinidad Carnival*, pp. 32–3.

29 Hill, *The Trinidad Carnival*, p. 34.

30 On the origins of the religio-cultural festival of Jonkunnu (also: Jonkonnu), Wynter, *Black Metamorphosis*, p. 556, notes that it owes its name to 'John Konny, Cabocero': an 'African merchant prince and partner in the slave trading enterprises of the Prussians', who was 'drawn in as an ancestral loa [= deity], a Lord too, of Life and Death. That he helped the Prussians to buy and sell slaves is not seen as an ethical minus.' Rather, 'John Konny is celebrated because he fought for his own stake and fought off the Dutch.'

31 Wynter, *Black Metamorphosis*, pp. 116–17.

32 Wynter, *Black Metamorphosis*, p. 187.

33 Wynter, *Black Metamorphosis*, p. 187.

34 Wynter, *We Must Learn to Sit Down Together and Talk About a Little Culture*, p. 261.

35 Wynter, *We Must Learn to Sit Down Together and Talk About a Little Culture*, p. 261.

36 Wynter, *Black Metamorphosis*, p. 218.

37 Wynter, *Black Metamorphosis*, p. 199.

38 Simone Browne, *Dark Matters: On Surveillance of Blackness* (Durham, NC: Duke University Press, 2015), p. 22.

39 Marshall, *American Trickster*, p. 1.

40 For some fascinating scholarship on the trickster figure in African oral traditions, see: Henry L. Gates Jr, *The Signifying Monkey: A Theory of Afro-American Literary Criticism* (New York: Oxford University Press, 1988), Emily Z. Marshall, *Anansi's Journey: A Story of Jamaican Cultural Resistance* (Kingston: University of the West Indies Press, 2012), and Marshall, *American Trickster*. Esu-Elegbara/Exú, the Yoruba trickster figure, reigns supreme here, featuring in the mythology of Nigeria

(Esu-Elegbara), Benin (Legba), Brazil (Exú), Cuba (Echu-Elegua), Haiti (Papa Legba) and New Orleans (Papa La Bas) – as the quintessential Afro-diasporic troublemaker and messenger of the Gods. In the English-speaking world, the lyrics of Oscar Brown Jr's *Signifying Monkey* offer a wonderful and unforgettable portrait of the trickster's legendary cunning. For a collection of Anancy stories, see Andrew Salkey, *Anancy's Score* (London: Bogle-L'Ouverture Publications, 1973).

41 Hollis Liverpool, *Rituals of Power and Rebellion: The Carnival Tradition in Trinidad and Tobago, 1763–1962* (Chicago: Research Associates School Times Publications, 2001); Jocelyn Guilbault, *Governing Sound: The Cultural Politics of Trinidad's Carnival Musics* (Chicago: University of Chicago Press, 2007).

42 Wynter, *Black Metamorphosis*, p. 187.

43 Kwesi Owusu and Jacob Ross, *Behind the Masquerade: The Story of Notting Hill Carnival* (London: Arts Media Group, 1988), p. 37.

44 Anonymous calypso, quoted in Charles S. Espinet and Harry Pitts, *Land of the Calypso: The Origin and Development of Trinidad's Folk Song* (Port of Spain: Guardian Commercial Printery, 1944), p. 66. This calypso tune is also found with minor variations in the lyrics, complementing or substituting the 'me' with 'we' (e.g. 'Can't beat we drum'), adding another verse (e.g. 'Can't have we Bacchanal') and sometimes omitting the last line in Trinidadian French Creole. See Owusu and Ross, *Behind the Masquerade*, p. 37 and Cedric J. Robinson, *Black Marxism: The Making of the Black Radical Tradition* (Chapel Hill: The University of North Carolina Press, 2020), p. 246 for such variations.

45 Owusu and Ross, *Behind the Masquerade*, p. 37.

46 Owusu and Ross, *Behind the Masquerade*, p. 37; Bridget Brereton, *Race Relations in Colonial Trinidad 1870–1900* (Cambridge: Cambridge University Press, 1979), p. 162.

47 The Canboulay processions were based on a 're-enactment of putting out fires in the cane fields (a task slaves were often called upon to carry out), and was in part an act of resistance and in part a harvest ritual' (Emily Z. Marshall, Max Farrar and Guy Farrar, 'Popular political cultures and the Caribbean carnival', *Soundings* 2017, no. 67 (2017), 34–49, at p. 36.

48 Susan Campbell, 'Calypso, and Class Struggle in Nineteenth Century Trinidad', *History Workshop*, no. 26 (1988), 1–27, at p. 14.

49 The legislation referenced here is the Habitual Criminals Act which applied not just to persons charged with offences, but also to 'the bands, which under different names infest the colony and are fruitful sources of

immorality and crime' as the *Trinidad Royal Gazette* reported with much sensationalist glee (Andrew Pearse, 'Carnival in Nineteenth Century Trinidad', *Caribbean Quarterly* 4, no. 3/4 (1956), 175–93, at p. 189).

50 Campbell, 'Calypso, and Class Struggle in Nineteenth Century Trinidad', p. 14. See also, Wynter, *Black Metamorphosis*, p. 189; Hill, *The Trinidad Carnival*, p. 59; and Pearse, 'Carnival in Nineteenth Century Trinidad', esp. p. 181, pp. 188–9 and p. 192.

51 Fatsis, 'From Overseer to Officer'; Lambros Fatsis, 'Beat(s) for Blame: UK Drill Music, "Race", and Criminal Justice', in P. Dale, P. Burnard and R. Travis Jr (eds), *Music for Inclusion and Healing in Schools and Beyond: Hip Hop, Techno, Grime, and More* (Oxford: Oxford University Press, 2023), pp. 19–36.

52 Wynter, *Black Metamorphosis*, p. 189.

53 Campbell, 'Calypso, and Class Struggle in Nineteenth Century Trinidad', p. 14.

54 Wynter, *Black Metamorphosis*, p. 189.

55 Campbell, 'Calypso, and Class Struggle in Nineteenth Century Trinidad', pp. 14–15, 26.

56 Hill, *The Trinidad Carnival*, p. 59.

57 Kevin Le Gendre, *Don't Stop the Carnival: Black Music in Britain* (Leeds: Peepal Press, 2018), p. 240.

58 Wynter, *Black Metamorphosis*, p. 189.

59 Wynter, *Black Metamorphosis*, p. 189.

60 Wynter, *Black Metamorphosis*, p. 189.

61 Hill, *The Trinidad Carnival*, p. 45.

62 *Don't Stop the Carnival*, popularised by Sonny Rollins and Harry Belafonte, has an illustrious history musically and historically too. Originally composed by Lord Invader in 1939, it was a response to the banning of carnival during World War II. For more discographic and historical details on, and an excellent rendition of, the song by the mighty Duke of Iron, see: https://archive.culturalequity.org/field-work/calypso-midnight-1946/new-york-city-1246/dont-stop-carnival-part-1 (accessed 16 June 2025). The original version can be heard here: www.youtube.com/watch?v=yhSlXliCG2I (accessed 16 June 2025).

63 Hill, *The Trinidad Carnival*, p. 45.

64 Hill, *The Trinidad Carnival*, p. 46.

65 A rare clip showing The Duke of Iron playing the cuatro/quatro to the tune of *Wild Indian* can be found here: www.youtube.com/watch?v=9TXFFlfyT_g (accessed 16 June 2025). You can also hear 'The

Duke' pay tribute to his trusty four-stringed companion in *The Duke of Calypso*, where he boasts about 'strumming chords on his quatro, it's the Duke of calypso' and about how 'the quatro will let you know, that is the Duke of calypso'.

66 Hill, *The Trinidad Carnival*, pp. 46–7.

67 Hill, *The Trinidad Carnival*, p. 49.

68 Hill, *The Trinidad Carnival*, p. 49.

69 Wynter is referring here to the discarded oil drums that were abandoned in British military bases on the island, with the conclusion of World War II. For a great photographic history of steel pan music, see: Cy Grant, *Ring of Steel: Pan Sound & Symbol* (London: Macmillan, 1999).

70 Wynter, *Black Metamorphosis*, p. 189.

71 Owusu and Ross, *Behind the Masquerade*, p. 45.

72 Hill, *The Trinidad Carnival*, p. 50.

73 Anonymous/uncredited calypso, quoted in Hill, *The Trinidad Carnival*, p. 50.

74 Quevedo, *Atilla's Kaiso*, pp. 57–8.

75 Quevedo, *Atilla's Kaiso*, p. 27.

76 Quevedo, *Atilla's Kaiso*, p. 61.

77 Quevedo, *Atilla's Kaiso*, p. 58.

78 Quevedo, *Atilla's Kaiso*, pp. 60, 63.

79 Quevedo, *Atilla's Kaiso*, p. 62.

80 Quevedo, *Atilla's Kaiso*, pp. 58–9.

81 Lyrics, transcribed by the author, a digital recording of Atilla's tune can be found at: https://bitingtick.blogspot.com/2016/07/banning-of-records-attila-hun.html (accessed 16 June 2025).

82 Quevedo, *Atilla's Kaiso*, p. viii.

83 Hill, *The Trinidad Carnival*, p. 67.

84 Quevedo, *Atilla's Kaiso*, p. ix.

85 This observation is made in the spirit of Stuart Hall's, 'Race, Articulation and Societies Structured in Dominance', in *Sociological Theories on Race and Colonialism* (Paris: UNESCO, 1980), pp. 305–45, at p. 341, ubiquitously cited remark that 'class relations' can also function as 'race relations', with '[r]ace' being 'the modality in which class is "lived", the medium through which class relations are experienced, the form in which it is appropriated and "fought through"'.

86 Lord Protector aka Chinee Patrick Jones, *Class Legislation*. Although this tune was recorded in the 1920s, Protector claimed, in an interview, to have written the first political kaiso/calypso – also noting that he was

charged with sedition as a result of his song. This short interview with Lord Protector, which also features him singing a few verses, can be found online at: www.youtube.com/watch?v=_-WoYMcOTaI (accessed 16 June 2025).

87 Quevedo, *Atilla's Kaiso*, p. 45.

88 Lewis R. Gordon, 'Decolonizing Philosophy', *The Southern Journal of Philosophy* 57 (2019), 16–36, at p. 17.

89 Jalal Al-i Ahmad, *Occidentosis: A Plague from the West* (Berkeley: Mizan Press, 1984).

90 Quevedo, *Atilla's Kaiso*, p. 45.

4 'Salvation 'tis a joyful sound': A concluding soda

1 The title of this section is a quote from Frederick Douglass, *My Bondage and My Freedom* (New York and Auburn: Miller, Orton & Mulligan, 1855), p. 52.

2 Douglass, *My Bondage and My Freedom*, p. 99.

3 Amílcar Cabral, *Return to the Source* (New York: Monthly Review Press, 1973), p. 43.

4 Frederick Douglass, *Narrative of the Life of Frederick Douglass, an American Slave* (Boston: Published at the Anti-Slavery Office, 1846), pp. 13–4.

5 Cyril L.R. James, *C.L.R. James and Revolutionary Marxism: Selected Writings of C.L.R. James 1939–1949* (Atlantic Highlands, NJ: Humanities Press, 1994), p. 77.

6 James, *C.L.R. James and Revolutionary Marxism*, p. 77.

7 Scott, *The Common Wind*.

8 Wynter, *Black Metamorphosis*, p. 71.

9 Scott, *The Common Wind*.

10 See also, Linebaugh and Rediker, *The Many-Headed Hydra*.

11 Douglass, *My Bondage and My Freedom*, p. 447.

12 Gilroy, *The Black Atlantic*, p. 4.

13 A diagram can be found at the website of the National Maritime Museum in Greenwich: www.rmg.co.uk/collections/objects/rmgc-object-254938 (accessed 16 June 2025). *Brooks/Brookes* became famous as a piece of anti-slavery propaganda, because of the way it depicted the brutal reality of the 'regulated slave trade' – as a copy of the Brook(e)s' plan refers to the cruelty of enslavement (Hakim Adi, *African and Caribbean People in Britain: A History* (London: Allen Lane, 2022), p. 87).

14 Brathwaite, *Folk Culture of the Slaves in Jamaica*, p. 13.

15 Brathwaite, *Folk Culture of the Slaves in Jamaica*, p. 7.
16 Brathwaite, *Folk Culture of the Slaves in Jamaica*, p. 7.
17 Gilroy, *The Black Atlantic*, p. 4.
18 Linebaugh, *The London Hanged*, p. 415.
19 Linebaugh, *The London Hanged*, p. 415.
20 Robinson, *Black Marxism*, p. 130. *Palenques* (Colombia, Ecuador, Cuba), *mocambos* and *quilombos* (Brazil) all refer to rural, mostly hillside, fugitive settlements that were set up by enslaved people in Latin America and the Caribbean to escape forced labour and create spaces of community, struggle and resistance. They are also known as *cumbes* (Venezuela), *garífunas* (Honduras and Guatemala), *cimarrones* (Mexico, Puerto Rico, Cuba) and maroons (Jamaica, Suriname) or *marrons* (Haiti). For a historical overview of marronage as a practice of struggle across Latin America and the Caribbean, see Givânia M. Da Silva and Bárbara O. Souza, 'Quilombos in Brazil and the Americas: Black Resistance in Historical Perspective', *Agrarian South*, 11:1 (2022), 112–33 and Flávio Gomes, 'Quilombos, Hotbeds of Afro-Brazilian Resistance', *UNESCO* (2024), https://courier.unesco.org/en/articles/quilombos-hotbeds-afro-brazilian-resistance (accessed 10 April 2025).
21 Robinson, *Black Movements in America*, p. 53.
22 Angela Y. Davis, 'Reflections on the Black Woman's Role in the Community of Slaves', *The Massachusetts Review*, 13:1/2 (1972), 81–100.
23 Robinson, *Black Marxism*, pp. 130–66; Robinson, 'An Inventory of Contemporary Black Politics'.
24 Gikandi, *Slavery and the Culture of Taste*, p. 264.
25 Vincent Brown, *Tacky's Revolt: The Story of an Atlantic Slave War* (Cambridge, MA: Belknap Press, 2020).
26 Victor S. Reid, *New Day* (New York: Alfred A. Knopf, 1949); Victor S. Reid, *Sixty-Five* (London; Harlow, Essex: Pearson Education, 1968).
27 Cyril L.R. James, *The Black Jacobins* (London: Penguin, 1980).
28 H.L.T. Quan, "It's Hard to Stop Rebels that Time Travel': Democratic Living and the Radical Reimagining of Old Worlds', in G.T. Johnson and A. Lubin (eds), *Futures of Black Radicalism* (London: Verso, 2017), pp. 173–93.
29 Fatsis and Lamb, *Policing the Pandemic*, pp. 45–77.
30 Orlando Patterson, *Slavery and Social Death: A Comparative Study* (Cambridge, MA: Harvard University Press, 1982).
31 For more information on Dunbar's Mississippi plantation, The Forrest, see: 'William Dunbar', *Monticello*, www.monticello.org/research-education/thomas-jefferson-encyclopedia/william-dunbar (accessed 16 June 2025).

32 Toni Morrison, *Playing in the Dark: Whiteness and the Literary Imagination* (New York: Vintage Books, 1992), p. 43.

33 Peter Gay, *John Locke on Education* (New York: Bureau of Publications, Teachers College, Columbia University, 1964), p. 1.

34 John Locke, *Two Treatises of Government* (London: Whitmore and Fenn and C. Brown, 1821), pp. 258, 194, 200, 339.

35 David Armitage, 'John Locke, Carolina, and the "'Two Treatises of Government'", *Political Theory*, 32:5 (2004), 602–27.

36 Locke, *Two Treatises of Government*, p. 1.

37 Sylvia Wynter, '1492: A New World View', in V. Lawrence and R. Nettleford (eds), *Race, Discourse, and the Origin of the Americas: A New World View* (Washington: Smithsonian Institution Press, 1995).

38 Robinson, *Black Marxism*, p. 66.

39 Robinson, *Black Movements in America*, p. 40.

40 Elizabeth Wilson, 'Le voyage et l'espace clos – Island and Journey as Metaphor: Aspects of Woman's Experience in the Works of Francophone Caribbean Women Novelists', in C.B. Davies and E.S. Fido (eds), *Out of the Kumbla: Caribbean Women and Literature* (Trenton, NJ: Africa World Press, 1990), pp. 45–58.

41 Robinson, *Black Marxism*, p. 241.

42 James, *The Black Jacobins*, p. 69.

43 James, *The Black Jacobins*, p. 15.

44 June Jordan, *Moving Towards Home: Political Essays* (London: Virago, 1989), p. 186.

Part II: Does it belong here? Policing Black music as 'out of place' in post-war Britain

1 Lamming, *The Pleasures of Exile*, p. 12. Lamming builds this wonderful book around the encounter and the power dynamics in the unequal relationship of Prospero and Caliban, from Shakespeare's *Tempest*, as a poetic critique of colonialism. Aimé Césaire would revisit this theme in his own play, *A Tempest*, in 1969 – nine years after Lamming's book was originally published. For more, see Aimé Césaire, *A Tempest*, trans. Richard Miller (New York: Theatre Communications Group, 2002).

2 The term 'West Indian' could and should be contested, lumping together – as it does – people and islands from the anglophone Caribbean that are not one and the same. It is nevertheless used here to denote how Caribbean people were identified as West Indians by white Britons, while also noting

how they came to adopt the term themselves. George Lamming, *The Pleasures of Exile*, p. 214, explains: 'No Barbadian, no Trinidadian, no St Lucian, no islander from the West Indies sees himself as a West Indian until he encounters another islander in foreign territory. It was only when the Barbadian childhood corresponded with the Grenadian or the Guianese childhood in important details of folk-lore, that the wider identification was arrived at. In this sense, most West Indians of my generation were born in England. The category West Indian, formerly understood as a geographical term, now assumes cultural significance.'

3 For details on the history of these three ships and for a fascinating look at passenger lists detailing who boarded them, see: *Ormonde, Almanzora, Windrush*, The National Archives, https://beta.nationalarchives.gov.uk/ explore-the-collection/stories/ormonde-almanzora-windrush/ (accessed 16 June 2025).

4 Adi, *African and Caribbean People in Britain*, p. 387.

5 Adi, *African and Caribbean People in Britain*, p. 389.

6 David Olusoga, *Black and British: A Forgotten History* (London: Pan Books, 2016), p. 467.

7 Tony Kushner, *The Battle of Britishness: Migrant Journeys, 1685 to the Present* (Manchester: Manchester University Press, 2012), p. 164.

8 Olusoga, *Black and British*, p. 493.

9 Edward Kamau Brathwaite, *History of the Voice* (London: New Beacon Books, 1984), p. 8.

10 Brathwaite, *History of the Voice*, p. 8.

11 Nation language is the term Brathwaite coined 'in contrast to *dialect*'. The word 'dialect' has been bandied about for a long time, and it carries very pejorative overtones. Dialect is thought of as 'bad English'. Dialect is 'inferior English'. Dialect is the language used when you want to make fun of someone. Caricature speaks in dialect'. Nation language on the other hand, 'is the language which is influenced very strongly by the African model, the African aspect of our new World/Caribbean heritage. English it may be in terms of some of its lexical features. But in its contours, its rhythm and timbre, its sound explosions, it is not English, even though the words, as you hear them, might be English to a greater or lesser degree' (Brathwaite, *History of the Voice*, p. 13). In a characteristic passage, Brathwaite points out how the (iambic) pentameter used in English verse (= five pairs of syllables with an unstressed syllable followed by a stressed syllable), does not lend itself to describing the cultural and natural environment of the Caribbean. As he so memorably put it: 'The hurricane does not roar in pentameters'

and moves on to (rightly) praise legendary jazz trumpeter and poet, Shake Keane's (1979) *Volcano Suite* (Shake Keane, *The Volcano Suite: A Series of Five Poems* (St Vincent: Reliance Press, 1979); Brathwaite, *History of the Voice*, p. 12). For a brilliant biography of Shake Keane, see: Philip Nanton, *Riff: The Shake Keane Story* (London: Papillote Press, 2021). For similar accounts on Black English, especially from the perspective of the anglophone Caribbean, see: Beryl Gilroy, *Black Teacher* (London: Bogle L'Ouverture Press, 1976), pp. 41–2). For a passionate defence of Black English, from an African-American perspective, see: Jordan, *Civil Wars*, pp. 59–73). For a fantastic illustration of June Jordan's Black English politics in action, see her beautiful novel *His Own Where*, which was written entirely in Black English and is a must-read as a utopian vision for urban conviviality (June Jordan, *His Own Where* (New York: Crowell, 1971)). On the more musical side of things, Mighty Sparrow's *Dan is the Man* remains the best bitingly sarcastic critique of linguistic colonialism that I know.

12 Brathwaite, *History of the Voice*, p. 13.

13 Stuart Hall, *Old and New Identities, Old and New Ethnicities*, in *Culture, Globalization, and the World-System: Contemporary Conditions for the Representation of Identity*, ed. A.D. King (Minneapolis: University of Minnesota Press, 1997), 41–68, at p. 24.

14 Gurminder K. Bhambra, 'Locating Brexit in the Pragmatics of Race, Citizenship and Empire', in W. Outhwaite (ed.), *Brexit: Sociological Responses* (London: Anthem Press, 2017), pp. 91–100, at p. 92.

15 The fourteen territories are: Anguilla; Bermuda; British Antarctic Territory (BAT); British Indian Ocean Territory (BIOT); British Virgin Islands; Cayman Islands; Falkland Islands; Gibraltar; Montserrat; Pitcairn, Henderson, Ducie and Oeno Islands; Saint Helena, Ascension and Tristan da Cunha; South Georgia and the South Sandwich Islands; Turks and Caicos Islands; UK Sovereign Base Areas. For geographical information compiled by the Permanent Committee on Geographical Names (PCGN), see: https://assets.publishing.service.gov.uk/media/5fdca611e90e07452a1c44de/ UKOTs_Information_Paper.pdf (accessed 16 June 2025).

16 Lambros Fatsis, 'When the Exception Makes the Rules: Public Order Policing in the Aftermath of Covid-19', in Anna Di Ronco and Rosella Selmini (eds), *Criminalisation of Dissent in Times of Crisis* (London: Palgrave, 2024).

17 Linebaugh, *The London Hanged*, p. 416.

18 W.E.B. Du Bois, 'Of the Culture of White Folk', *The Journal of Race Development*, 7:4 (1917), 434–47, at p. 437.

19 James, *The Black Jacobins*, p. 51.
20 Joan Riley, *The Unbelonging* (London: Women's Press, 1985).
21 Kushner, *The Battle of Britishness*, p. 186.
22 The term 'UK soundsystem reggae' is employed here to refer to reggae music played in and by UK soundsystem collectives. I am therefore not suggesting, or implying, that the music that was played was reggae made in the UK but that it was played here. For more information/details about soundsystems and soundsystem culture, read on or see: Lambros Fatsis, 'Arresting Sounds: What UK Soundsystem Culture Teaches Us about Police Racism and Public Life', in M. Charles and M.W. Gani (eds), *Black Music in Britain in the 21st Century* (Liverpool: Liverpool University Press, 2023), pp. 181–97, at pp. 183–5.
23 Paul Gilroy, 'Working with "Wogs": Aliens, Denizens and the Machinations of Denialism', *Communication, Culture and Critique*, 15:2 (2022), 122–38, at p. 122.
24 Fatsis, 'Policing the Union's Black'.

5 'If you brown, they say you can't stick around': Policing and (cr)immigration in post-war Britain

1 The title of this chapter is borrowed from the lyrics of Lord Kitchener's, *If You Brown*. You can listen to it in full at the Honest Jon's Records Bandcamp page: https://honestjonsrecords.bandcamp.com/track/if-you-brown (accessed 16 June 2025). All the other tunes mentioned above are to be found in the, currently, eight-volume compilation series that Honest Jon's has released since 2002 – also featured on the label's Bandcamp page.
2 The newsreel film in question is available from the British Pathé's online archive and can be accessed at: www.britishpathe.com/asset/84440 (accessed 16 June 2025) The original recorded version of *London is the Place For Me*, can be heard here: https://honestjonsrecords.bandcamp.com/track/london-is-the-place-for-me (accessed 16 June 2025).
3 While Paul Gilroy's liner notes are only available as an accompaniment to the compilation album (in LP format), you can listen to and find out more about the compilation series, here: https://honestjons.com/shop/artist/London_Is_The_Place_For_Me/release/2_Calypso_And_Kwela_Highlife_And_Jazz_From_Young_Black_London (accessed 16 June 2025).
4 To listen to *If You Brown*, go to: https://honestjonsrecords.bandcamp.com/track/if-you-brown (accessed 16 June 2025).

5 To listen to *If You're Not White You're Black*, go to: https://honestjon srecords.bandcamp.com/track/if-youre-not-white-youre-black (accessed 16 June 2025).

6 To listen to *My Landlady*, go to: https://honestjonsrecords.bandcamp. com/track/my-landlady (accessed 16 June 2025).

7 *Bulldog Don't Bite Me* is a traditional tune sung primarily by fishermen about boat-owners who would set their dogs on them, if the catch was too small. Applied to a British context, however, this version by multi-instrumentalist-turned-calypsonian Al(bon) Timothy encourages a different reading that makes Britain the bulldog whose bite is to be feared so much. I owe this interpretation to my conversations with Laura Rennie, whose current PhD thesis thoughtfully and eloquently expands on this point. You can listen to *Bulldog Don't Bite Me* here: https://honestjon srecords.bandcamp.com/track/bulldog-dont-bite-me (accessed 16 June 2025).

8 To listen to *Drink-A-Rum* in full, go to: https://honestjonsrecords.band camp.com/track/drink-a-rum (accessed 16 June 2025).

9 Winthrop R. Holder, '"Notting Eh Strange": Black Stalin Speaks!', *Small Axe*, 5:1 (2001), 140–58, https://doi.org/10.1353/smx.2001.0006, at pp. 140–1; Stuart Hall, 'Calypso Kings', *Guardian* (28 June 2002), www. theguardian.com/culture/2002/jun/28/nottinghillcarnival2002.nottingh illcarnival (accessed 29 July 2024); Hugh Hodges, 'Kitchener Invades England: The London Calypsos of Aldwyn Roberts', *Wasafiri*, 20:45 (2005), 24–30.

10 Simon Gikandi, *Writing in Limbo: Modernism and Caribbean Literature* (Ithaca, NY: Cornell University Press, 1992), pp. 15–20 at p. 96.

11 Toni Cade Bambara, 'Preface', in Julie Dash (ed.), *Daughters of the Dust: The Making of an African American Woman's Film* (New York, NY: New Press, 1992), p. xii.

12 Donald Hinds, *Journey to an Illusion: The West Indian in Britain* (London: Bogle L'Ouverture, 1966).

13 Peter Fryer, *Staying Power: The History of Black People in Britain* (London: Pluto Press, 1984), p. 1.

14 Sam Selvon, *The Lonely Londoners* (Toronto: TSAR, 1991), p. 124.

6 (Don't) Welcome to Britain

1 Olusoga, *Black and British*, p. 491.

2 Olusoga, *Black and British*, p. 491.

3   Olusoga, *Black and British*, pp. 491–2.

4   Olusoga, *Black and British*, p. 492.

5   Olusoga, *Black and British*, p. 492.

6   Olusoga, *Black and British*, pp. 492–3.

7   Olusoga, *Black and British*, p. 495.

8   Olusoga, *Black and British*, p. 495.

9   Olusoga, *Black and British*, p. 498.

10 Preeti Dhillon, *The Shoulders We Stand On: How Black and Brown People Fought for Change in the United Kingdom* (London: Dialogue Books, 2023), p. 86.

11 Winston N. Trew, *Black for a Cause ... Not Just Because ...: The Case of the 'Oval 4' and the Story of Black Power in Britain* (London: Trew Books, 2015), p. 203.

12 Trew, *Black for a Cause*, pp. 203, 216.

13 Powell's nauseating racist rant can be read in full at Channel 4 News, 'Rivers of Blood speech' (2008), www.channel4.com/news/articles/dis patches/rivers+of+blood+speech/1934152.html (accessed 16 June 2025).

14 Ambalavaner Sivanandan, 'From Resistance to Rebellion: Asian and Afro-Caribbean Struggles in Britain', *Race & Class*, 23:2–3 (1981), 111–52, at p. 129.

15 Dhillon, *The Shoulders We Stand On*, p. 37.

16 Dhillon, *The Shoulders We Stand On*, p. 33.

17 Dhillon, *The Shoulders We Stand On*, pp. 60–1, 67.

18 Nadine El-Enany, *(B)ordering Britain: Law, Race and Empire* (Manchester: Manchester University Press, 2019); Goodfellow, 2020).

19 Amelia Gentleman, *The Windrush Betrayal: Exposing the Hostile Environment* (London: Faber & Faber, 2019).

20 This account of post-war immigration legislation in Britain, has been woven together by borrowing from: Olusoga, *Black and British*, pp. 490–519; Fryer, *Staying Power*, pp. 372–81, and Adi, *African and Caribbean People in Britain*, pp. 327–8, at p. 510; Luke de Noronha, *Deporting Black Britons: Portraits of Deportation to Jamaica* (Manchester: Manchester University Press, 2020).

21 Yvette Cooper, 'Home Secretary Launches new Border Security Command', UK Government (2024), www.gov.uk/government/news/home-secretary-launches-new-border-security-command (accessed 16 June 2025).

22 More info on the Rwanda scheme is provided by The Right to Remain: www.righttoremain.org.uk/what-we-know-about-the-rwanda-act-and-tre aty-so-far (accessed 16 June 2025), one of the 270 charities and expert

organisations that called on Peers (= members of the House of Lords) to reject the Rwanda Bill.

7 Racism runs riot

1 Edward Pilkington, *Beyond the Mother Country: West Indians and the Notting Hill White Riots* (London: Bloomsbury, 2021).

2 Fryer, *Staying Power*, pp. 298–9.

3 Jacqueline Jenkinson, *Black 1919: Riots, Racism and Resistance in Imperial Britain* (Liverpool: Liverpool University Press, 2009); Le Gendre, *Don't Stop the Carnival*, p. 94.

4 Fryer, *Staying Power*, p. 298.

5 Fryer, *Staying Power*, pp. 391–9; Institute of Race Relations (IRR), *Policing Against Black People* (London: Institute of Race Relations, 1987).

6 Olusoga, *Black and British*, p. 496; Adi, *African and Caribbean People in Britain*, p. 395.

7 Pilkington, *Beyond the Mother Country*, pp. 41–51.

8 C.L.R. James, *Spheres of Existence: Selected Writings* (London: Allison & Busby, 1980), pp. 245–55.

9 Pilkington, *Beyond the Mother Country*, p. 47.

10 Learie Constantine, *Colour Bar* (London: Stanley Paul and Co. Ltd, 1954).

11 Pilkington, *Beyond the Mother Country*, pp. 47–8.

12 Du Bois, *Black Reconstruction*, p. 700.

13 Pilkington, *Beyond the Mother Country*, p. 69.

14 Dhillon, *The Shoulders We Stand On*, p. 89.

15 The hurricane quotes here come from Grace Nichols's poem *Hurricane Hits England*, recited and discussed in this recording: 'Grace Nichols: I Have Crossed an Ocean', *Bloodaxe Books* (2010), https://vimeo.com/11987216 (accessed 16 June 2025).

16 British Pathé, *Pathe Reporter Meets (1948)*, www.youtube.com/watch?v=QDH4IBeZF-M (accessed 16 June 2025).

17 To watch the film *Our Jamaican Problem*, visit British Pathé, *Our Jamaican Problem* (1955), www.youtube.com/watch?v=A2VyKtfByXk (accessed 16 June 2025).

18 Ida B. Wells-Barnett, *On Lynchings: Southern Horrors; A Red Record; Mob Rule in New Orleans* (New York: Arno Press, 1969).

19 Pilkington, *Beyond the Mother Country*.

20 Paul Gilroy, *Black Britain: A Photographic History* (London: Saqi Books, 2007), p. 152.

21 A beautiful documentary on Count Suckle and Duke Vin (aka 'The Tickler'), UK's sound system pioneers, is available from Gusto Films: *Count Suckle and Duke Vin*, https://gustofilms.com/duke-vin-and-the-birth-of-ska (accessed 16 June 2025); for the trailer: https://vimeo.com/774368 (accessed 16 June 2025).

22 Ishmahil Blagrove, *Carnival: A Photographic and Testimonial History of the Notting Hill Carnival* (London: Ricenpeas, 2014), p. 46; Le Gendre, *Don't Stop the Carnival*, pp. 239–40.

23 The reference here is to referring to Little Rock, Arkansas where nine African American students were prevented from attending a racially segregated school, under the instructions of Orval Faubus, the Governor of Arkansas – who inspired Charles Mingus's protest tune against him, namely: *Fables of Faubus*. You can hear this gem of a tune here: www.youtube.com/watch?v=m2nBEoPHaDM (accessed 16 June 2025). Mark Olden, *Murder in Notting Hill* (Winchester: Zero Books, 2011).

24 Joseph A. Hunte, *Nigger Hunting in England?* (London: West Indian Standing Conference, 1966), p. 12.

25 Gilroy, 'Working with "Wogs"', pp. 122–3.

26 Linton Kwesi Johnson, *Selected Poems* (London: Penguin, 2022), p. 20.

27 The story of the Mangrove is now known thanks to Steve McQueen's (2020) *Mangrove*. However, a much better documentary precedes it. Made in 1973 by John La Rose (poet, activist and co-founder of the George Padmore Institute, co-owner of New Beacon Books and Press and leading member of the Caribbean Artists Movement) and filmmaker Franco Rosso, who also made the essential movie, *Babylon* in 1980), *Mangrove Nine* is available from the George Padmore Institute, www.georgepadmoreinstitute.org/news-and-events/mangrove-nine-documentary-1973 (accessed 16 June 2025). A sample of Altheia Jones-LeCointe's comments used by Kano in *Hoodies All Summer*, is taken from that documentary.

28 Dhillon, *The Shoulders We Stand On*, pp. 118–19.

29 The Fasimba was the youth wing of the South East London's Parents' Organisation, set up in 1969 by a group of concerned parents with the state of mis-education their children received in British schools (Bernard Coard, *How the West Indian Child is Made Educationally Sub-normal in the British School System: The Scandal of the Black Child in Schools* (London: New Beacon Books, 1971). The name comes from the Fasimba regiment of Shaka Zulu, king of the Zulu Kingdom in South Africa (Trew, *Black for a Cause*, pp. 148, 78).

30 Trew, *Black for a Cause*.

31 Winston N. Trew, 'He Didn't Just Steal Mailbags, He Stole Lives', *Proof*, 6 (2024), 25–9.

32 Fryer, *Staying Power*, p. 392; Derek Humphry, *Police Power and Black People* (London: Panther, 1972), p. 108.

33 Maureen Cain, *Society and the Policeman's Role* (London: Routledge, 1973), p. 19.

34 Blagrove, *Carnival*, pp. 122–55.

35 Blagrove, *Carnival*, p. 154 (emphasis added).

36 Dhillon, *The Shoulders We Stand On*, pp. 240, 255–6.

37 Institute of Race Relations (IRR), 'Police against black people', *Race & Class*, 20:4 (1979), 413–16; Fatsis, 'Policing the Union's Black'.

38 Trew, *Black for a Cause*; John Narayan, 'British Black Power: The Anti-imperialism of Political Blackness and the Problem of Nativist Socialism', *The Sociological Review*, 67:5 (2019), 945–67; Dhillon, *The Shoulders We Stand On*. For an indicative list of groups, campaigns and movements of that time, see Dhillon, *The Shoulders We Stand On*, pp. 329–30.

39 For a sonic account of the New Cross Massacre, Johnny Osbourne's (1981) *13 Dead (Nothing Said)* remains essential listening, just like Menelik Shabazz's (1982) *Blood Ah Go Run* remains essential viewing – alongside John La Rose's, *The New Cross Massacre Story* (London: George Padmore Institute, 2020), authoritative account of the New Cross Massacre Action Committee's struggle for justice.

40 Tony Jefferson, 'Policing the Riots: From Bristol and Brixton to Tottenham, via Toxteth, Handsworth, etc.', *Criminal Justice Matters*, 87:1 (2012), 8–9 at p. 8.

41 Stuart Hall, Chas Critcher, Tony Jefferson et al., *Policing the Crisis: Mugging, the State and Law and Order* (London: Macmillan, 1982); Paul Gilroy, *There Ain't No Black in the Union Jack* (London: Routledge, 2002); Fatsis, 'Policing the Union's Black'.

42 A transcript of that interview is available at the Margaret Thatcher Foundation: www.margaretthatcher.org/document/103485 (accessed 16 June 2025).

43 A digital copy of the *Vagrancy Act (1824)* is available at: www.legislation.gov.uk/ukpga/Geo4/5/83/enacted?view=plain (accessed 16 June 2025).

44 Clare Demuth, *'Sus': A Report on the Vagrancy Act 1824* (London: Runnymede Trust, 1978).

45 La Rose, *The New Cross Massacre Story*, p. 46.

46 Leslie G. Scarman, *The Scarman Report: Report of an Inquiry* (Harmondsworth: Penguin Books, 1986), p. 209.

47 Scarman, *The Scarman Report*, p. 209.

48 Olusoga, *Black and British*, p. 516.

49 John Clare, 'Eyewitness in Brixton', in John Benyon (ed.), *Scarman and After: Essays Reflecting on Lord Scarman's Report, The Riots, and Their Aftermath* (Oxford: Pergamon Press, 1984), pp. 46–53, at p. 52.

50 Special Branch, *Political Extremism and the Campaign for Police Accountability Within the Metropolitan Police District* (London: London Metropolitan Police, 1983), pp. 36–7.

51 For a brilliant documentary on the 1985 uprisings, see the Ceddo Film Collective's (1985) *The People's Account*.

52 Johnson, *Selected Poems*, p. 94.

53 APC (Association for a People's Carnival), *'Police Carnival' 1989: A Report on the Notting Hill Carnival* (London: APC, 1989).

54 APC, *'Police Carnival' 1989*, p. 1.

55 Tanzil Chowdhury, 'Policing the "Black party": Racialized Drugs Policing at Festivals in the UK', in K. Koram (ed.), *The War on Drugs and the Global Colour Line* (London: Pluto Press, 2019), pp. 48–65.

56 Demuth, *'Sus'*.

57 Elliott-Cooper, *Black Resistance to British Policing*, p. 159.

58 Paul Gilroy, *Between Camps: Race, Identity and Nationalism at the End of the Colour Line* (London: Allen Lane, 2000), p. 49.

59 MacFarlane's poem can be accessed at: https://poetrysociety.org.uk/poems/joy-gardner-1993 (accessed 16 June 2025).

60 William Macpherson, *The Stephen Lawrence Inquiry* (London: HMSO, 1999).

61 Stuart Hall, 'From Scarman to Stephen Lawrence', *History Workshop Journal*, 48 (1999), 187–97.

62 Kwame Ture and Charles Hamilton, *Black Power: The Politics of Liberation* (London: Vintage, 1967).

63 Raphael Schlembach, *Spycops: Secrets and Disclosure in the Undercover Policing Inquiry* (Bristol: Policy Press, 2024), pp. 25, 30.

64 Lambros Fatsis, 'Racism Runs Riot', *The British Society of Criminology Blog (2024)*, https://thebscblog.wordpress.com/2024/08/21/racism-runs-riot/ (accessed 21 August 2024).

65 Fatsis, 'When Police Racism is Denied'.

66 Renato Rosaldo, *Culture and Truth: The Remaking of Social Analysis* (Boston, MA: Beacon Press, 1989).

67 Paul Gilroy, *Postcolonial Melancholia* (New York, NY: Columbia University Press, 2005).

68 Pilkington, *Beyond the Mother Country*, p. 68.

69 Pilkington, *Beyond the Mother Country*, p. 146.

70 Adi, *African and Caribbean People in Britain*, pp. 24–5.

71 Samuel Estwick, *Considerations on the Negroe Cause Commonly So Called, Addressed to the Right Honourable Lord Mansfield, Lord Chief Justice of the Court of King's Bench, &c.* (London: Printed for J. Dodsley, 1788), p. 47.

72 Césaire, *Discourse on Colonialism*, p. 36.

73 Du Bois, *The World and Africa*, p. 23.

74 Roger Mais, *Now We Know* (University of the West Indies, Mona Library Digital Collections, 1944), http://contentdm64-srv.uwimona.edu.jm/cdm/ref/collection/RogerMS/id/1575 (accessed 7 August 2024).

75 Oscar R. Dathorne, 'Roger Mais: The Man On The Cross', *Studies in the Novel*, 4:2 (1972), 275–83, at p. 277.

76 For an example, consider this speech by (Sir) Winston Churchill at a banquet of West Indies sugar planters in London, on 20 July 1939: 'Our possession of the West Indies … gave us the strength, the support, but especially the capital, the wealth, at a time when no other European nation possessed such a reserve, which enabled us to come through that great struggle of the Napoleonic Wars, the keen competition of the eighteenth and nineteenth centuries, and enabled us … to lay the foundation of that commercial and financial leadership … which enabled us to make our great position in the world' (Fryer, *Aspects of British Black History*, p. 10).

77 Susan D. Pennybacker, *From Scottsboro to Munich: Race and Political Culture in 1930s Britain* (Oxford: Princeton University Press, 2009), p. 96.

78 Carol Anderson, 'From Hope to Disillusion: African Americans, the United Nations, and the Struggle for Human Rights, 1944–1947', *Diplomatic History*, 20:4 (1996), 531–63 at p. 539.

79 Hannah Arendt, *The Origins of Totalitarianism* (London: Penguin Books, 1975).

80 Zygmunt Bauman, *Modernity and the Holocaust* (Ithaca, NY: Cornell University Press, 2000).

81 Alfie Hancox, 'The Left Must Stop Whitewashing the NHS', *Discover Society* (2020), https://archive.discoversociety.org/2020/10/07/viewpoint-the-left-must-stop-whitewashing-the-nhs/ (accessed 29 July 2024).

82 Ian Sinclair, 'Retrieved from the Memory Hole: British Intervention in Greece in the 1940s', *openDemocracy* (2017), www.opendemocracy.net/en/opendemocracyuk/retrieved-from-memory-hole-british-intervention-in-greece-in-1940s (accessed 5 August 2024).

83 Gilroy, *There Ain't No Black in the Union Jack*, pp. 86, 140.

8 'It gets me 'fraid when Babylon raid'

1 Peter Fryer, *Mrs Grundy: Studies in English Prudery* (London: Dennis Dobson, 1963), p. 15.
2 Fryer, *Mrs Grundy*, p. 223.
3 Fryer, *Mrs Grundy*, p. 224.
4 Fryer, *Mrs Grundy*, p. 224.
5 Fryer, *Mrs Grundy*, p. 226.
6 Adi, *African and Caribbean People in Britain*, p. 321.
7 Pilkington, *Beyond the Mother Country*, pp. 61–2, 46.
8 For recorded examples of what soundsystem sessions sound like, visit: www.whocorkthedance.com (accessed 16 June 2025).
9 Hip-hop and rap are interrelated, but they are often mistaken for or reduced to each other despite subtle differences that set them apart. Hip-hop describes a music genre that involves heavy, 'fat'/'phat' rhythms/beats that are taken/sampled from chunks of pre-recorded music tracks which are blended with other sampled bits of sound, be it vocals, horns, or spoken word. Rap usually refers to the practice of rhyming over beats/pre-recorded tracks and could be described as the lyrical/rhymed component of hip-hop.
10 Gilroy, *The Black Atlantic*, p. ix.
11 For a taste of the entire sweep of Jamaican music, listen to Linton Kwesi Johnson's ten-part history of Jamaican music for BBC Radio 6: www.bbc.co.uk/programmes/b00sl252/episodes/player (accessed 16 June 2025), or a similar broadcast for radiobubble featuring MC Trooper on the mic and Boulevard Soundsystem (= this book's author) on the turntables, www.mixcloud.com/lambrosfatsis/history-of-jamaican-music-feat-mc-tr ooper-part-1 (accessed 16 June 2025) (Part I) and www.mixcloud.com/lambrosfatsis/history-of-jamaican-music-pt2-feat-boulevard-soundsystem-mc-trooper (accessed 16 June 2025) (Part II).
12 Lloyd Bradley, *Bass Culture: When Reggae Was King* (London: Serpent's Tail, 2001), pp. 427–8; Gilroy, *There Ain't No Black in the Union Jack*, pp. 95–104, 115–16, 128; Gilroy, *Black Britain*, p. 152; Paul Ward, 'Sound System Culture: Place, Space and Identity in the United Kingdom, 1960–1989', *Historia Contemporánea*, 57:2 (2018), 349–76; Campbell, *Rasta and Resistance*, p. 200.
13 Cecil Gutzmore, 'Carnival, the State and the Black Masses in the United Kingdom', in Clive Harris and Winston James (eds), *Inside Babylon: The Caribbean Diaspora in Britain* (London: Verso, 1993), pp. 207–12, at p. 208,

Transpontine, '"Mek" It Blow: Police Raid New Cross Jah Shaka Blues Dance', *Transpontine Blog* (2015), http://transpont.blogspot.com/2015/10/mek-it-blow-police-raid-new-cross-jah.html (accessed 12 August 2024).

14 Bradley, *Bass Culture*, p. 428.

15 John Brown, *Policing by Multi-Racial Consent: The Handsworth Experience* (London: Bedford Square, 1982), pp: 9, 6.

16 In John Brown's (1982) *Shades of Grey* report that is quoted here and discussed below, the author alternates between the words 'criminal' (pp. 9 and 31) and 'criminalised' (pp. 6 and 46). The *Shades of Grey* report is included in John Brown's book that is cited here.

17 Contrary to popular usage, no references are made to 'Rastafarianism' out of respect for and faithfulness to the political vocabulary of Rastafari philosophy which rejects '-isms' and 'schisms', especially when applied to the Rasta movement itself.

18 Campbell, *Rasta and Resistance*, p. 194.

19 Horace Campbell and Barry Chevannes, 'Reviews', *Caribbean Quarterly*, 26:4 (1980), 86–95, at p. 86.

20 Brown, *Policing by Multi-Racial Consent*, pp. 1–54.

21 W.E.B. Du Bois, *John Brown* (Philadelphia: G.W. Jacobs & Company, 1909).

22 Ernest Cashmore and Barry Troyna, *Black Youth in Crisis* (London: Allen & Unwin, 1982), p. 33.

23 Campbell and Chevannes, 'Reviews', p. 87.

24 Campbell and Chevannes, 'Reviews', p. 86; Ernest Cashmore, *Rastaman: The Rastafarian Movement in England* (London: Unwin Paperbacks, 1983), pp. 10, 2.

25 Cashmore, *Rastaman*, p. 2.

26 Cashmore, *Rastaman*, p. 26.

27 Cashmore, *Rastaman*, p. 56.

28 Cashmore, *Rastaman*, p. 176.

29 Cashmore, *Rastaman*, p. 102.

30 Cashmore, *Rastaman*, pp. 3, 99, 116.

31 Lawrence, in Centre for Contemporary Cultural Studies (CCCS), *The Empire Strikes Back: Race and Racism in 70s Britain* (London: Hutchinson, 1982), p. 129.

32 Ken Pryce, *Endless Pressure: A Study of West Indian Lifestyles in Bristol* (Bristol: Bristol Classical Press, 1986), p. 155.

33 Barry Chevannes, *Rastafari: Roots and Ideology* (New York, NY: Syracuse University Press, 1994).

34 Césaire, *Discourse on Colonialism*, p. 32.

35 Herbie Miller, 'Brown Girl in the Ring: Margarita and Malungu', *Caribbean Quarterly*, 53:4 (2007), 47–110, at p. 53.

36 Gilroy, CCCS, *The Empire Strikes Back*, p. 146.

37 Lawrence, in CCCS, *The Empire Strikes Back*, p. 47.

38 Owusu and Ross, *Behind the Masquerade*, p. 51.

39 Kwesi Owusu, *Black British Culture and Society: A Reader* (London: Routledge, 2000), p. 11.

40 Trew, *Black for a Cause*, p. 199.

41 Transpontine, '"Mek" It Blow'.

42 Owusu, *Black British Culture and Society*, p. 11.

43 Footage analysed here is available at Saffron Saffron's YouTube channel: www.youtube.com/watch?v=66r5B573vOE&t=3s (accessed 16 June 2025).

44 George Steiner and Antoine Pire, *Barbarie de l'Ignorance* (Bordeaux: Le Bord de l'Eau, 1998), pp. 44–6, 50–7.

45 Aislinn Simpson and Jessica Salter, 'Cambridge Academic Says He Would Not Tolerate Jamaican Neighbours', *Telegraph* (31 August 2008), www.telegraph.co.uk/news/uknews/2656774/Cambridge-academic-says-he-wo uld-not-tolerate-Jamaican-neighbours.html (accessed 12 August 2024).

46 Kei Miller, 'The Banning of the Drums; or "How to be a Good Nigger in Jamaica"', *Under the Saltire Flag* (2014), https://web.archive.org/web/20210803075838/https://underthesaltireflag.com/2014/07/13/the-ba nning-of-the-drums-or-how-to-be-a-good-nigger-in-jamaica/ (archived 3 August 2021, accessed 5 June 2021).

47 Just like above, the footage analysed here is available at Saffron Saffron's YouTube channel: www.youtube.com/watch?v=vownU4oXEyA (acce-ssed 16 June 2025).

48 Walter Rodney, *The Groundings With My Brothers* (London: Bogle-L'Ouverture Publications, 1983), pp. 12–16; Miller, 'Brown Girl in the Ring', p. 55.

49 The names of Dennis Brown, Freddie McGregor, Alton Ellis, Horace Andy, Sugar Minott, Johnny Clarke, John Holt, Gregory Isaacs, Errol Dunkley and Ken Boothe quickly come to mind – as do UK soundsys-tems that borrow their names from Jamaican recording studios (Channel One), virtuoso engineers (King Tubby's Sound System), record produc-ers (Clement 'Coxsone' Dodd) and record shops like Peckings Studio 1 which specialises in, releases and experiments with records from the legendary Studio One and Treasure Isle studios and labels. Such an ongo-ing cultural dialogue between UK and JA is also seen in the fruitful

collaboration of many Jamaican musicians with their Black British counterparts (e.g. Vin Gordon's trombone licks on Aswad's *Warrior Charge*),
the role of record producers from Prince Buster to Bunny 'Striker' Lee
who would travel back and forth to keep the tunes flowing and the countless 'dubplate specials' that Jamaican artists continue to record for DJs and
selectors in the UK.

50 Charles Tilly, 'War Making and State Making as Organized Crime', in
P. Evans, D. Rueschemeyer and T. Skocpol (eds), *Bringing the State Back
In* (Cambridge: Cambridge University Press, 1985), pp. 170–86, at pp. 169,
171, 181.

51 Judith Shklar, 'Torturers', *London Review of Books* (1986), www.lrb.co.uk/
the-paper/v08/n17/judith-shklar/torturers (accessed 12 August 2024).

52 Peter Drucker, *Management Challenges for the 21st Century* (New York:
Harper Collins, 1999), p. 74.

53 Paula Chakravartty and Denise Ferreira da Silva, 'Accumulation,
Dispossession, and Debt: The Racial Logic of global Capitalism – An
Introduction', *American Quarterly*, 64:3 (2012), 361–85, https://doi.org/
10.1353/aq.2012.0033.

54 Alan Travis, 'Oliver Letwin Blocked Help for Black Youth after 1985
Riots', *Guardian* (30 December 2015), www.theguardian.com/politi
cs/2015/dec/30/oliver-letwin-blocked-help-for-black-youth-after-1985-riots
(accessed 9 August 2024).

55 Fatsis, 'Policing the Union's Black'.

56 Gilroy, *There Ain't No Black in the Union Jack*, pp. xxiii, 140.

57 Hall et al., *Policing the Crisis*.

58 Stuart Hall, 'The Great Moving Right Show', *Marxism Today*, January
1979, 14–20, at p. 16.

59 Hall et al., *Policing the Crisis*, p. 132.

60 Gilroy, *There Ain't No Black in the Union Jack*, p. 129.

61 Gilroy, *There Ain't No Black in the Union Jack*, p. 129.

62 Gilroy, *There Ain't No Black in the Union Jack*, pp. 87, 90.

63 Gilroy, *There Ain't No Black in the Union Jack*, pp. 89, 87.

64 Robert Mark, *In the Office of Constable* (London: Collins, 1978),
p. 255.

65 Fortune, *Black and White*, p. 103 (original emphasis).

66 'Poli-tricks' is a play on words, drawn from the political vocabulary of
Rastafari – whose rejection of professional(ised), corporate, electoralist,
representative politics is encapsulated in this memorable word. An indicative example, in sonic form, is to be found in Cornell Campbell's roots

reggae gem *Righteous Rastaman*, with an irresistible dub by King Tubby on the flip side of the 7" single. For a brilliant introduction to the liberation theology and radical philosophy of Rastafari, see: Chevannes, *Rastafari: Roots and Ideology*; and Campbell, *Rasta and Resistance*.

67 Charles W. Chesnutt, *The Marrow of Tradition* (Boston: Houghton, Mifflin and Company, 1901), p. 90.

68 Linton K. Johnson, 'Jamaican Rebel Music', *Race and Class*, 17:4 (1976), 397–412.

Part III: Isn't it criminal? Black music as 'Out of Order' in contemporary Britain

1 For a full reference to Kim Howells' statement, see: Fiachra Gibbons, 'Minister labelled racist after attack on rap 'idiots'', *Guardian* (6 January 2003), www.theguardian.com/uk/2003/jan/06/ukguns.immigrationpol icy1 (accessed 1 July 2024).

2 Hartman, *Lose Your Mother*, p. 129.

3 Fortune, *Black and White*, p. 172.

4 Fanon, *The Wretched of the Earth*.

5 W.E.B. Du Bois, *Darkwater: Voices from Within the Veil* (New York: Harcourt Brace and Howe, 1920), p. 36 (emphasis added).

6 Arday, Jason, *Cool Britannia and Multi-Ethnic Britain: Uncorking the Champagne Supernova* (London: Routledge, 2021).

7 Michael Keith, *Race, Riots and Policing: Lore and Disorder in a Multi-Racist Society* (London: Routledge, 1993).

8 Gus John, *Taking a Stand: Gus John Speaks on Education, Race, Social Adion & Civil Unrest 1980–2005* (Manchester: Gus John Partnership, 2006), p. 107.

9 Paul Gilroy, 'Multiculture in Times of War', *Critical Quarterly*, 48:4 (2006), 27–45, at p. 40.

10 Gilroy, *After Empire*, p. xvi, p. 105.

11 Gilroy, *After Empire*.

12 Gilroy, 'Multiculture in Times of War'.

13 Patrick Wolfe, 'Settler Colonialism and the Elimination of the Native', *Journal of Genocide Research*, 8:4 (2006), 387–409, at p. 390.

14 For a more detailed argument and definition(s) of racism, see: Part IV of this book.

15 Sivamohan Valluvan, 'Conviviality and Multiculture: A Post-integration Sociology of Multi-ethnic Interaction', *YOUNG*, 24:3 (2016), 204–21.

16 Suzanne Hall, *City, Street and Citizen: The Measure of the Ordinary* (London: Routledge, 2012); Suzanne M. Hall, 'Super-diverse Street: A "Trans-ethnography" Across Migrant Localities', *Ethnic and Racial Studies*, 38:1 (2013), 22–37.

17 Horace R. Cayton and St Clair Drake, *Black Metropolis* (London: Jonathan Cape, 1946), p. 97.

18 Macpherson, *The Stephen Lawrence Inquiry*.

19 Bhikhu Parekh, *The Future of Multi-Ethnic Britain: The Parekh Report* (London: Profile Books, 2000).

20 Michael Keith, 'From Punishment to Discipline? Racism, Racialization and the Policing of Social Control', in M. Cross and M. Keith (eds), *Racism, the City and the State* (London: Routledge, 1993), 193–209, at p. 201.

21 Schlembach, *Spycops*, pp. 25, 30.

22 Samuel P. Huntington, 'The Clash of Civilizations?', *Foreign Affairs*, 72:3 (Summer 1993), 22–50.

23 Bernard Lewis, 'The Roots of Muslim Rage', *Atlantic Monthly* (September 1990).

24 Edward W. Said, 'The Clash of Ignorance', *Nation* (22 October 2001), www.thenation.com/article/archive/clash-ignorance (accessed 21 August 2024); Edward W. Said, 'The Clash of Definitions', in E. Qureshi and M.A. Sells (eds), *The New Crusades: Constructing the Muslim Enemy* (New York: Columbia University Press, 2003), 68–87.

    For similar critiques of neo-Orientalist, civilisationist discourses in the media, politics and academia, see: Edward W. Said, *Covering Islam: How the Media and the Experts Determine How We See the Rest of the World* (New York: Vintage, 1997); Eqbal Ahmad, 'Terrorism: Theirs and Ours', in K.L. Carrington and S. Griffin (eds), *Transforming Terror: Remembering the Soul of the World* (Berkeley: University of California Press, 2011), 53–8; Mahmood Mamdani, *Good Muslim, Bad Muslim: America, the Cold War, and the Roots of Terror* (New York: Pantheon, 2004); Mahmood Mamdani, 'Whither Political Islam? Understanding the Modern Jihad', *Foreign Affairs* (2005), www.foreignaffairs.com/reviews/whither-political-islam (accessed 26 August 2024); Susan Buck-Morss, *Thinking Past Terror: Islamism and Critical Theory on the Left* (London: Verso, 2003).

25 Asim Qureshi, *I Refuse to Condemn: Resisting Racism in Times of National Security* (Manchester: Manchester University Press, 2020); Suhaiymah Manzoor-Khan, *Tangled in Terror: Uprooting Islamophobia* (London: Pluto Press, 2022).

26 Paul Gilroy, "'My Britain is fuck all": Zombie Multiculturalism and the Race Politics of Citizenship', *Identities*, 19:4 (2012), 380–97, at p. 384.

27 Gilroy, "'My Britain is fuck all"', p. 384.

28 For an explanation of how the word 'white' is approached in this book, see this book's postscript on 'whiteness'.

29 Casey, *An Independent Review*.

30 Paul Gilroy, 'The Myth of Black Criminality', in P. Scraton (ed.), *Law, Order and the Authoritarian State: Readings in Critical Criminology* (London: Open University Press, 1987), 47–56.

31 Paul Gilroy, 'A New Crime, But the Same Old Culprits', *Guardian* (8 January 2003), www.theguardian.com/uk/2003/jan/08/ukguns.com ment (accessed 22 August 2024).

32 Fatsis, 'Grime: Criminal Subculture or Public Counterculture?'; Lambros Fatsis, 'Policing the Beats: The Criminalisation of UK Drill and Grime Music by the London Metropolitan Police', *The Sociological Review*, 67:6 (2019), 1300–16.

33 Tilman Schwarze and Lambros Fatsis, 'Copping the Blame: The Role of YouTube Videos in the Criminalisation of UK Drill Music', *Popular Music*, 41:4 (2022), 463–80.

34 For some indicative and insightful work on some of these genres, see: Georgina Cook, *Drumz of the South: The Dubstep Years (2004–2007)* (London: Velocity Press, 2021); Brian Belle-Fortune, *All Crews: Journeys Through Jungle/Drum and Bass Music* (London: Vision Publishing, 2004); Caspar Melville, *It's a London Thing: How Rare Groove, Acid House and Jungle Remapped the City* (Manchester: Manchester University Press, 2019); Julia Toppin in Monique Charles with Mary W. Gani, *Black Music in Britain in the 21st Century* (Liverpool: Liverpool University Press, 2023), pp. 89–104, and Alex De Lacey, '"Let Us Know You're Locked": Pirate Radio Broadcasts as Historical and Musical Artefact', *Popular Music History*, 12:2 (2020), 194–214. For a more panoramic view of Black music in contemporary Britain, see: Charles and Gani, *Black Music in Britain*, and William L. Henry and Matthew Worley, *Narratives from Beyond the UK Reggae Bassline: The System is Sound* (London: Palgrave, 2021). For a good history of pirate radio in Britain, see John Hind and Steve Mosco, *Rebel Radio: The Full Story of British Pirate Radio* (London: Pluto Press, 1987).

9 To be Black is a crime

1 Tilly, 'War Making and State Making as Organized Crime'; Michael Sorkin, *Indefensible Space: The Architecture of the National Insecurity State* (London: Routledge, 2008).

2 Patrick Wintour and Vikram Dodd, 'Blair Blames Spate of Murders on Black Culture', *Guardian* (12 April 2007), www.theguardian.com/poli tics/2007/apr/12/ukcrime.race (accessed 26 August 2024).

3 New Statesman, 'From the Archive: Tony Blair is Tough on Crime, Tough on the Causes of Crime' (2015), www.newstatesman.com/uncatego rized/2015/12/archive-tony-blair-tough-crime-tough-causes-crime (accessed 26 August 2024).

4 Home Affairs Committee, *Young Black People and the Criminal Justice System* (London: The Stationery Office, 2007), p. 368.

5 Tony Thompson, 'Homegrown Gangs Shoot to Power on Our Violent Streets', *Guardian* (26 August 2001), www.theguardian.com/uk/2001/ aug/26/london (accessed 27 August 2024).

6 Patrick Williams, 'Criminalising the Other: Challenging the Race-Gang Nexus', *Race & Class*, 56:3 (2015), 18–35.

7 Michael Woodiwiss and Dick Hobbs, 'Organized Evil and the Atlantic Alliance: Moral Panics and the Rhetoric of Organized Crime Policing in America and Britain', *British Journal of Criminology*, 49:1 (2008), 106–28.

8 Equality and Human Rights Commission (EHRC), *Is Britain Fairer? The State of Equality and Human Rights* (2018), www.equalityhumanrights. com/sites/default/files/is-britain-fairer-2018-pre-lay.pdf?fbclid=IwAR3qW Z3rVULJKMWT_ndlIla906EqrIwkv-jE_9KGcWCjlseEU_FHM7pJY8g (accessed 28 August 2024), p. 7.

9 Office of the United Nations High Commissioner for Human Rights (OHCHR), 'UN Expert Laments UK's "Doubling Down on Failed Anti-Poor Policies"' (2019), www.ohchr.org/en/press-releases/2019/05/ un-expert-laments-uks-doubling-down-failed-anti-poor-policies (Accessed 28 August 2024).

10 Office of the United Nations High Commissioner for Human Rights (OHCHR), 'Statement on Visit to the United Kingdom, by Professor Philip Alston, United Nations Special Rapporteur on Extreme Poverty and Human Rights' (2018), www.ohchr.org/sites/default/files/Documents/ Issues/Poverty/EOM_GB_16Nov2018.pdf (Accessed 28 August 2024), p. 18.

11 Jess McQuail and Olivier De Schutter, 'UN Rapporteur on Extreme Poverty: 'UK Policies Continue to Inflict Misery'", *Big Issue* (9 November 2023), www.bigissue.com/opinion/un-extreme-poverty-uk-policies-olivi er-de-schutter-just-fair (accessed 28 August 2024).

12 Robert Booth, 'UK "in Violation of International Law" over Poverty Levels, Says UN Envoy', *Guardian* (5 November 2023), www.theguardian. com/society/2023/nov/05/uk-poverty-levels-simply-not-acceptable-says-un-envoy-olivier-de-schutter (accessed 28 August 2024).

13 Edwin H. Sunderland, *Principles of Criminology* (Chicago: J.B. Lippincott Company, 1947), p. 11.

14 Nils Christie, *Crime Control as Industry: Towards Gulags, Western Style?* (London: Routledge, 1993), p. 21.

15 Louk H.C. Hulsman, 'Critical Criminology and the Concept of Crime', *Contemporary Crises*, 10:1 (1986), 63–80, at p. 71 (original emphasis).

16 Robert Reiner, *Crime* (London: Polity, 2016), p. 6.

17 Hulsman, 'Critical Criminology and the Concept of Crime', p. 71.

18 Frederick Douglass, *Address of Hon. Fred. Douglass, Delivered before the National Convention of Colored Men, at Louisville, Ky., September 24, 1883* (Louisville: Courier-Journal Job Printing Company, 1883), p. 5.

19 Sunita Toor, 'New "Racisms" and Prejudices? The Criminalisation of "Asian"', in Mike Duggan and Matt Cowburn (eds), *Values in Criminology and Criminal Justice* (Bristol: Policy Press, 2015), pp. 93–108, at p. 94.

20 Danny Dorling, David Gordon, Paddy Hillyard, Christina Pantazis, Simon Pemberton and Steve Tombs, *Criminal Obsessions: Why Harm Matters More Than Crime* (London: Centre for Crime and Justice Studies, 2008).

21 Wole Soyinka, 'Telephone Conversation', in George Lamming (ed.), *Cannon Shot and Glass Beads* (London: Picador, 1974), pp. 153–4, at p. 153.

22 Frederick Douglass, *The Life and Writings of Frederick Douglass, Volume 5: (Supplementary Volume) 1844–1860* (New York: International Publishers, 1975), p. 250.

23 Eric Klinenberg, *Palaces for the People: How to Build a More Equal and United Society* (London: The Bodley Head, 2018), p. 59.

24 Home Office, *Crime and Disorder Act* (London: HMSO, 1998).

25 Peter Squires, *ASBO Nation: The Criminalisation of Nuisance* (Bristol: Bristol University Press, 2008).

26 Elizabeth Burney, *Crime and Banishment: Nuisance and Exclusion in Social Housing* (Winchester: Waterside Press, 1999).

27 Geoffrey Pearson, *Hooligan: A History of Respectable Fears* (London: Macmillan, 1983).

28 Labour Party, *A Quiet Life: Tough Action on Criminal Neighbours* (London: Labour Party, 1995); Labour Party Study Group, *Crime: A Challenge to Us All (The Longford Report)* (London: Labour Party, 1964).

29 Michael Tonry, *Punishment and Politics: Evidence and Emulation in the Making of English Crime Control Policy* (Cullompton: Willan Publishing, 2004).

30 John Pitts, 'Korrectional Karaoke: New Labour and the Zombification of Youth Justice', *Youth Justice*, 1:2 (2001), 3–16.

31 Peter Squires and Dawn E. Stephens, *Rougher Justice: Anti-Social Behaviour and Young People* (Cullompton: Willan Publishing, 2005).

32 Paul Garon, 'Psychiatry's White Problem: Racism as Therapy', *Race Traitor*, no. 9, Summer 1998, pp. 73–86, at p. 83.

33 Alexandra Topping, 'Rinse FM Pirate Radio Station Goes Legit', *Guardian* (10 October 2010), www.theguardian.com/music/2010/oct/10/rinse-fm-ofcom-licence (accessed 28 August 2024); Matheus Sanchez, 'Asbo Bars Pirate DJ from the Rooftops', *Evening Standard* (13 April 2012), www.standard.co.uk/hp/front/asbo-bars-pirate-dj-from-the-rooftops-7173468.html (accessed 28 August 2024).

34 Richard Bramwell, *UK Hip-Hop, Grime and the City: The Aesthetics and Ethics of London's Rap Scene* (Abingdon: Routledge, 2015), pp. 11, 51.

35 Fatsis, 'Grime: Criminal Subculture or Public Counterculture?'

36 Michel Foucault, *Discipline and Punish: The Birth of the Prison* (London: Allen Lane, 1977), p. 277.

37 Prince's Trust, *No Ball Games* (London: Prince's Trust, 2004).

38 Mike Davis, *City of Quartz: Excavating the Future in Los Angeles* (New York: Vintage Books, 1992), pp. 226, 223.

39 Davis, *City of Quartz*, p. 226.

40 Mark A. Carrigan and Lambros Fatsis, *The Public and Their Platforms: Public Sociology in an Era of Social Media* (Bristol: Bristol University Press, 2021), p. 22–9.

41 Dan Hancox, 'Skepta's Mission', *The Fader* (2015), www.thefader.com/2015/06/04/skepta-cover-story-konnichiwa-interview (accessed 29 August 2024).

42 For good critical discussions on 'broken windows' policing, see: Dorothy E. Roberts, 'Race, Vagueness, and the Social Meaning of Order-Maintenance Policing', *The Journal of Criminal Law & Criminology*, 89:3 (1999), 775–836; Amy McArdle and Tony Erzen, *Zero Tolerance: Quality*

of Life and the New Police Brutality in New York City (New York: New York University Press, 2001); Bernard Harcourt, *Illusion of Order: The False Promise of Broken Windows Policing* (Cambridge, MA: Harvard University Press, 2001); Jordan T. Camp and Christina Heatherton, *Policing the Planet: Why the Policing Crisis Led to Black Lives Matter* (London: Verso, 2016); Vitale, *The End of Policing* and Klinenberg, *Palaces for the People*.

43 David Sibley, 'The Racialisation of Space in British Cities', *Soundings*, 10 (1998), 119–27, at p. 123.

44 Sibley, 'The Racialisation of Space in British Cities', p. 127.

45 Fatsis, 'Grime: Criminal Subculture or Public Counterculture?', pp. 449–50; Fatsis, 'Policing the Beats', pp. 1306–8.

10 Looking for 'crime' in grime

1 London Metropolitan Police Service, *Promotion Event Risk Assessment Form 696* (2008).

2 London Metropolitan Police Service, *Promotion Event Risk Assessment Form 696* (2009), p. 1.

3 BBC News, 'Megaman's Controversial Career' (2006), http://news.bbc.co.uk/1/hi/entertainment/4481112.stm – :~:text=He and other members performed,he has now been cleared (accessed 16 September 2024).

4 BBC News, 'Garage Star Stabbed in Cyprus' (2003), news.bbc.co.uk/1/hi/entertainment/3055770.stm – :~:text=Up-and-coming garage music,Ayia Napa on Monday evening (accessed 16 September 2024); Hugh Muir, 'Rapper Who Killed Producer for "Disrespect" Gets 30 Years', *Guardian* (3 November 2006), www.theguardian.com/uk/2006/nov/03/ukguns.music news (accessed 16 September 2024); Independent, 'How Form 696 Could Pull the Plug on the Capital's Music Scene' (2008), www.independent.co.uk/arts-entertainment/music/news/how-form-696-could-pull-the-plug-on-the-capitals-music-scene-1028240.html (accessed 16 September 2024); Dan Hancox, 'Public Enemy No 696', *Guardian* (21 January 2009), www.theguardian.com/culture/2009/jan/21/police-form-696-garage-music (accessed 4 September 2024).

5 Jonathan Ilan, 'The Industry's the New Road': Crime, Commodification and Street Cultural Tropes in UK Urban Music', *Crime, Media, Culture*, 8:1 (2012), 39–55, at p. 46.

6 Bramwell, *UK Hip-Hop, Grime and the City*, p. 127; Channel 4 News, 'UK Drill Music Gang Banned from Making Violent Music' (2018),

www.youtube.com/watch?v=KXXob4hka4g (accessed 16 September 2024); *Independent*, 'How Form 696 Could Pull the Plug on the Capital's Music Scene'; Tim Jonze, 'Rapper Giggs's Tour Cancelled After Police Warning', *Guardian* (23 February 2010), www.theguardian.com/music/2010/feb/23/rapper-giggs-tour-cancelled (accessed 16 September 2024).

7 Hannah Ellis-Petersen, 'Met to Review Risk Assessment Form "Stifling" Grime and Garage Scenes', *Guardian* (21 September 2017), www.theguardian.com/music/2017/sep/21/met-to-review-risk-assessment-form-696-stifling-grime-garage-scenes (accessed 16 September 2024).

8 Jamie Grierson, 'Croydon Bar Accuses Police of Banning Jamaican Bashment Music', *Guardian* (11 March 2016), www.theguardian.com/uk-news/2016/mar/11/croydon-bar-accuses-police-banning-jamaican-bashment-music?CMP=share_btn_url (accessed 16 September 2024).

9 Bramwell, *UK Hip-Hop, Grime and the City*, p. 63.

10 London Metropolitan Police Service, *Promotion Event Risk Assessment Form 696*; UK Music, 'UK Music Welcomes Decision to Scrap Unloved Form 696' (2017), www.ukmusic.org/news/uk-music-welcomes-decision-to-scrap-unloved-form-696 (accessed 21 November 2017).

11 *Noisey, The Police vs Grime Music – A Noisey Film* (2014), www.youtube.com/watch?v=eW_iujPQpys (accessed 16 September 2024).

12 London Metropolitan Police Service, 'Decision Made Following Consultation'.

13 London Metropolitan Police Service, 'Decision Made Following Consultation'.

14 See, e.g. Hinton Rowan Helper, *The Impending Crisis of the South: How to Meet It* (New York: Burdick Brothers, 1857).

15 Bernard, Jesse, 'Form 696 is Gone – So Why is Clubland Still Hostile to Black Londoners?', *Guardian* (31 January 2018), www.theguardian.com/music/2018/jan/31/form-696-is-gone-so-why-is-clubland-still-hostile-to-black-londoners (accessed 16 September 2024); Fatsis, Lambros, 'Now That Grime Is "Pop", When Will the Panic about Drill Music Stop?', *Discover Society* (2019), https://archive.discoversociety.org/2019/08/07/viewpoint-now-that-grime-is-pop-when-will-the-panic-about-drill-music-stop/ (accessed 16 September 2024).

16 Latoya Reisner and Kamila Rymajdo, 'The 0161 Rap Gap: The Marginalisation of Black Rap Musicians in Manchester's Live Music Scene', *Popular Music*, 41:4 (2022), 481–94.

17 Laura Hill, 'Leeds Councillor Claims Grime Music is Associated With Trouble as Norman bar Brawl is Investigated', *Yorkshire Evening Post*

(17 April 2019), www.yorkshireeveningpost.co.uk/news/politics/leeds-cou ncillor-claims-grime-music-is-associated-with-trouble-as-norman-bar-bra wl-is-investigated-483019 (accessed 29 May 2019).

18 House of Commons Digital, Culture, Media and Sport Committee, *Live Music: Government Response to the Committee's Ninth Report of Session 2017–19, Eighth Special Report of Session 2017–19* (London: House of Commons, 2019), p. 2.

19 Simon Wheatley, *Don't Call Me Urban! The Time of Grime* (Carmarthen: McNidder & Grace, 2011); Nikhaela Wicks, 'You Wanna Come to the "Urban" Night Tomorrow … It's the Wrong Night Tonight": Black Consumers as Both "Wanted" and "Unwanted" in the Night-Time Economy', *Conflict and Society*, 8:1 (2022), 20–37.

20 Lee Barron, 'The Sound of Street Corner Society: UK Grime Music as Ethnography', *European Journal of Cultural Studies*, 16 (2013), 531–47; Bramwell, *UK Hip-Hop, Grime and the City*; Richard Bramwell, 'Council Estate of Mind: The British Rap Tradition and London's Hip-Hop Scene', in J.A. Williams (ed.), *The Cambridge Companion to Hip-Hop* (Cambridge: Cambridge University Press, 2015), pp. 256–62; Ilan, 'The Industry's the New Road'; Dan Hancox, *Stand Up Tall: Dizzee Rascal and the Birth of Grime* (Amazon Media EU, Kindle Edition, 2013); Dan Hancox, 'The Drill and Knife Crime Story is a Classic Chicken-and-Egg Dilemma', *Vice* (2018), www.vice.com/en/article/drill-knife-crime-violence-london-long-read (accessed 16 September 2024).

21 Fatsis, 'Policing the Union's Black'.

22 Laudable though the ideals of Clause IV were, arguing for common ownership of the means of production, distribution and exchange (Aisha Gani, 'Clause IV: A Brief History', *Guardian* (9 August 2015), www.theguardian.com/politics/2015/aug/09/clause-iv-of-labour-party-constitution-what-is-all-the-fuss-about-reinstating-it (accessed 4 September 2024)), they take little away from the fact they were drafted by Sidney Webb – whose eugenicist politics are well documented even in the mainstream liberal press (Jonathan Freedland, 'Eugenics and the Master Race of the Left – Archive, 1997', *Guardian* (1 May 2019), www.theguardian.com/politics/from-the-archive-blog/2019/may/01/eugenics-founding-fathers-british-so cialism-archive-1997 (accessed 4 September 2024).

23 Yusef Bakkali, 'Dying to Live: Youth Violence and the Munpain', *The Sociological Review*, 67:6 (2019), 1317–32.

24 Joy White, *Terraformed: Young Black Lives in the Inner City* (London: Repeater Books, 2020).

25 Monique Charles, 'Grime Labour: Grime Politics Articulates New Forms of Cross-Race Working-Class Identities', *Soundings: A Journal of Politics and Culture*, 68 (2018), 40–52; Jessica Perera, 'The Politics of Generation Grime', *Race & Class*, 60 (2018), 82–93; Fatsis, 'Grime: Criminal Subculture or Public Counterculture?', p. 454; Dan Bulley et al., *After Grenfell: Violence, Resistance and Response* (London: Pluto Press, 2019).

26 Dan Hancox, 'Pow!: Anthem for Kettled Youth', *Guardian* (3 February 2011), www.theguardian.com/music/2011/feb/03/pow-forward-lethal-biz zle-protests (accessed 4 September 2024).

27 The comparison between the two dates, is intended as a way of linking and thinking about the Broadwater Farm uprisings of 1985 and 2011 as similar, both having been prompted by the police murder of Cynthia Jarett in 1985 and Mark Duggan in 2011. See Part II of this book for more details and also see, or rather watch, George Amponsah's 2015 documentary *The Hard Stop*, Fahim Alam's (2013) *Riots Reframed* and Ken Fero's (2020) *Ultraviolence*.

28 The full album and Gilroy's introduction to it, can be accessed at: https:// planet.mu/releases/red-white-zero/ (accessed 16 June 2025).

29 For a 'forensic' account of the police killing of Mark Duggan, see: Foren-sic Architecture, 'The Killing of Mark Duggan' (2021), https://foren sic-architecture.org/investigation/the-killing-of-mark-duggan (accessed 6 September 2024). For a critical reading of Duggan's murder by the Met, see Fatsis and Lamb, *Policing the Pandemic*, pp. 98–9.

30 Stafford Scott, 'If the Rioting Was a Surprise, People Weren't Looking', *Guardian* (8 August 2011), www.theguardian.com/commentisfree/2011/ aug/08/tottenham-riots-not-unexpected (accessed 4 September 2024).

31 Paul Lewis, 'Tottenham Riots: A Peaceful Protest, Then Suddenly All Hell Broke Loose', *Guardian* (7 August 2011), www.theguardian.com/uk/2011/ aug/07/tottenham-riots-peaceful-protest (accessed 16 September 2024).

32 Guardian, 'David Cameron on the Riots: "This Is Criminality Pure and Simple" – Video' (2011), www.theguardian.com/politics/video/2011/aug/09/ david-cameron-riots-criminality-video (accessed 16 September 2024).

33 Starkey is known for his racist views, resulting in the termination of his honorary fellowship at Fitzwilliam College at Cambridge University and his visiting professorship at Canterbury Christ Church University after claiming that: 'Slavery was not genocide otherwise there wouldn't be so many damn blacks in Africa or Britain would there?' (Rory Sullivan, 'David Starkey Loses Two University Positions After Saying Slavery Didn't Constitute Genocide', *Independent* (3 July 2020), www.independent.

co.uk/news/uk/home-news/david-starkey-fired-racist-slavery-cambridge-university-canterbury-christ-church-a9599831.html (accessed 4 September 2024)), BBC News, 'England Riots: "The Whites Have Become Black" Says David Starkey' (2011), www.bbc.co.uk/news/av/uk-14513517 (accessed 16 September 2024).

34 Zygmunt Bauman, 'On Consumerism Coming Home to Roost', in *A Chronicle of Crisis: 2011–2016 (Social Europe, 2017)*, https://socialeurope.eu/wp-content/uploads/2022/01/Zygmunt-Bauman-A-Chronicle-of-Crisis-Print-2017.pdf (accessed 16 September 2024), pp. 51–3.

35 David Harvey, 'Feral Capitalism Hits the Streets' (2011), https://davidharvey.org/2011/08/feral-capitalism-hits-the-streets/ (accessed 16 September 2024).

36 BBC News, 'England Riots: "The Whites Have Become Black"'.

37 Julia Day and Owen Gibson, 'Cameron Raps Radio 1 DJ for Violent Lyrics', *Guardian* (8 June 2006), www.theguardian.com/politics/2006/jun/08/uk.conservatives (accessed 16 September 2024).

38 Lethal Bizzle, 'David Cameron Is a Donut', *Guardian* (8 June 2006), www.theguardian.com/commentisfree/2006/jun/08/davidcameronisadonut (accessed 16 September 2024).

39 Hancox, 'Pow!: Anthem for Kettled Youth'.

40 HM Government, *Ending Gangs and Youth Violence: A Cross-Government Report* (London: HM Stationery Office, 2011), p. 3.

41 HM Government, *Ending Gangs and Youth Violence*, p. 4.

42 Simon Hallsworth and Tara Young, 'Gang Talk and Gang Talkers: A Critique', *Crime, Media, Culture*, 4:2 (2008), 175–95.

43 Patrick Williams and Becky Clarke, *Dangerous Associations: Joint Enterprise, Gangs and Racism: An Analysis of the Processes of Criminalisation of Black, Asian and Minority Ethnic Individuals* (London: Centre for Crime and Justice Studies, 2016).

44 Claire Alexander, *(Re)thinking 'Gangs'* (London: Runnymede Trust, 2008), p. 7.

45 Office of the United Nations High Commissioner for Human Rights (OHCHR), 'UN Rights Expert Hails UK for Anti-Racism Action but Raises Serious Concerns over Immigration Policy, Prevent Programme and Brexit' (2018), www.ohchr.org/en/press-releases/2018/05/un-rights-expert-hails-uk-anti-racism-action-raises-serious-concerns-over?LangID=E&NewsID=23074 (accessed 16 September 2024).

46 Michael Shiner, Zoe Carre, Rebekah Delsol, and Niamh Eastwood, *The Colour of Injustice: 'Race', Drugs and Law Enforcement in England and*

Wales (London: Stopwatch, 2018), www.stop-watch.org/what-we-do/
research/the-colour-of-injustice-race-drugs-and-law-enforcement-in-eng
land-and-wales (accessed 16 September 2024), p. 2.

47 Patrick Williams, *Being Matrixed: The (Over)policing of Gang Suspects in
London* (London: Stopwatch, 2018), www.stop-watch.org/what-we-do/
projects/the-gangs-matrix (Accessed 16 September 2024), p. 5.

48 To access the relevant data on the 'Crime, justice and the law' section of
the Race Disparity Unit, go to: www.ethnicity-facts-figures.service.gov.
uk/crime-justice-and-the-law.

49 'Met to Overhaul Racist Gangs Matrix After Landmark Legal Challenge',
Liberty (2022), www.libertyhumanrights.org.uk/issue/met-to-overhaul-rac
ist-gangs-matrix-after-landmark-legal-challenge/ – :~:text=The Metropolitan
Police Service has,of the Matrix was unlawful (accessed 16 September 2024).

50 'Harms of Gangs Matrix Set to Be Repeated, Groups Warn', *Liberty*
(2024), www.libertyhumanrights.org.uk/issue/harms-of-gangs-matrix-set-
to-be-repeated-groups-warn/ – :~:text=Awate Suleiman, a claimant in,to
get to this point (Accessed 16 September 2024).

51 Liberty, 'Harms of Gangs Matrix Set to Be Repeated'.

52 Jasbinder S. Nijjar, 'Echoes of Empire: Excavating the Colonial Roots
of Britain's "War on Gangs"', *Social Justice*, 45:2/3 (2018), 147–62, at
p. 150.

53 Gilroy, 'The Myth of Black Criminality', p. 117.

54 Stuart Hall, *The Hard Road to Renewal: Thatcherism and the Crisis of the
Left* (London: Verso, 2021), p. 3.

55 David Downes, *Law and Order: Theft of an Issue* (London: Fabian Society,
1983).

56 Laura Trevelyan, 'Bill Bratton to Advise at UK Gang Conference', *BBC
News* (10 October 2011), www.bbc.co.uk/news/uk-15229199 (accessed
6 September 2024).

57 Peter B. Kraska, 'Militarization and Policing – Its Relevance to 21st
Century Police', *Policing: A Journal of Policy and Practice*, 1:4 (2007),
501–51; Go, *Policing Empires*.

58 Hall et al., *Policing the Crisis*, p. 306; see also: Fatsis and Lamb, *Policing
the Pandemic*, esp. pp. 60–1; Fatsis, 'When the Exception Makes the
Rules'.

59 Hinton Rowan Helper, *The Negroes in Negroland; The Negroes in America;
and Negroes Generally* (New York: G.W. Carleton, 1868), p. ix.

11 Blaming Drill for making people kill

1 Shingi Mararike, Tom Harper and Andrew Gilligan, 'Drill, the "Demonic"' Music Linked to Rise in Youth Murders', *The Times* (8 April 2018), www.thetimes.com/uk/article/drill-the-demonic-music-linked-to-rise-in-youth-murders-obkbh3csk (accessed 16 September 2024); John Simpson, '"Drill" Music: A Nihilistic Genre Filled with Boasts of Death and Violence', *The Times* (2018), www.thetimes.com/uk/politics/article/drill-music-a-nihilistic-genre-filled-with-boasts-of-death-and-violence-g7p736tcj (accessed 16 September 2024).

2 'The Knife Crime Rap: Everything You Should Know About Drill Music', *Sunday Times Magazine* (5 May 2019), p. 1.

3 Sam Knight, 'The Soundtrack to London's Murders', *The New Yorker* (20 April 2018), www.newyorker.com/news/letter-from-the-uk/the-soundtrack-to-londons-murders (accessed 21 November 2018).

4 Sian Boyle, 'Soundtrack to Murder', *Daily Mail* (2021), www.dailymail.co.uk/news/article-9585461/Soundtrack-murder-time-gangland-drill-track-Number-One.html (accessed 20 July 2021).

5 Kevin Hurley, 'Police Are Absolutely Right to Target Drill Rappers … Their Toxic Words Are Responsible for Far Too Many Deaths in Britain', *RT* (2021), www.rt.com/op-ed/511838-uk-police-drill-rap/ (accessed 6 February 2022).

6 'Met Police Chief Calls on YouTube to Take Down Drill Music to Curb Gang Crime', *LBC* (2018), www.lbc.co.uk/radio/presenters/nick-ferrari/met-police-chief-calls-on-youtube-drill-music/ (accessed 16 September 2024).

7 Amnesty International, 'UK: The Killing of Jean Charles de Menezes' (2005), www.amnesty.org/en/wp-content/uploads/2021/06/eur45032200 5en.pdf (accessed 16 September 2024).

8 Fatsis, 'When Police Racism is Denied'.

9 BBC News, 'Cressida Dick: Sadiq Khan Intimidated Met Chief into Quitting – Report' (2022), www.bbc.co.uk/news/uk-england-london-62766240 (accessed 16 September 2024).

10 Sean Morrison, 'London Crime: Gang Members "to be Treated like Terror Suspects" under New Measures to Tackle Violence', *Evening Standard* (30 May 2018), www.standard.co.uk/news/crime/london-gang-members-to-be-treated-like-terror-suspects-under-new-measures-to-tackle-violent-crime-a3850626.html (accessed 16 September 2024); Ciaran Thapar, 'Treating Drill Rappers like Terrorists is a Colossal Mistake', *New*

Statesman (2018), www.newstatesman.com/culture/music/2018/06/treat ing-drill-rappers-terrorists-colossal-mistake (accessed 16 September 2024); *Telegraph*, 'Police to Treat Gangs Like Terror Suspects With Tough New Laws', (2018), www.telegraph.co.uk/news/2018/05/30/police-treat-gangs-like-terror-suspects-tough-new-laws (Accessed 16 September 2024).

11 Justin Davenport, Robin De Peyer, Adebola Lamuye and Owen Sheppard, 'Met Police Chief Cressida Dick Declares War on 190 Gangs Behind Violence in London', *Evening Standard* (8 November 2018), www.standard.co.uk/news/crime/met-police-chief-cressida-dick-declares-war-on-190-gangs-behind-violence-in-london-a3984691.html (acc essed 16 September 2024).

12 HM Government, *Serious Violence Strategy* (London: HM Stationery Office, 2018), p. 79.

13 HM Government, *Serious Violence Strategy*, p. 9.

14 Hancox, 'The Drill and Knife Crime Story Is a Classic Chicken-and-Egg Dilemma' (original emphasis).

15 London Assembly, *Police and Crime Committee Meeting*, 17 November 2021 at 10 am, https://webcasts.london.gov.uk/Assembly/Event/Index/f546d1a1–66c0–452a–961e-d0d1booddebe?in=2021–11–17T11%3A58%3A13.788Z (accessed 16 September 2024), 02:15:18 to 02:19–40.

16 Eithne Quinn, 'Lost in Translation? Rap Music and Racial Bias in the Courtroom', *Policy@Manchester Blogs* (2018), http://blog.policy.manches ter.ac.uk/posts/2018/10/lost-in-translation-rap-music-and-racial-bias-in-th e-courtroom/ (accessed 16 September 2024).

17 Wil Crisp and Vikram Dodd, 'Met Police Profiling Children "on a Large Scale", Documents Show', *Guardian* (3 June 2022), www.theguardian.com/uk-news/2022/jun/03/met-police-project-alpha-profiling-children-do cuments-show (accessed 16 September 2024).

18 Michael Railton, 'Analysing Gang-Related Music Linked to Serious Violence', *College of Policing* (2022), www.college.police.uk/article/ana lysing-gang-related-music-linked-serious-violence (accessed 16 September 2024).

19 Wil Crisp and Vikram Dodd, 'Met Police Did Not Consult Us on Children's Data Project, Say Youth Violence Experts', *Guardian* (5 June 2022), www.theguardian.com/uk-news/2022/jun/05/met-police-childre n-data-project-alpha-youth-violence (accessed 16 September 2024).

20 Lizzie Dearden, 'Police Targeting Drill Music Videos in Controversial Crackdown on Social Media That "Incites Violence"', *Independent* (29 May 2018), www.independent.co.uk/news/uk/crime/drill-music-stabbin

gs-london-youtube-violence-police-knife-crime-gangs-a8373241.html (accessed 16 September 2024).

21 Fatsis, 'Policing the Beats', p. 1303; Ciaran Thapar, 'I Want to Tell People That Prison Life is Super Dead': Digga D on Rap Stardom Amid Police Restrictions', *Guardian* (30 June 2023), www.theguardian.com/music/2023/jun/30/digga-d-back-to-square-one-interview (accessed 16 September 2024).

22 Shereener Browne and Anthony Hudson, 'Kill Drill: The Death of Freedom of Expression?', *Index on Censorship* (2018), www.indexoncensorship.org/2018/06/kill-drill-the-death-of-freedom-of-expression/#1 (accessed 16 September 2024). In my experience as an expert witness for the defence in cases that rely on drill music material as 'evidence', I have witnessed prosecutors argue that rappers should give the police a notice period of 76 hours before posting their music online, while also ceding control of their social media handles to the police. The verdict on this trial is still pending at the time of writing, but it indicates the prosecutorial zeal to further suppress drill. Given that the defendant is one of the most popular drill artists in the UK, if the judge sides with the prosecution this could set a very dangerous precedent for other rappers who risk being subjected to even more draconian – if not entirely vindictive – restrictions on what they can say or do in/with their music.

23 Crown Prosecution Service (CPS), *Sentencing – Ancillary Orders* (2024), www.cps.gov.uk/legal-guidance/sentencing-ancillary-orders – :%7E:text= The CBO is an order,Drinking Banning Order on conviction (accessed 16 September 2024).

24 Crown Prosecution Service (CPS), *Criminal Behaviour Orders: Legal Guidance* (2018), www.cps.gov.uk/legal-guidance/criminal-behaviour-orders (accessed 16 September 2024).

25 HM Government, *Serious Violence Strategy*, pp. 80, 87.

26 Mayor's Office for Policing and Crime (MOPAC), *Gangs* (2016), www.london.gov.uk/sites/default/files/mopac_challenge_gangs_2_february_20 16_-_presentation.pdf (accessed 16 September 2024); see also: Roger Grimshaw and Matt Ford, *Young People, Violence and Knives: Revisiting the Evidence and Policy Discussions* (London: Centre for Crime and Justice Studies, 2018), p. 9.

27 Amnesty International, 'Trapped in the Matrix: Secrecy, Stigma, and Bias in the Met's Gangs Database' (2018), www.amnesty.org.uk/files/reports/Inside%20the%20matrix.pdf (accessed 16 September 2024); Williams, *Being Matrixed.*

28 Youth Justice Legal Centre, 'ICO Finds Gangs Matrix Breached Data Protection Laws' (2018), http://yjlc.uk/resources/legal-updates/ico-finds-gangs-matrix-breached-data-protection-laws – :~:text=serious breaches of data protection laws with the potential to,confusion amongst those using it (accessed 28 May 2025).

29 Clarke, 2018.

30 OHCHR, 2018.

31 Youth Violence Commission, *Interim Report* (2018), www.yvcommission. com/_files/ugd/ad2256_a0f38547a4134e0cb923905486bcc186.pdf (accessed 16 September 2024), p. 5.

32 Peter Squires, 'The Knife Crime "Epidemic" and British Politics', *British Politics*, 4:1 (2009), 127–57.

33 Home Affairs Select Committee (HASC), *Knife Crime: Seventh Report of Session 2008–09*, HC 112 (2 June 2009) (London: The Stationery Office, 2009), p. 6.

34 Lambros Fatsis, 'Thinking about Knife Crime Beyond Dangerous Myths and Comfortable Untruths', *The British Society of Criminology Blog* (2019), http://thebscblog.wordpress.com/2019/02/11/Thinking-about-knife-crime-beyond-dangerous-myths-and-comfortable-untruths (accessed 16 September 2024); Lambros Fatsis, Jonathan Ilan, Habib Kadiri, Abenaa Owusu-Bempah, Eithne Quinn, Michael Shiner, and Peter Squires, 'Missing the Point: How Policy Exchange Misunderstands Knife Crime in the Capital', *Identities Blog* (2021), www.identitiesjournal.com/blog-collection/missing-the-point-how-policy-exchange-misunderstands-knife-crime-in-the-capital (accessed 16 September 2024); Elaine Williams and Peter Squires, *Rethinking Knife Crime Policing, Violence and Moral Panic?* (London: Palgrave, 2021); Bhattacharyya et al., *Empire's Endgame*, pp. 30–40.

35 Williams and Squires, *Rethinking Knife Crime*, pp. 5, 9 & 7.

36 Crown Prosecution Service (CPS), *Gang Related Offences – Decision Making In* (2021), www.cps.gov.uk/legal-guidance/gang-related-offences-decision-making (accessed 16 September 2024).

37 Criminal Justice Act (CJA), *Criminal Justice Act 2003 – Explanatory Notes* (2003), www.legislation.gov.uk/ukpga/2003/44/notes/division/4/11/1 – :~: text=Section 104 restricts the admissibility,undermined the co-defendant%27s defence (accessed 16 September 2024).

38 Crown Prosecution Service (CPS), *Crown Prosecution Service Joint Enterprise Pilot 2023: Data Analysis* (2023), www.cps.gov.uk/publication/crown-prosecution-service-joint-enterprise-pilot-2023-data-analysis (accessed 16 September 2024).

39 A campaign that is implied here is the Art Not Evidence campaign (https://artnotevidence.org (accessed 16 June 2025)), but there is also the Prosecuting Rap project (https://sites.manchester.ac.uk/prosecuting-rap (accessed 16 June 2025)) that explores and opposes how rap music is used in court, in Britain. In the interest of full disclosure, I am core member of both groups.

40 Crown Prosecution Service, *Gang Related Offences*.

41 Railton, 'Analysing Gang-Related Music'.

42 Tony Ward and Shahrzad Fouladvand, 'Bodies of Knowledge and Robes of Expertise: Expert Evidence about Drugs, Gangs and Human Trafficking', *Criminal Law Review*, 6 (2021), 442–60; Lambros Fatsis, 'When Cops Analyse Drill, but Get It Wrong Still', *StopWatch* (2022), www.stop-watch.org/news-opinion/when-cops-analyse-drill-but-get-it-wrong-still (accessed 16 September 2024).

43 Andrea L. Dennis, 'Poetic (In)Justice? Rap Music Lyrics as Art, Life, and Criminal Evidence', *The Columbia Journal of Law & the Arts*, 31 (2007), 1–41; Erik Nielson and Andrea L. Dennis, *Rap on Trial: Race, Lyrics, and Guilt in America* (New York: New Press, 2019); Jonathan Ilan, 'Digital Street Culture Decoded: Why Criminalizing Drill Music Is Street Illiterate and Counterproductive', *British Journal of Criminology*, 60 (2020), 994–1013.

44 Expert Witness Services, *Urban Street Gangs & Slang*, www.expertwitnessservices.co.uk/service-page/urban-street-gangs-slang (accessed 16 June 2025).

45 Will Pritchard, '"I Wanted to Show Their Innocence": Teenage Drill Rappers Take Centre Stage in Bold New Play', *Guardian* (4 November 2022), www.theguardian.com/music/2022/nov/04/uk-drill-project-barbican-interview (accessed 16 September 2024).

46 Much of this is well known in legal circles and I am personally aware of it all, having served as an expert witness for the defence in cases involving both officers that were satirised by *The UK Drill Project* and the 'Professor' in question. For more public information on how cops and 'Profs' work together to criminalise drill rappers, you can read this post from one such 'expert's' blog: Tony Thorne, 'The Words on the Streets', *Language and Innovation* (2022), https://language-and-innovation.com/2022/05/26/the-words-on-the-streets/ (accessed 16 June 2025).

47 Henry L. Gates Jr, 'Foreword', in A. Bradley and A. DuBois (eds), *The Anthology of Rap* (New Haven: Yale University Press, 2010), pp. xxvi, xxv.

48 Dennis, 'Poetic (In)Justice?'; Forrest Stuart, *Ballad of the Bullet: Gangs, Drill Music and the Power of Online Infamy* (Princeton: Princeton University Press, 2020), p. 195.

49 Dennis, 'Poetic (In)Justice?'

50 Williams and Clarke, *Dangerous Associations*.

51 Fatsis et al., 'Missing the Point'.

52 See, e.g. Hallsworth and Young, 'Gang Talk and Gang Talkers'; Hannah Smithson, Rob Ralphs and Patrick Williams, 'Used and Abused: The Problematic Usage of Gang Terminology in the United Kingdom and Its Implications for Ethnic Minority Youth', *The British Journal of Criminology*, 53:1 (2013), 113–12.

53 See, e.g. Alexander, *(Re)thinking 'Gangs'*; Anthony Gunter, *Race, Gangs and Youth Violence: Policy, Prevention and Policing* (Bristol: Policy Press, 2017); Abenaa Owusu-Bempah, 'Race and Policing in Historical Context: Dehumanization and the Policing of Black People in the 21st Century', *Theoretical Criminology*, 21:1 (2017), 23–34, Patrick Williams and Becky Clarke, 'The Black Criminal Other as an Object of Social Control', *Social Sciences*, 7:234 (2018), 1–14; Nijjar, 'Echoes of Empire', *Social Justice*; Fatsis, 'When Police Racism is Denied'; Fatsis, 'Grime: Criminal Subculture or Public Counterculture?'; Coretta Phillips, Rod Earle, Alpa Parmar et al., 'Dear British Criminology: Where Has All the Race and Racism Gone?', *Theoretical Criminology*, 24:3 (2020), 427–46; Becky Clarke and Patrick Williams, '(Re)producing Guilt in Suspect Communities: The Centrality of Racialisation in Joint Enterprise Prosecutions', *International Journal for Crime, Justice and Social Democracy*, 9 (2020), 116–29; Sandra Paul, *Tackling Racial Injustice: Children and the Youth Justice System: A Report by JUSTICE* (London: Justice, 2021); Keir Monteith, Eithne Quinn, Andrea L. Dennis, Remi Joseph-Salisbury, Erica Kane, Franklyn Addo, and Claire McGourlay, *Racial Bias and the Bench: A Response to the Judicial Diversity & Inclusion Strategy (2020–25)*, Simon Fellowship Report, University of Manchester, 2022. https://documents.manchester. ac.uk/display.aspx?DocID=64125 (accessed 16 September 2024).

54 Fatsis, 'When the Exception Makes the Rules'.

55 Hallsworth and Young, 'Gang Talk and Gang Talkers'.

56 David Conn, 'One Death, 11 jailed Teenagers: Was a Moss Side Murder Trial Racist?', *Guardian* (5 June 2021), www.theguardian.com/ world/2021/jun/05/one-death-11-jailed-teenagers-was-a-moss-side-trial-ra cist#:~:text=He%20then%20sentenced%20the%2011,that%20only%20on e%20carried%20out (accessed 16 September 2024).

57 The judge's summing up was shared with me as part of my personal e-mail communication with Keir Monteith KC, Barrister at Garden Court Chambers, who acted for the families of some of the defendants.

58 Roxy Legane, 'How Do Text Messages Turn Into a Prison Sentence For Black Boys?', *Guardian* (7 December 2022), www.theguardian.com/commentisfree/2022/dec/07/crime-black-skin-ademola-adedeji-gang-court (accessed 16 September 2024).

59 Helen Pidd, 'Fury in Manchester as Black Teenagers Jailed as Result of Telegram Chat', *Guardian* (1 July 2022), www.theguardian.com/uk-news/2022/jul/01/fury-in-manchester-as-black-teenagers-jailed-as-result-of-telegram-chat#:~:text=They%20were%20jailed%20for%20taking,evidence%20of%20%20E2%80%9Cthought%20policing%E2%80%9D (accessed 16 September 2024).

60 Aamna Mohdin, 'Manchester 21-year-old's Conviction Quashed After Rap Video Evidence Refuted', *Guardian* (15 January 2025), www.theguardian.com/uk-news/2025/jan/15/manchester-conviction-quashed-rap-video-evidence-refuted (accessed 10 April 2025).

61 Unfortunately, the judgements for these two cases aren't freely available, but they can be accessed online via LexisNexis or the Westlaw UK database.

62 Eithne Quinn, Joy White and John Street, 'Introduction to Special Issue: Prosecuting and Policing Rap', *Popular Music*, 41:4 (2022), 419–26, https://doi.org/10.1017/S0261143022000642, p. 2; Steve Swann, 'Drill and Rap Music on Trial', *BBC News* (2021), www.bbc.co.uk/news/uk-55617706 (accessed 16 September 2024).

63 See also: Lambros Fatsis, 'Stop Blaming Drill For Making People Kill', *British Society of Criminology Blog* (2021), thebscblog.wordpress.com/2021/10/18/stop-blaming-drill-for-making-people-kill (accessed 16 September 2024); Fatsis et al., 'Missing the Point'.

64 Abenaa Owusu-Bempah, 'The Irrelevance of Rap', *Criminal Law Review*, 2 (2022), 130–51; Abenaa Owusu-Bempah, 'Prosecuting rap: What Does the Case Law Tell Us?', *Popular Music*, 41:4 (2022), 427–45, https://doi.org/10.1017/S0261143022000575

65 Robin D.G. Kelley, 'Kickin' Reality, Kickin' Ballistics: "Gangsta Rap" and Post-industrial Los Angeles', in W. Perkins (ed.), *Droppin' Science: Critical Essays on Rap Music and Hip Hop Culture* (Philadelphia, PA: Temple University Press, 1996), pp. 183–300; Adam Krims, *Rap Music and the Poetics of Identity* (Cambridge: Cambridge University Press, 2000); Cheryl Keyes, *Rap Music and Street Consciousness* (Chicago, IL: University

NOTES

of Illinois Press, 2004); Bakari Kitwana, *Why White Kids Love Hip-Hop: Wankstas, Wiggers, Wannabes and the New Reality of Race in America* (New York: Basic Civitas Books, 2005); Charis E. Kubrin, 'Gangstas, Thugs and Hustlas: Identity and the Code of the Street in Rap Music', *Social Problems*, 52 (2005), 360–78; Andrew Deveraux, 'What Chew Know About Down the Hill?: Baltimore Club Music, Subgenre Crossover, and the New Subcultural Capital of Race and Space', *Journal of Popular Music Studies*, 19 (2007), 311–41; Ilan, 'The Industry's the New Road', p. 47; Charis E. Kubrin and Erik Nielson, 'Rap on Trial', *Race and Justice*, 4:3 (2014), 185–211; Bramwell, *UK Hip-Hop, Grime and the City*; Bramwell, 'Council Estate of Mind'; Richard Bramwell, 'Freedom Within Bars: Maximum Security Prisoners' Negotiations of Identity Through Rap', *Identities*, 25:4 (2018), 475–94; Fatsis, 'When Police Racism is Denied'; Fatsis, 'Grime: Criminal Subculture or Public Counterculture?'; Ilan, 'Digital Street Culture Decoded'; Adam Lynes, Craig Kelly and Emma Kelly, 'Thug Life: Drill Music as Periscope into Urban Violence in the Consumer Age', *British Journal of Criminology*, 60 (2020), 1201–19; Fatsis, 'Sounds Dangerous', Fatsis, 'Beat(s) for Blame', pp. 19–36; Owusu-Bempah, 'The Irrelevance of Rap'; Owusu-Bempah, 'Prosecuting Rap'.

66 Carrie B. Fried, 'Who's Afraid of Rap: Differential Reactions to Music Lyrics', *Journal of Applied Social Psychology*, 29:4 (1999), 705–21; Adam Dunbar, Charis E. Kubrin and Nicholas Scurich, 'The Threatening Nature of "Rap" Music', *Psychology, Public Policy and Law*, 22 (2016), 280–92; Adam Dunbar and Charis E. Kubrin, 'Imagining Violent Criminals: An Experimental Investigation of Music Stereotypes and Character Judgments', *Journal of Experimental Criminology*, 14:4 (2018), 507–28; Nicholas Stoia, Kyle Adams and Kevin Drakulich, 'Rap Lyrics as Evidence: What Can Music Theory Tell Us?', *Race and Justice*, 8:4 (2018), 330–65; Nielson and Dennis, *Rap on Trial*.

67 Clarke and Williams, '(Re)producing Guilt in Suspect Communities'; Susie Hulley and Tara Young, 'Silence, Joint Enterprise and the Legal Trap', *Criminology & Criminal Justice* (2021), 1–19. https://doi.org/10.1177/1748895821991622.

68 Helen Mills, Matt Ford and Roger Grimshaw, 'The Usual Suspects: Joint Enterprise Prosecutions Before and After the Supreme Court Ruling', *Centre for Crime and Justice Studies* (2022) (archived at web.archive.org/web/20220429201412/https://www.crimeandjustice.org.uk/sites/crimeandjustice.org.uk/files/The%20usual%20suspects%2C%20April%202022.pdf, accessed 12 April 2024); Nisha Waller, 'Gang Narratives and Broken

285

Law: Why Joint Enterprise Still Needs Fixing', *Centre for Crime and Justice Studies* (2022), www.crimeandjustice.org.uk/resources/gang-narratives-and-broken-law-why-joint-enterprise-still-needs-fixing (accessed 16 September 2024).

69 Quinn et al., 'Introduction to Special Issue', p. 2.

70 Brown, 'The Politics of Penal Excess'.

71 Helen Pidd, 'Manchester MP to write to minister over 'guilty by association' verdicts', *Guardian* (4 July 2022), www.theguardian.com/law/2022/jul/04/manchester-mp-to-write-to-minister-over-guilty-by-association-verdicts (accessed 9 January 2024).

72 Jay Bernard, *Joint*, London Literature Festival (2021), www.youtube.com/watch?v=Qp8lYHohGzg (accessed 12 February 2021).

73 Shirley Halperin and Ethan Shanfeld, 'RAP Act introduced in Congress would bar the use of lyrics as evidence in court proceedings', *Variety* (2022), www.variety.com/2022/music/news/rap-lyrics-crimimal-evidence-congress-bill-legislation-1235327683 (accessed 9 January 2023).

74 The New York Senate Bill S7527, nicknamed: the "Rap on trial" Bill (Nancy Dillon, 'New York Lawmakers Introducing Bill to Limit Rap Lyrics As evidence in Criminal Trials', *Rolling Stone* (2021), www.rollingstone.com/music/music-news/ny-state-senators-bill-legislation-rap-lyrics-evidence-criminal-trials-1258767 (accessed 29 March 2022); Tara Joshi, 'Spitting Innocence: The Use and Abuse of Drill Lyrics in Court', *Rolling Stone* (2022), www.rollingstone.co.uk/politics/features/prosecuting-uk-drill-rap-lyrics-court-20131 (accessed 16 September 2024), '[e]stablishes an assumption of the inadmissibility of evidence of a defendant's creative or artistic expression', unless prosecutors can 'affirmatively prove that the evidence is admissible by clear and convincing evidence'. The full text can be accessed at: www.nysenate.gov/legislation/bills/2021/s7527. Section 352.2(a) of the California Evidence Code, which became law on 1 January 2023, restricts the admissibility of creative expression.

75 Quinn et al., 'Introduction to Special Issue', pp. 419–20.

76 Thomas Kingsley, 'Criminologists Slam "Misleading" Policy Exchange Report Linking Drill Music to Youth Violence', *Independent* (13 November 2021), www.independent.co.uk/news/uk/home-news/policy-exchange-report-youth-violence-b1955691.html (accessed 16 September 2024).; Fatsis et al., 'Missing the Point'; Fatsis, 'Stop Blaming Drill for Making People Kill'.

77 Aneesa Ahmed, '"It Risks Miscarriages of Justice": MPs Oppose Rap Lyrics Being Used as Evidence in UK Trials', *Guardian* (22 November

2023), www.theguardian.com/music/2023/nov/22/mps-call-for-change-in-rap-lyrics-being-used-as-evidence-in-uk-trials-nadia-whittome-kim-jo hnson-shami-chakrabarti-annie-mac (accessed 16 September 2024).

78 For more details, see Keir Monteith KC, Audrey Cherry-Mogan and Shina Animashaun, 'Art Not Evidence Launches Campaign to Stop Rap Lyrics Being Used as Evidence', *Garden Court Chambers* (2023), www.gar dencourtchambers.co.uk/art-not-evidence-launches-campaign-to-stop-ra p-lyrics-being-used-as-evidence (accessed 28 May 2025).

79 Jeremy Ball and Caroline Lowbridge, 'CPS to Review Guidance on Using Drill Music as Evidence', *BBC News* (2022), www.bbc.co.uk/news/uk-england-nottinghamshire-60070345 (accessed 21 April 2024).

80 Crown Prosecution Service (CPS), 'Pioneering "Gangs" Unit Set Up to Tackle Those Who "Live by Crime"' (2022), www.cps.gov.uk/west-mid lands/news/pioneering-gangs-unit-set-tackle-those-who-live-crime (accessed 12 January 2023).

81 Langston Hughes, *The Collected Poems of Langston Hughes, 1902–1967* (New York: Knopf, 1997), p. 31.

82 Such a compendium of FAQs exists, courtesy of the Art Not Evidence campaign against the criminalisation of drill – that I am proud to be a core member of and a contributor to its FAQs section too: Art not evidence: http://driftime.notion.site/FAQ-1c26e89ocded428ea8f9bb9f3f2f9 dof (accessed 16 June 2025).

83 Lambros Fatsis, 'Decriminalising Rap Beat by Beat: Two Questions in Search of Answers', in E. Peters (ed.), *Music in Crime, Resistance, and Identity* (London: Routledge, 2023); Fatsis, 'Sounds Dangerous', pp. 30–1.

12 But isn't Rap violent and misogynistic?

1 '808s' refer to the loud bass drum beats created by and composed with the 808 or TR-808 Rhythm Composer – an analogue drum machine that has been a staple ingredient in the making of 'phat'/fat/heavy hip-hop beats/rhythms. For a brilliant, original, imaginative and promising 'take' on '808s' as tools for knowledge production, see Katherine McKittrick and Alexander G. Weheliye, '808s and Heartbreak', *Propter*, 2:1 (2017), 13–42. For an overall defence of Black music(s) as 'Black method', or as episte-mology in sound, see Katherine McKittrick, *Dear Science and Other Stories* (Durham, NC: Duke University Press, 2021). See also: Fatsis, 'Sounds Dangerous' and Fatsis, 'Arresting Sounds'.

2 Fatsis, 'Policing the Beats', p. 1302–3.

3   Fatsis, 'Policing the Beats', p. 1303.

4   BBC, *Radio 1Xtra: Gangs, Drill and Prayer*, www.bbc.co.uk/iplayer/epi sode/p065zhf8/1xtra-gangs-drill-and-prayer (accessed 16 June 2025).

5   Ciaran Thapar, 'UK drill & youth violence: The final word', *Trench* (2018), www.trenchtrenchtrench.com/features/uk-drill-and-youth-viole nce-the-final-word (accessed 16 September 2024); Dan Hancox, *Inner City Pressure: The Story of Grime* (London, UK: HarperCollins, 2018).

6   Hancox, *Inner City Pressure*, pp. 304–5.

7   For some insightful commentary on purging violence in and through rap(ping), see: Cecil Brown, *Stagolee Shot Billy* (Cambridge, MA: Harvard University Press, 2004), p. 221.

8   Charles Nicholl, *The Chemical Theatre* (London: Routledge, 1980), p. 142.

9   Jabari Evans, '"We [mostly] Carry Guns for the Internet": Visibility, Labour, Social Hacking and Chasing Digital Clout by Black Male Youth in Chicago's Drill Rap Scene', *Global Hip Hop Studies*, 1/2 (2020), 227–47; Stuart, *Ballad of the Bullet*; Schwarze and Fatsis, 'Copping the Blame'.

10 Eithne Quinn, *Nuthin' But a G Thang: The Culture and Commerce of Gangsta Rap* (New York: Columbia University Press, 2005).

11 While I recognise the reality that rap music cannot be understood in 'exclu-sively racial/ ethnic terms' (Anthony Gunter and Paul Watt, 'Grafting, Going to College and Working on Road: Youth Transitions and Cultures in an East London Neighbourhood', *Journal of Youth Studies*, 12:5 (2009), 515–29, p. 520), especially in the context of contemporary urban mul-ticulture, the (kin)aesthetic, linguistic and musical codes that define it are nevertheless informed by, and borrow from, Black or Afro- diasporic culture(s). Indeed, road culture would be, as well as sound, radically different if this was not so.

12 Fried, 'Who's Afraid of Rap', p. 716.

13 Dunbar, Kubrin and Scurich, 'The Threatening Nature of "Rap" Music', p. 288.

14 Dunbar and Kubrin, 'Imagining Violent Criminals', p. 521.

15 Nielson and Dennis, *Rap on Trial*, p. 114.

16 Nielson and Dennis, *Rap on Trial*, p. 114.

17 Robin D.G. Kelley, *Race Rebels: Culture, Politics and the Black Working Class* (New York: Free Press, 1994), p. 191; see also: Lawrence W. Levine, *Black Culture and Black Consciousness: Afro-American Folk Thought From Slavery to Freedom* (Oxford: Oxford University Press, 1977), pp. 412–13.

18 Zora N. Hurston, *They Don't Know Us Negroes and Other Essays* (London: HarperCollins, 2022), p 54; David Toop, *Rap Attack #3:*

African Rap to Global Hip Hop (London: Serpent's Tail, 2000), p. 34; Quinn, *Nuthin' But a G Thang*; Nielson and Dennis, *Rap on Trial*. For good discussions of such heroic 'badman' figures in African-American folklore in particular, see: Brown, *Stagolee Shot Billy* and Kelley, *Race Rebels*, pp. 183–301.

19 Angela Y. Davis, *Blues Legacies and Black Feminism: Gertrude "Ma" Rainey, Bessie Smith, and Billie Holiday* (New York: Pantheon Books, 1998), pp. 23–4.

20 Davis, *Blues Legacies and Black Feminism*, p. 23.

21 William C. Banfield, 'Some Aesthetic Suggestions for a Working Theory of the "Undeniable Groove"', in A.M.S. Nelson (ed.), *This Is How We Flow* (Columbia, SC: University of South Carolina Press, 1999), pp. 31–45, at p. 36.

22 Edward P. Thompson, 'Rough Music Reconsidered', *Folklore*, 103:1 (1992), 3–26.

23 Kassandra L. Hartford, 'Beyond the Trigger Warning: Teaching Operas that Depict Sexual Violence', *Journal of Music History Pedagogy*, 7:1 (2016), 19–34.

24 Toop, *Rap Attack #3*, p. 15.

25 Nielson and Dennis, *Rap on Trial*, p. 30.

26 Toop, *Rap Attack #3*, p. 166.

27 Toop, *Rap Attack #3*, p. 170.

28 Gates, *The Signifying Monkey*, pp. xix–xx.

29 E.g. London Assembly, *Police and Crime Committee Meeting*, 02:15:18 to 02:19–40.

30 Casey, *An Independent Review*.

31 Willie Horton was an African-American prisoner in Massachusetts who, while released on a furlough programme, raped a white woman from Maryland and stabbed her boyfriend. This case became a cause célèbre, but it was also cynically exploited by President George Bush in his 1988 presidential election campaign to generate support for a law-and-order agenda that reproduced racist stereotypes of 'blackness' as a synonym of violence, aggression, and criminality. Tricia Rose, 'Never Trust a Big Butt and a Smile', *Camera Obscura*, 23 (1990), 108–31, p. 108.

32 bell hooks, *We Real Cool: Black Men and Masculinity* (London: Routledge, 2004).

33 Kimberlé W. Crenshaw, 'Beyond Racism and Misogyny: Black Feminism and 2 Live Crew', in D.T. Meyers (ed.), *Feminist Social Thought: A Reader* (London: Routledge, 1997), pp. 245–63.

34   Rose, 'Never Trust a Big Butt and a Smile'; Tricia Rose, *Black Noise: Rap Music and Black Culture in Contemporary America* (Hanover: Wesleyan University Press, 1994); Tricia Rose, *The Hip Hop Wars: What We Talk about When We Talk about Hip Hop-and Why It Matters* (New York: Basic Books, 2008).

35   Imani Perry, 'It's My Thang and I'll Swing It the Way That I Feel!', in Gail Dines and Jean M. Humez (eds), *Gender, Race and Class in Media* (Thousand Oaks, CA: Sage, 1995), pp. 524–30; Imani Perry, *Prophets of the Hood: Politics and Poetics in Hip Hop* (Durham, NC: Duke University Press, 2004).

36   bell hooks, *Outlaw Culture: Resisting Representations* (London: Routledge, 2006), p. 135.

37   Rotem Kahalon et al., 'The Madonna-Whore Dichotomy Is Associated with Patriarchy Endorsement: Evidence from Israel, the United States, and Germany', *Psychology of Women Quarterly*, 43:3 (2019), 348–67.

38   Sigmund Freud, *New Introductory Lectures on Psychoanalysis* (New York: Norton & Co., 1933).

39   Cesare Lombroso, *The Female Offender* (New York: Philosophical Library, 1958).

40   Peter J. Burgard, *Nietzsche and the Feminine* (London: University Press of Virginia, 1994), p. 4.

41   Rose, *The Hip Hop Wars*, p. 5.

42   hooks, *Outlaw Culture*, p. 135.

43   hooks, *Outlaw Culture*, p. 135.

44   hooks, *Outlaw Culture*, p. 143.

45   hooks, *Outlaw Culture*, p. 135.

46   hooks, *Outlaw Culture*, p. 143.

47   hooks, *Outlaw Culture*, p. 139.

48   hooks, *Outlaw Culture*, p. 139.

49   hooks, *Outlaw Culture*, p. 140.

50   hooks, *Outlaw Culture*, p. 140.

51   hooks, *Outlaw Culture*, p. 140.

52   hooks, *Outlaw Culture*, p. 141.

53   Gloria T. Hull, Patricia B. Scott and Barbara Smith, *All the Women Are White, All the Blacks Are Men, But Some of Us Are Brave* (New York: The Feminist Press, 1982). For a masterly discussion of how blackness is theorised, constructed and fictionalised as property, object or what she calls a 'surrogate' through which the white imagination asserts itself, see Morrison, *Playing in the Dark*, p. 26.

54 Pratibha Parmar and Jackie Kay, 'Frontiers. Pratibha Parmar and Jackie Kay Interview Audre Lorde Nielsen and Dennis, 2019: 30', in S. Grewal (ed.), *Charting the Journey: Writings by Black and Third World Women* (London: Sheba, 1988), pp. 121–31, at p. 125.

55 Mary Wollstonecraft, *Vindication of the Rights of Women* (Harmondsworth: Penguin Books, 1985), pp. 310–1.

56 Hortense J. Spillers, *Black, White, and in Color* (Chicago: University of Chicago Press, 2003), p. 159.

57 Spillers, *Black, White, and in Color*, p. 160.

58 Alice Walker, 'Coming Apart', in L. Lederer (ed.), *Take Back the Night: Women on Pornography* (New York: William Morrow and Company, 1980), pp. 95–104 at p. 100.

59 Walker, 'Coming Apart', p. 100.

60 For further discussion on womanism, see: Chikwenye O. Ogunyemi, 'Womanism: The Dynamics of the Contemporary Black Female Novel in English', *Signs*, 11:1 (1985), 63–80; Katie G. Cannon, *Black Womanist Ethics* (Atlanta: Scholars Press, 1988); Geneva Smitherman, 'A Womanist Looks at the Million Man March', in H.R. Madhubuti and M. Karenga (eds), *Million Man March/Day of Absence* (Chicago: Third World Press, 1996), pp. 104–7; Patricia Hill Collins, *Fighting Words: Black Women and the Search for Justice* (Minneapolis: University of Minnesota Press, 1998 and Clenora Hudson-Weems, 'Africana Womanism', in O. Nnaemeka (ed.), *Sisterhood, Feminisms, and Power: From Africa to the Diaspora* (Trenton, NJ: Africa World Press, 1998), pp. 149–62.

61 Aileen Moreton-Robinson, *Talkin' Up to the White Woman: Indigenous Women and Feminism* (St Lucia: University of Queensland Press, 2020).

62 Joan Morgan, *When Chickenheads Come Home to Roost: A Hip-Hop Feminist Breaks It Down* (New York: Simon & Schuster, 1999); Marlo David, 'More than Baby Mamas: Black Mothers and Hip-Hop Feminism', in G.D. Pough et al. (eds), *Home Girls Make Some Noise: Hip Hop Feminism Anthology* (Mira Loma: Parker Publishing, 2007), pp. 345–67; Whitney A. Peoples, '"Under Construction": Identifying Foundations of Hip-Hop Feminism and Exploring Bridges between Black Second-Wave and Hip-Hop Feminisms', *Meridians*, 8:1 (2008), 19–52.

63 Gwendolyn D. Pough et al. (eds), *Home Girls Make Some Noise: Hip Hop Feminism Anthology* (Mira Loma, CA: Parker Publishing), pp. 345–67.

64 Aisha Durham, Brittney C. Cooper, and Susana M. Morris, 'The Stage Hip-Hop Feminism Built: A New Directions Essay', *Signs*, 38:3 (2013), 721–37.

65 Patricia Hill Collins, *Black Feminist Thought: Knowledge, Consciousness and the Politics of Empowerment* (Revised Tenth Anniversary Edition) (London: Routledge, 2000), p. 85.

66 Carolyn Cooper, 'Sweet & Sour Sauce: Sexual Politics in Jamaican Dancehall Culture', *The Sixth Jagan Lecture*, presented at York University, 22 October 2005, www.yorku.ca/cerlac/wp-content/uploads/sites/259/2016/08/Cooper.pdf (accessed 18 September 2024), p. 1.

67 Cooper, 'Sweet & Sour Sauce', p. 1, see also: Cooper, *Noises in the Blood* and Cooper, *Sound Clash*, Jamaican Dancehall Culture at Large.

68 Cooper, 'Sweet & Sour Sauce', p. 3.

69 Cooper, 'Sweet & Sour Sauce', p. 3.

70 In contemporary Britain, 'on road', 'the roads', 'road life' and 'road culture' – all referring to a "UK- specific form of street culture" (Bakkali, 'Dying to Live', pp. 13– 17) – represent a spatial and cultural reality, that is lived both as a social cul-de-sac and as an avenue for transgression (Simon Hallsworth and Daniel Silverstone, '"That's Life Innit": A British Perspective on Guns, Crime and Social Order', *Criminology & Criminal Justice*, 9:3 (2009), 359–77) through musical expression, dress codes and common patterns of speech (Gunter and Watt, 'Grafting, Going to College and Working on Road'; Yusef Bakkali, 'Road Capitals: Reconceptualising Street Capital, Value Production and Exchange in the Context of Road Life in the UK', *Current Sociology*, 70:3 (2022), 419–35). For a discussion of the criminalisation of 'road culture' through drill music, see: Lambros Fatsis, 'The Road, in Court: How UK Drill Music Became a Criminal Offence', in J. Levell, T. Young and R. Earle (eds), *Exploring Urban Youth Culture Outside of the Gang Paradigm: Critical Questions of Youth, Gender and Race On-Road* (Bristol: Bristol University Press, 2023), pp. 100–14.

71 Oliver, *Deeping It*.

72 Steiner and Pire, *Barbarie de l'Ignorance*, p. 45. I have attempted to translate from French to the best of my limited ability. The original passage reads as follows: 'ce qu'il y a de plus meurtrier dans los civilisations urbaines. Le rap, c'est la voix même de la violence, de la brutalisation de l'individu' (Steiner and Pire, *Barbarie de l'Ignorance*, p. 45).

73 I am greatly indebted to Sudip Sen for this observation. So much so, that I am lovingly borrowing, if not brazenly hijacking, his own words here.

Part IV: Sounds radical: Black critique(s) of White reason

1　Du Bois, *Black Reconstruction*, pp. 725–6.
2　hooks, *Outlaw Culture*, p. 142.
3　Monique Charles, 'MDA as a Research Method of Generic Musical Analysis for the Social Sciences: Sifting Through Grime (Music) as an SFT Case Study', *International Journal of Qualitative Methods*, 17 (2018), 1–11, at p. 7.
4　Agawu, 'Representing African Music'; Agawu, *Audible Empire*, pp. 334–55.
5　Bebey, *African Music*, p. 92, p. vi.
6　James W. Johnson, *The Autobiography of an Ex-Coloured Man* (New York: Random House, 1989), pp. 72–3.
7　Browning, *Samba: Resistance in Motion*, pp. 12, 1.
8　Lambros Fatsis, 'Becoming Public Characters, Not Public Intellectuals: Notes Towards an Alternative Conception of Public Intellectual Life', *European Journal of Social Theory*, 21:3 (2018), 267–87.
9　Patricia Hill Collins, *Black Feminist Thought: Knowledge, Consciousness and the Politics of Empowerment* (London: Routledge, 1991), p. 100.
10　Spillers, *Black, White, and in Color*, p. 442.
11　Léopold S. Senghor, *Liberté I, Négritude et Humanisme* (Paris: Seuil, 1964), p. 288.
12　Stuart Hall, 'What Is This "Black" in Black Popular Culture?', *Social Justice*, 20:1/2 (1993), 104–14, p. 109.

13　Who feels it, knows it: Black radical thought in sound

1　Gilroy, *The Black Atlantic*, p. ix.
2　Gilroy, *The Black Atlantic*, p. 127.
3　Gilroy, *The Black Atlantic*.
4　Gilroy, *Between Camps*, p. 337.
5　Gilroy, *The Black Atlantic*, p. 4; Brathwaite, *Folk Culture of the Slaves in Jamaica*, pp. 7, 13.
6　Kehinde Andrews, 'The Problem of Political Blackness: Lessons from the Black Supplementary School Movement', *Ethnic and Racial Studies*, 39:11 (2016), 2060–78 at pp. 2063–4.
7　Hall, 'What Is This "Black" in Black Popular Culture?'
8　Sonjah Stanley Niaah, *DanceHall: From Slave Ship to Ghetto* (Ottawa: University of Ottawa Press, 2010).
9　Spillers, *Black, White, and in Color*, pp. 1–64.

10 Spillers, *Black, White, and in Color*, p. 5.
11 Edward Kamau Brathwaite, *The Arrivants: A New World Trilogy* (Oxford: Oxford University Press, 1973).
12 Bambara, *Deep Sightings and Rescue Missions*, p. 145.
13 Bambara, *Deep Sightings and Rescue Missions*, p. 107.
14 Gilroy, *Between Camps*, p. 123.
15 Stuart Hall, 'Africa is Alive and Well in the Diaspora: Cultures of Resistance: Slavery, Religious Revival and Political Cultism in Jamaica', in Paul Gilroy and Ruth Wilson Gilmore (eds), *Selected Writings on Race and Difference* (Durham: Duke University Press, 2021), pp. 161–94.
16 Clyde A. Woods, *Development Arrested: The Blues and Plantation Power in the Mississippi Delta* (London: Verso), 2017, p. 288.
17 Hill, *The Trinidad Carnival*, p. 115.
18 Juliette Bowles, 'A Rap on Rhythm', in A.M.S. Nelson (ed.), '*This is How We Flow*' (Columbia, South Carolina: University of South Carolina Press, 1999), pp. 5–14, at p. 6.
19 Wynter, *We Must Learn to Sit Down Together and Talk About a Little Culture*, p. 246.
20 Amiri Baraka, *Black Music* (New York: Akashic Books, 2010), pp. 19; 209.
21 Baraka, *Black Music*, p. 214.
22 Browning, *Samba: Resistance in Motion*, pp. xi, 12.
23 Ntozake Shange, *Dance We Do: A Poet Explores Black Dance* (Boston: Beacon Press, 2020), p. 53.
24 Wynter, *Black Metamorphosis*, p. 546.
25 Wynter, *Black Metamorphosis*, p. 140.
26 Brathwaite, *Folk Culture of the Slaves in Jamaica*, p. 13 (original emphasis)].
27 For a book-length critique of the written word as the dominant medium for thinking and scholarship that is also a defence of 'the orally transmitted expressive culture of Afro-Americans', see Levine, *Black Culture and Black Consciousness*, p. ix.
28 Hartman, *Lose Your Mother*, pp. 174–5.
29 Spillers, *Black, White, and in Color*, p. x.
30 Hartman, *Wayward Lives, Beautiful Experiments*, p. 345.
31 Griots in West Africa are often likened to storytellers who inform listeners about the world through their music. Bebey, *African Music*, p. 24 describes the griot as 'a living archive of his people's traditions' who '"knows everything that is going on', despite belonging to 'one of the lowest castes in the social hierarchy'. The West African griot then is a 'historian praise-singer, entertainer, intermediary in disputes and notably, the initiator of major

decisions made in times of crisis. In other words, the griot had the power
to intervene as the social critic of society' (Galina Chester and Tunde
Jegede, *The Silenced Voice: Hidden Music of the Kora* (London: Diabaté
Kora Arts, 1987), p. 16).

32 Brathwaite, *History of the Voice*, pp. 18–19.
33 Kwesi Owusu, *Storms of the Heart: An Anthology of Black Arts and Culture*
(London: Camden Press, 1988), p. 215; see also: Keith Owusu, *The Struggle
for Black Arts in Britain* (London: Comedia, 1986), pp. 127–50; Chester
and Jegede, *The Silenced Voice*, p. 27 and Édouard Glissant, *Caribbean
Discourse: Selected Essays* (Charlottesville: University Press of Virginia,
1989), esp. pp. 248–9.
34 Wynter, *Black Metamorphosis*, p. 521.
35 Wynter, *Black Metamorphosis*, p. 521; Jürgen Habermas, *Knowledge and
Human Interests* (Boston: Beacon Press, 1978), p. 301.
36 Bebey, *African Music*, p. vi.
37 Alejo Carpentier, *Music in Cuba* (London: University of Minnesota Press,
2001), p. 229.
38 Lambros Fatsis, 'Grime: Criminal Subculture or public Counterculture?
A Critical Investigation into the Criminalization of Black Musical
Subcultures in the UK', *Crime Media Culture*, 15:3 (2019), 447–61, at
pp. 452–6.
39 Wynter, *Black Metamorphosis*, p. 218.
40 McKittrick, *Dear Science and Other Stories* pp. 50–1.
41 Fatsis and Lamb, *Policing the Pandemic*, pp. 75–7.
42 Eric J. Hobsbawm, *The Jazz Scene* (London: Weidenfeld & Nicholson,
1989), p. 34.
43 Hobsbawm published his jazz criticism under the pseudonym Francis
Newton, as a nod to trumpeter Frankie Newton who is most famous
perhaps for his opening, plaintive solo on Billie Holiday's anti-lynching
classic: *Strange Fruit*.
44 Kelley, 'Kickin' Reality, Kickin' Ballistics', p. 134.
45 Quevedo, *Atilla's Kaiso*, p. 28.
46 Jeff Chang, *Can't Stop Won't Stop: A History of the Hip-Hop Generation*
(London: Picador, 2005), p. 251.
47 Hill, *The Trinidad Carnival*, p. 69.
48 *Melody Maker*, 'N[*****]ers with Attitude', 4 November 1989, p. 33.
49 Robinson, '"The First Attack Is an Attack on Culture"', p. 230.
50 Kelley, 'Kickin' Reality, Kickin' Ballistics', p. 121.
51 Fatsis, 'From Overseer to Officer'.

52 Toni Cade Bambara, *The Salt Eaters* (New York, NY: Vintage, 1992), p. 119 (italics added).

53 Gates, *The Signifying Monkey*, p. 22.

54 Baldwin, *The Cross of Redemption*, p. 148.

55 Collins, *Black Feminist Thought*, p. 230.

56 It should be noted that 'Traneing' is not the invention of Coltrane's fans, but a word that John Coltrane himself coined in *Traneing In*, the album and the title track that defined St John Coltrane's collaboration with pianist Red Garland and his trio. The reference to John Coltrane's saintly status here is intended here as a sign of reverence to the tenor and soprano saxophone wizard, but also a reference to his elevation to sainthood by the Saint John Coltrane Church in San Francisco. For a musical tribute to John Coltrane's as a musical and spiritual sainthood, listen to avant-garde saxophonist Byard Lancaster's *Saint John Coltrane*.

57 Mari J. Matsuda, 'Looking to the Bottom: Critical Legal Studies and Reparations', *Harvard Civil Rights-Civil Liberties Law Review*, 22:3 (1987), 323–99 at p. 388.

58 Frank Kofsky, *John Coltrane and the Jazz Revolution of the 1960s* (New York: Pathfinder, 1998), p. 435.

59 Steven Feld, 'Acoustemology', in David Novak and Matt Sakakeeny (eds), *Keywords in Sound* (Durham, NC: Duke University Press, 2015).

60 Les Back, 'Let a Thousand Stones Roll: Living and Thinking with Music', in T. Johansson and T. Söderman (eds), *Låt alla stenar rulla – lärande, estetik, samhälle. En vänbok till Ove Sernhede* (Göteborg: Daidalos, 2016), pp. 119–37.

61 Ntozake Shange, *I Live in Music* (New York: Welcome Enterprises, 1994).

62 Douglass, *Narrative of the Life of Frederick Douglass*, p. 14.

14 Who knows it, feels it: Learning about criminal injustice from the policing of Black music(s)

1 Noura Erakat, *Justice for Some: Law and the Question of Palestine* (Stanford, CA: Stanford University Press, 2019).

2 Sarah Ahmed, 'Evidence', *feministkilljoys* (2016), https://feministkilljoys.com/2016/07/12/evidence/ (accessed 4 October 2024).

3 Fatsis and Lamb, *Policing the Pandemic*, esp. pp. 96–100; Fatsis, 'When the Exception Makes the Rules'.

4 John O. Calmore, 'Critical Race Theory, Archie Shepp, and fire Music: Securing an Authentic Intellectual Life in a Multicultural World', *Southern California Law Review*, 65:5 (1992), 2129–230 at p. 2184.

5 Derrick Bell, 'Racial Realism', *Connecticut Law Review*, 24:2 (1992), pp. 363–80, at p. 364.

6 Anatole France, *The Red Lily* (New York: Dodd-Mead & Company, n.d.), p. 91.

7 Jerrard Winstanley, *Fire in the Bush* (London: Printed for Giles Calvert, 1650), p. 29.

8 John M. Moore, 'Built for Inequality in a Diverse World: The Historic Origins of criminal Justice', *Papers from the British Criminology Conference*, 16 (2016), 38–56; John M. Moore, '"law", "order", "justice", "crime": Disrupting Key Concepts in Criminology Through the Study of Colonial History', *The Law Teacher*, 54:4 (2020), 489–502.

9 Wynter, *Black Metamorphosis*, p. 17.

10 Hall, 'Race, Articulation and Societies Structured in Dominance', p. 341.

11 Robinson, *Black Marxism*; Oliver C. Cox, *Caste, Class, and Race* (New York: Doubleday and Company, 1948); Oliver C. Cox, *The Foundations of Capitalism* (New York: Philosophical Library, 1959); Oliver C. Cox, *Capitalism and American Leadership* (New York: Philosophical Library, 1962); Oliver C. Cox, *Capitalism as a System* (New York: Philosophical Library, 1964); Oliver C. Cox, 'Marxism: Looking Backward and Forward: Essay 6', *Monthly Review*, 26:2 (1974), 58; Harold Wolpe, *Race, Class and the Apartheid State* (London: James Currey, 1988); Neville Alexander, *Against Racial Capitalism: Selected Writings* (London: Pluto Press, 2023); Lambros Fatsis, 'Racial Capitalism: A Guide for the Naysayer', in: J.I. Fúnez-Flores, S.J. Ndlovu-Gatsheni, A.C. Díaz Beltrán, S. Bakshi, L. Laó-Montes and F. Rios (eds), *Sage Handbook of Decolonial Theory* (London: Sage, 2025), pp. 522–32.

12 Hulsman, 'Critical Criminology and the Concept of Crime'.

13 Hartman, *Wayward Lives, Beautiful Experiments*, p. 62.

14 Césaire, *Discourse on Colonialism*, p. 32.

15 Sigmund Freud, *Civilization and Its Discontents* (London: The Hogarth Press, 1930), p. 94.

16 Michel Foucault, *Power/Knowledge: Selected Interviews and Other Writings 1972–1977* (New York: Pantheon Books, 1980), p. 47.

17 Hartman, *Wayward Lives, Beautiful Experiments*, p. 107.

18 George Jackson, *Soledad Brother: The Prison Letters of George Jackson* (Harmondsworth: Penguin, 1971), p. 42.

19 Dane Archer and Rosemary Gartner, *Violence and Crime in Cross-National Perspective* (New Haven: Yale University Press, 1984).

20 Jordan, *Civil Wars*, p. 48.

21 Jordan, *Civil Wars*, p. 180.

22 Toop, *Rap Attack #3*, p. 58.

23 Jackson, *Soledad Brother*, p. 154.

24 London Assembly, *Police and Crime Committee Meeting*, at 2:17:56.

25 Fatsis and Lamb, *Policing the Pandemic*.

26 David Hare, *Asking Around* (London: Faber & Faber, 1993), p. 97.

27 Hubert L. Dreyfus and Paul Rabinow, *Michel Foucault: Beyond Structuralism and Hermeneutics* (Chicago: The University of Chicago Press, 1983), p. 139.

28 Dreyfus and Rabinow, *Michel Foucault: Beyond Structuralism and Hermeneutics*, p. 139.

29 Toni Morrison, *Love* (Toronto: Vintage Canada, 2005), p. 5.

30 Fatsis and Lamb, *Policing the Pandemic*, pp. 21–2, 28–34.

31 Ian Loader, *Revisiting the Police Mission. Policing Insight Paper 2, The Strategic Review of Policing in England and Wales* (The Police Foundation, 2020), https://police-foundation.org.uk/policingreview2022/ (accessed 4 October 2024), p. 10.

32 David H. Bayley, *Police for the Future* (Oxford: Oxford University Press, 1996), pp. 3, 10.

33 Michel Foucault, *Security, Territory, Population: Lectures at the Collège de France 1977–1978* (London: Palgrave Macmillan, 2009), p. 441.

34 Jackson, *Soledad Brother*, p. 42.

35 Steve Martinot and Jason Sexton, 'The Avant-Garde of White Supremacy', *Social Identities*, 9:2 (2003), 169–81, at p. 173.

36 Martinot and Sexton, 'The Avant-Garde of White Supremacy', p. 172.

37 Frank Wilderson, 'The Prison Slave as Hegemony's (Silent) Scandal', *Social Justice*, 30:2 (2003), 18–27, at p. 20.

38 James Baldwin, *No Name in the Street* (New York: Vintage Books, 2007), p. 149.

39 Charles W. Mills, *The Racial Contract* (London: Cornell University Press, 1999).

40 see also: Rinaldo Walcott, 'The Problem of the Human: Black Ontologies and 'the Coloniality of Our Being', in Svenja Broeck and Christian Junker (eds), *Postcoloniality – Decoloniality – Black Critique: Joints and Fissures* (Frankfurt: Campus Verlag, 2014), pp. 93–105.

41 Mills, *The Racial Contract*, p. 87.

42 For a book-length discussion of this theme in the form of essays and poems, see: Claudia Rankine, *Just Us: An American Conversation* (London: Penguin Books, 2020).

43 Levine, *Black Culture and Black Consciousness*, pp. 445, 1.

44 W.E.B. Du Bois, 'The Color Line Belts the World, October 20, 1906', *W.E.B. Du Bois Papers* (MS 312), Special Collections and University Archives, University of Massachusetts Amherst Libraries.

45 Du Bois, *Darkwater*, p. 39.

46 Frantz Fanon, *Toward the African Revolution* (London: Penguin Press, 1970), pp. 84, 46.

47 Walter Benjamin, 'On the Concept of History', in Howard Eiland and Michael W. Jennings (eds), *Selected Writings, Volume 4: 1938–1940* (Cambridge, MA: Harvard University Press, 2003), p. 392.

48 Césaire, *Discourse on Colonialism*, p. 36, p. 41.

49 Arendt, *The Origins of Totalitarianism*, p. 182.

50 Michel Foucault, '"Society Must Be Defended" Lectures at the Collège de France, 1975–76' (New York: Picador, 2003), p. 103.

51 Fanon, *Toward the African Revolution*, pp. 41–54.

52 Beryl Gilroy, *The Green Grass Tango* (Leeds: Peepal Tree Press, 2001), p. 14.

53 Fanon, *Toward the African Revolution*, p. 48.

54 Fanon, *Toward the African Revolution*, p. 47.

55 Fanon, *Toward the African Revolution*, pp. 47, 46.

56 Fanon, *Toward the African Revolution*, p. 43.

57 Fanon, *Toward the African Revolution*, pp. 49–50.

58 Gilroy, *After Empire*, p. 42.

59 Ruth W. Gilmore, *Golden Gulag: Prisons, Surplus, Crisis and Opposition in Globalizing California* (Berkeley: University of California Press, 2007), pp. 28, 24.

60 Paul Robeson, *Here I Stand* (Boston: Beacon Press, 1958), p. 78 (original emphasis].

61 Césaire, *Discourse on Colonialism*, p. 42.

62 Wynter, *Black Metamorphosis*, p. 223.

63 Sylvia Wynter, 'Unsettling the Coloniality of Being/Power/Truth/ Freedom: Towards the Human, After Man, Its Overrepresentation – An Argument', *CR: The New Centennial Review*, 3:3 (2003), 257–337; Walcott, 'The Problem of the Human'; Aníbal Quijano, 'Coloniality of Power and Eurocentrism in Latin America', *International Sociology*, 15:2 (2000), 215–32; Walter D. Mignolo, *Local Histories/Global Designs: Coloniality,*

Subaltern Knowledges, and Border Thinking (Princeton: Princeton University Press, 2000); Walter D. Mignolo, 'Delinking: The Rhetoric of Modernity, the Logic of Coloniality and the Grammar of Decoloniality', *Cultural Studies*, 21:2–3 (2007), 449–514; Walter D. Mignolo, 'Epistemic Disobedience, Independent Thought and Decolonial Freedom', *Theory, Culture & Society*, 26:7–8 (2009), 159–81.

64 Jamaica Kincaid, *A Small Place* (New York: Farrar, Straus, Giroux, 2000), p. 54.

65 Glissant, *Caribbean Discourse*, p. 2.

66 Fanon, *Toward the African Revolution*, p. 93.

67 W.E.B. Du Bois, 'The African Roots of War', in Ato Getachew and James Pitts (eds), *W.E.B. Du Bois: International Thought* (Cambridge: Cambridge University Press, 2022), pp. 22–35, at pp. 24–5.

68 Donna Haraway, 'Situated Knowledges: The Science Question in Feminism and the Privilege of Partial Perspective', *Feminist Studies*, 14:3 (1988), 575–99.

69 W.E.B. Du Bois, *Dusk of Dawn: An Essay Toward an Autobiography of a Race Concept* (Oxford: Oxford University Press, 2007), p. 34.

70 Hartman, *Lose Your Mother*, p. 133.

71 Du Bois, *Black Reconstruction*.

72 Hartman, *Lose Your Mother*, p. 6.

73 June Jordan, *Directed By Desire: The Collected Poems of June Jordan* (Washington: Copper Canyon Press, 2007), pp. 17, 67.

Postscript

1 James, *Spheres of Existence*, p. 187.

2 Fryer, *Aspects of British Black History*, p. 5.

3 Wolfe, 'Settler Colonialism and the Elimination of the Native', p. 387.

4 Joel Olson, *The Abolition of White Democracy* (Minnesota, MN: University of Minnesota Press, 2004), p. 43.

5 Rodney, *The Groundings With My Brothers*, p. 16.

6 Du Bois, *Darkwater*, p. 30.

7 James Baldwin, 'The White Man's Guilt', in Toni Morrison (ed.), *James Baldwin: Collected Essays* (New York: The Library of America, 1998), pp. 722–7, at p. 723.

8 Alice Walker, *In Search of Our Mothers' Gardens: Womanist Prose* (New York: Harcourt Brace Jovanovich, 1983), p. 128.

9 Baldwin, *The Cross of Redemption*, p. 137.

10 Ambalavaner Sivanandan, *Catching History on the Wing: Race, Culture and Globalisation* (London: Pluto Press, 2008), p. xviii.

11 Marie Liboiron, *Pollution is Colonialism* (Durham, NC: Duke University Press, 2021), pp. 53–4.

12 Baldwin, *The Cross of Redemption*, p. 137.

13 Zora N. Hurston, *Dust Tracks on a Road* (New York: Arno Press, 1969), p. 239.

Glossary

1 Uvanney Maylor, 'What is the Meaning of "Black"? Researching "Black" Respondents', *Ethnic and Racial Studies*, 32:2 (2009), 369–87, at p. 373.

2 Andrews, 'The Problem of Political Blackness', pp. 2063–4.

3 The full text of *The Combahee River Collective Statement* can be found at: https://americanstudies.yale.edu/sites/default/files/files/Keyword%20Coalition_Readings.pdf (accessed 16 June 2025).

4 Hull, Scott, and Smith, *All the Women Are White*, pp. 13–22.

5 Ronald Hyam, *Empire and Sexuality* (Manchester: Manchester University Press, 1990), p. 2. A qualifying footnote is required here to clarify that in quoting Hyam, I do not share his tendency to downplay the brutally exploitative nature of concubinage. I simply quote him for the pithy way in which he (at least) acknowledged it. For indicative critiques of Hyam's position – especially his dubious conclusion that 'sexual interaction between the British and non-Europeans probably did more long-term good than harm to race relations' (Hyam, *Empire and Sexuality*, p. 215): see, Helen Bradford, 'Sex, Lies and Englishmen', *South African Historical Journal*, 26:1 (1992), 209–14 and Richard A. Voeltz, 'The British Empire, Sexuality, Feminism and Ronald Hyam', *European Review of History*, 3:1 (1996), 41–4.

6 Catherine Hall, 'Gendering Property, Racing Capital', *History Workshop Journal*, 78:1 (2014), 22–38, at pp. 35–6.

7 Sita Balani, *Deadly and Slick: Sexual Modernity and the Making of Race* (London: Verso, 2023); Catherine Hall, *White, Male and Middle Class: Explorations in Feminism and History* (Cambridge: Polity Press, 1992).

8 William Quigley, 'Letter to a Law Student Interested in Social Justice', *Depaul Journal for Social Sciences*, 1:1 (2007), 7–28, at p. 15.

9 Patricia J. Williams, *The Alchemy of Race and Rights* (London: Virago, 1993), p. 139.

10 Williams, *The Alchemy of Race and Rights*, p. 138.

11 Steven Lukes, *Liberals and Cannibals: The Implications of Diversity* (London: Verso, 2003).

12 Elkins, *Legacy of Violence*, p. 12.

13 Elkins, *Legacy of Violence*, p. 12.

14 Bertrand Russell, *The Good Citizen's Alphabet* (London: Tate, 2017).

15 Martin Legassick and Don Hemson, 'Foreign Investment and the Reproduction of Racial Capitalism in South Africa', *Anti-Apartheid Movement*, September (1976), 2–16.

16 Robinson, *Black Marxism*.

17 Robin D.G. Kelley, 'What Did Cedric Robinson Mean by Racial Capitalism?', *Boston Review* (2017), www.bostonreview.net/articles/robin-d-g-kelley-introduction-race-capitalism-justice/ (accessed 14 August 2024).

18 St Clair Drake, *Black Folk Here and There: An Essay in History and Anthropology, Volume 2* (New York: Diasporic Africa Press, 2014), p. xi.

19 Robinson, *Black Marxism*, pp. 9–28.

20 Drake, *Black Folk Here and There*, p. 226.

21 Fatsis, 'Racial Capitalism'.

22 W.E.B. Du Bois, *W.E.B. Du Bois Speaks: Speeches and Addresses: 1890–1919* (New York: Pathfinder Press, 1970), p. 124.

23 Du Bois, *W.E.B. Du Bois Speaks*, p. 75.

24 Gurminder K. Bhambra, 'Brexit, Empire, and Decolonization', *History Workshop* (2018), www.historyworkshop.org.uk/empire-decolonisation/brexit-empire-and-decolonization (accessed 16 June 2025).

25 John Donne, 'Meditation 17', in *Devotions Upon Emergent Occasions* (Cambridge: Cambridge University Press, 1823), p. 98.

Index

abolition democracy 191–2
Abolition of Slavery Bill 20–1
abolitionist thinking 11
Adams, Rolan, killing of 81
aesthetic dissonance 25
aesthetic judgement 96
African diaspora 4
African drumming 26
    policing 34–9, 43
    role of 54–5
    suppression of 6, 52
African rhythms, criminalisation 3
Afro-Cuban music 4
Afro-diasporic culture 165–6, 169
Age of Reason 53
Ali, Altab, murder of 78
alienness, cultural 86
Aliens Act, 1905 72
anti-colonial theory 190–1
anti-gang initiatives 107, 109–10,
        121, 123–6, 129–31
anti-racist struggles 78–81
anti-slavery advocates 50–1
Anti-social Behaviour Crime and
        Policing Act 2014 130

Antisocial Behaviour Orders
    (ASBOs) 113–17
Arouca riots, 1891 42
Àsìkò music 4
Association for a People's Carnival
    81
Asylum Immigration (Appeals) Act,
    1993 70
Atilla the Hun (Raymond
    Quevedo), Banning of Records
    45–7, 160
Awate 124–5

bad character, as form of evidence
    137–43
Baldwin, James 172, 184, 213
Bambaataa, Afrika 150, 181
Bambara, Toni Cade 30–1, 167
belonging and unbelonging 7, 61,
    96, 99, 182, 192
Black Atlantic, the 5, 166
Black criminality 7, 98–9, 100–1,
    107, 109–17, 121–2, 143,
    159
    rap subgenres 4, 8

Black cultural expression 4–5, 15, 54, 125
Black music
    context 54–5
    danger of 26–33
diasporic forms of Black music-making 5
    hate of 27
    thinking with 9
Black on Black crime 107, 110, 112
Black People's Day of Action 79
Black performative practices 39
Black Power 77
Black radical feminist thought 11
Black resistance 15
Black studies 11
Black-music-as-knowledge 165–74
Blackness 98–9, 166–7, 189
    as criminal category 8
    criminalisation of 172
    and criminality 7, 107, 109–17, 121–2, 143, 159
    and danger 3
    fear-inducing image of 121
    war on 126–7
Blair, Tony 109–10, 114, 126
blues music 4, 149
Bovell, Dennis, arrest 94
Brathwaite, Edward Kamau 32, 50, 57–8, 64, 166–7, 168, 168–9
Brazil 2–3, 34, 51
Brexit referendum campaign 70, 100
Bristol Bus Boycott 68
British Black Power Movement 78
British bulldog ideology 64
British Empire 59–61, 83, 84–5
British Nationality Act, 1948 57, 59, 67
British Nationality Act, 1981 70

British Overseas Territories (BOTs) 59
Brixton Riots 79–80

Callaghan, James 68, 69–70
calypso 7, 64
calypso/*kaiso* 6, 15, 26, 39, 39–47, 198–9
Cameron, David 121, 122–3, 126
Campbell, Cornell 98–9
Canboulay riots, 1881 40–2
capitalism 17, 19–20, 23, 49, 54–6, 61, 121, 177, 208, 210
capitalist coloniality 24
capoeira 2–3
Caribbean, the 6, 22, 34
    African drumming ban 37–9
    colonial curriculum 58–9
    colonial rule 39–47
    slave codes 36–9
Carnival 3, 15, 26, 34, 39–44, 76, 81
Casey Review 82–3, 106
Cashmore, Ernest 91–3
Césaire, Aimé 84, 178, 186, 189
Chaggar, Gurdip Singh, murder of 78
Churchill, Winston 67, 84
citizenship 7, 57, 69, 70
Cochrane, Kelso 76
Code Noir 35
Collins, Patricia Hill 172
colonial imperial capitalism 61
colonial imperialism 24, 31, 102, 105, 175, 184, 186, 189, 192
colonial rule 6, 32
colonialism 6, 14, 22, 25, 186–7, 190

colour bar, the 74–5
Colquhoun, Patrick 22–3
Coltrane, John 172–3
Commission for Racial Equality 69
Commonwealth Immigrants Act, 1962 68
Commonwealth Immigrants Act, 1971 69
Consolidated Act, 1787 36–7
Constantine, Learie 74–5
Cool Britannia 104, 106
'cop-italism' 20, 54–5, 55
crime 7–8, 177–80
    conceptualisation 112–13
    history of 179
    racialisation 113
    sensationalisation 178–9
Crime and Disorder Act 1998 113–14
Criminal Behaviour Orders (CBOs) 129–30
Criminal Justice Act 2003 137, 140
criminalisation 5, 15, 26, 48, 177, 189
    African rhythms 3
    Blackness 172
    calypso/*kaiso* 39–47
    Carnival 39–44
    and crime 178
    of dissent 46–7
    immigration 63–5, 71
    noise 35
    racialised 4
    rap 152, 158–9
    rap subgenres 7–9
    UK drill 107
    UK grime 107, 118–27

criminality 98–9, 100–1
    and Blackness 7, 107, 109–17, 121–2, 143, 159
    rap subgenres 4, 8
criminological historiography 14, 22
'crimmigration' 63–5, 71, 102
Crown Prosecution Service (CPS) 41, 128–9, 135, 140

dance 6, 40, 168
De Menezes, Jean Charles, killing of 128
De Schutter, Olivier 111–12
discrimination 23, 68, 69, 71, 74–5, 80, 105
dissent, criminalisation of 46–7
Douglass, Frederick 48–9, 173
drapetomania 52
Drill Music Translation Cadre 129–30
Du Bois, W.E.B. 22, 61, 84, 84–5, 185–6, 190, 191, 191–2, 213
Duggal, Rohit, killing of 81
Duggan, Mark, killing of 121
Dunbarton Oaks Conference 85

education 53, 58–9, 112, 189–90, 192, 194, 209
Emancipation Act 20–1
Empire Windrush 57–8, 63–4, 65, 66–7
Ending Gangs and Youth Violence programme 123
enemy within, tropes 99
Enlightenment, the 53, 190
'En-whitenment' 47, 53, 190, 214
Equality and Human Rights Commission 111
Equiano, Olaudah 50, 51

Eurocentrism 161–2
European Volunteer Workers 67

Fanon, Frantz 23–4, 104, 186, 188, 190
Fascism 84–5, 183
feminism 155–7
Fortune, T. Thomas 101–2
Foucault, Michel 179, 183, 186–7
Francis, Joshua, killing of 77
freedom struggles 43, 48–56
Fryer, Peter 20, 212

Gammal, Ahmed el, death in police custody 82
gang-related music 131, 132–7
Gardner, Joy, death of 81–2
Garvey, Amy Ashwood 76–7
general election, 2024 71
Gilroy, Beryl 64
Gilroy, Paul 50, 63–4, 76, 100, 101, 121, 166
Goveia, Elsa 22, 36–7
Graham, Vincent, death in police custody 81
Greater London Council, Police Committee 80
Groce, Cherry, killing of 81
gun violence 110–11

Haiti 37, 51
Haitian Revolution 52, 55
Hall, Stuart 59, 100–1, 167
Handsworth, Birmingham 91
Hartman, Saidiya 8, 168, 179–80, 191, 192
Hassan, Tunay, death in police custody 81
hate, of Black music 27

Hegel, Georg W.F. 27
Hill, Erroll 37, 42, 45–7
hip-hop 21, 89, 103, 140, 141, 150, 170, 181, 204–6, 210
hip-hop feminism 157
historical truth 191
hooks, bell 152, 154
House of Commons Digital, Culture, Media and Sport Committee 119–20
House, Stephen 129, 151, 181
Hughes, Langston 2, 141–2
Human Rights Act 140
Hume, David 30
Hunte, Joseph A. 77
Huntington, Samuel 106
Hurston, Zora Neal 214

ideological justifications 5–6
immigration 57–8
  controls 68
  criminalisation 63–5, 71
  discouragement of 66–8
  legislation 61
  limitation 70
  trade union policy 75
imperial–colonial context 3, 4, 13–15, 18–25, 32, 83
imperial–colonial symbolism 58–61
imperialism 35, 102
imperialist nostalgia 83
industrial working class, emergence of 20
industrialisation 17–18
Information Commissioner's Office (ICO) 130
injustice 4, 10, 11, 83, 164, 173, 175–93, 210, 228
  and Black criminality 143, 159

law as source of 176–7
normal(ised) 186
racial 175, 185, 210
and racism 184–93
inner-city problems 100
Institute of Race Relations 78, 80
intellectual craftscape 165–74
international dimension 4
intruders from without tropes 99
invasion, language of 70–2

Jackson, George 180, 181, 183
Jamaica 36–7, 37, 51, 88
Jamaica Slave Act, 1664 35
Jamaican dancehall 157–8
James, C.L.R. 49, 55, 74, 215
Jarrett, Cynthia, police killing of 81
jazz 43, 87, 171
Jefferson, Thomas 29
Johnson, Linton Kwesi 77, 81, 94
joint enterprise convictions 137–9
Jones, Claudia 76, 76–7
Jordan, June 23, 180–1
Jordan, Louis, *Saturday Night Fish Fry* 1

Kano, *This is England* 120
Kant, Immanuel 30
Kingston Trio, *Bad Man's Blunder* 147–8
knife crime 130–1
knowledge-making 9–10, 161–2, 164, 165–74
Krept & Konan, *Ban Drill* 160
KRS-One, *Sound of Da Police* 21

labour shortages 66, 74
Lamming, George 64, 101
language 10–11

law
administration 177
fairness 175
as source of injustice 176–7
Law for Regulating Negroes and Slaves at Night Time, 1731 35
law-and-order agendas 107
lawfare 175
Lawrence, Stephen, murder of 14, 81, 82
Le Gendre, Kevin 41–2
legislation 35–6, 53, 61, 68–70, 71–2, 113–14, 129, 177
Lewisham, Battle of 78
Linebaugh, Peter 22, 51
Liverpool, race riot 74
Locke, John 36, 53–4
London 63–4
Colombo Club 97
Imperial Hotel 74–5
Olympic Games, 2012 70
superdiversity 105
London Metropolitan Police 17, 20, 21, 21–2, 82–3, 118–19, 124–5, 129, 181
Lord Kitchener
Drink-A-Rum 64
If You Brown 64
If You're Not White You're Black 64
London is the Place for Me 63
My Landlady 64
lynch mobs 74, 191
lyrics 133–4, 140–1, 145–8

McCurbin, Clinton, death in police custody 81
MacFarlane, Roy 81–2
Macpherson Report 82, 105

McQuail, Jess 111–12
Mais, Roger 84
Maldonaldo, Adal, *La Mambopera* 3
Manchester 10, the 135, 135–6, 139
Mangrove Nine trial 77
marabi music 4
Martinot, Steve 183–4
Marx, Karl 19, 20, 26
Mighty Terror, *Life in Britain* 63
Miller, Herbie 91–2
Mills, Charles 183–4
misogyny and sexism 8, 144, 151–5
monarchy, the 59–60
Morant Bay Rebellion, 1865 52
Moss Side 11, the 135
multiculturalism 105–6
multi-racist Britain 104
music-making criteria, Western 27–8, 47
Myal 37

N[*****] Hunting in England report 77
National Front 70, 78
National Health Service Act 1948 85
New Cross Fire 78–9
The New Cross Massacre Action Committee 79
New Labour 104, 105–6, 106, 107, 110, 113, 114, 120, 126
New Orleans 1–2
Newman, Kenneth 80
Newport race riot 73–4
noise 15, 24, 27, 96, 171, 182, 192
  Black music dismissed as 5
  contextualisation 27–9
  criminalisation 35
Notting Hill Carnival 78, 81

Notting Hill race riots 68, 75–7
Nottingham race riots 68
Nugent, Lady 27

Occidentosis 47
offensiveness 31–2
Oluwale, David, death 77
Olympic Games, London, 2012 70
Operation Domain 129
Operation Swamp 79–80
Operation Vaken 70
oppression 4, 14, 23, 26, 35, 43, 46, 52, 55, 71, 99, 101–2, 177, 188, 189, 191, 209, 213
oral culture 175
orature 168–9
Ormonde 57
Others and otherness 67, 86, 91–4, 101, 109, 111
Oval Four case 77

Parekh Report 105
patriality 69
Peach, Blair, killing of 78
Peel, Sir Robert 17, 22, 23
Peterloo Massacre, 1819 18
The Piano (film) 154–5
Pilkington, Edward 73–4
pirate radio 114–15
poetic licence 145, 149
Police and Crime Committee Meeting of the London Assembly 151, 181
Police Gang Matrix 124–6, 130
police racism 10, 14, 23, 56, 77–83, 106–7, 186
police suppression 87–8
police violence 41, 77–83, 94, 186

policing
African drumming 34–9, 43
blood at its root 23
bureaucratic 117, 118–19
of calypso/*kaiso* 6
and crime 182–3
cultural function 182
as a disciplinary tool 15
fascism 183
heavy-handed 14
history 17–18
imperial-colonial context 18–23
imperial-colonial roots 13–14,
14–15, 34–47
insights 164, 175–93
institutionalised 23
international similarities 4
order maintenance function
181–7, 193
professionalised 17–18
and racism 183–4
rap 107
slavery 21–2, 23
UK drill 159–60
UK reggae soundsystems 7, 90
Policing and Crime Act 2009 134–5
*Political Extremism and the
Campaign for Police
Accountability Within the
Metropolitan Police District*
(Special Branch) 80
poverty levels 111–12
Rivers of Blood speech 68–9, 122
Project Alpha 129–30, 132
Promotion Event Risk Assessment
Form 696 117, 118–19

Quevedo, Raymond (aka Atilla the
Hun) 45–7, 160

R v NHF [2022] EWCA Crim 859
136
R v Sode [2017] EWCA Crim 705
136–7
Race Disparity Unit 124–6
Race Relations Act, 1965 68
Race Relations Act, 1968 68
Race Relations Act, 1976 69–70
race riots 73–4
Liverpool 74
Newport 73–4
Notting Hill 68, 75–7
Nottingham 68
Tyneside 73
Race Today 95
racial injustice 175, 185, 210
racialisation, of crime 113
racialised criminalisation 4
racism and racist ideologies 3,
27–31, 55–6, 71–2, 85,
99–100, 101–2, 104–5
and aesthetic judgement 96
conceptualisation 187–9
as foundational doctrine
of Western civilisation
188
and injustice 184–93
institutional 23, 80, 82, 106–7,
128
and nationalism 100–1
origins 5
police 10, 14, 23, 56, 77–83,
106–7, 186
and policing 183–4
rejection of 39
Rivers of Blood speech (Powell)
68–9
and sexual violence 155
white feminism 155–7

racism and racist ideologies (*cont.*)
Windrush scandal 70–1
worldviews 192–3
racist humanism 30
radicalism 170–2
rap 89, 144–60
criminalisation 4, 102, 152, 158–9
lyrics 133–4, 140–1, 145–8
and misogyny 151–5
people's views of 147–8
personas 145–6
policing 107
subgenres 4, 7–9, 204–6
and violence 107, 146–51, 158–9
rap-causes-crime fiction 122–3
Rastafarians 90, 91–4, 97, 98–9
realpolitik 45–6
rhythm 28, 162, 167
River Thames Police 22
Rivers of Blood speech (Powell) 68–9, 122
Roach, Colin, killing of 80
Robinson, Cedric 26, 55
Romeo, Max 97–9
One Step Forward 104
Rose, Tricia 152, 153
Royal Commission on Criminal Procedure 78
Royal Irish Constabulary 22
rule of law 176

Safety of Rwanda (Asylum and Immigration) Bill, 2024 71
samba 4
saturation policing 79–80
Scarman Report on the 'Brixton Disorders' 80
Selvon, Sam 64–5

Senghor, Léopold 163
sensationalisation 178–9
Sepulveda, Ginés de 29–30
Sepulveda syndrome 29–30
Serious Violence Strategy 129
Sexton, Jared 183–4
Shades of Grey report 90, 91
shebeens/blues dances 1
Sims, Aseta, death 77
Singh, Kenneth, murder of 78
slave codes 177
slave laws 34–9
slave narratives 50–1
slave rebellions 37, 52–4
slave ships 50
slave trade 20–1, 50, 166, 177
slavery and enslavement 5
abolition 20–1
afterlife of 192
denial of agency 39
as economic category 19
freedom struggles 48–56
ideological justifications 5–6
policing 21–2, 23, 34–9
revolutionary activity 49–50
self-legitimising theories and ideologies 53–4
Slimzee, DJ 115
So Solid Crew 118–19
social control 14, 55, 176, 193
social disorder 7–8
spatial politics 116–17
Special Patrol Group (SPG) 79–80
Starkey, David 121–2
state power 44, 99, 178
state violence 179, 180
steel bands 40, 43–4
steelpan music 28
Steiner, George 96, 158

Stephen Lawrence Inquiry 82
stereotypes 30–1, 117, 147, 189
Stokley, Jim 128–9
Stono Rebellion (aka Cato's
    Conspiracy), 1739 52
stop and search 124
Stormzy, *WickedSkengman 5* 148–9
structural disadvantage 111–12
sus laws 79–80
suspect populations 23

Tacky's Revolt, 1760 52
tambour-bamboo bands 43
tea 60–1
Thatcher, Margaret 79–80, 83, 100
Theatres and Dance Halls
    Ordinance, Trinidad 44,
    45–7
The Times 74, 87
Timothy (Al), *Bulldog Don't Bite
    Me* 64
'traneing' 172–3
Trident 110–11
Trinidad 26, 39–47
Trinidad Legislative Council 45–7

UK drill 7–8, 14, 122–3, 144–5,
    150, 193
  anti-terrorism legislation against
    129
  artistic conventions 132–3
  criminalisation 107, 126–7,
    128–43
  as evidence of bad character
    137–43
  as gang-related music 131,
    132–7
  lyrics 133–4, 140–1
  and misogyny 151

playlist 207
policing 159–60
videos 129–30, 135–7, 141–2,
    144
and violence 146–7
The UK Drill Project 132–3
UK grime 7–8
  criminalisation 107, 118–27
  pirate radio 114–15
  playlist 207
UK Overseas Territories (UKOTs)
    59
UK soundsystem reggae 61, 86
  conceptualisation 88–9
  cultural threat 95–6
  danger 89–99
  law-breaking threat 95–6
  playlist 199–203
  policing 90, 94–100
  policing of 7
  spread of 88–9
  styles 89
United States of America
  Black Codes 35
  Carolina 36, 53
  Jim Crow 191
  Restoring Artistic Protection Act
    139
  slave codes 35–6
  slave patrol legislation 34
  soundsystem culture 89
  South Carolina 52
  violence 181
  Virginia 35–6
uprisings, 2011 121–3, 126
Utrecht, Treaty of 177

Vagrancy Act 1824 79–80
violation, and violence 180–1

violence 40–2, 73–86, 144
   anti-racist struggles 78–81
   causes of 179–81
   double standards 181
   as entertainment 181
   glorification of 8
   key flashpoints 73
   origins 74
   police 77–83, 94, 186
   rap and 107, 146–51, 158–9
   state 179, 180
   UK drill and 146–7
   US 181
   and violation 180–1
   white murderous rage 96–7
   white riots 73–4
   youth 124–6, 130–1
   see also race riots
virginity testing 70
Vodun (also: Vodou, Voodoo) 37,
   55

War on Terror 106
welfare state 85
West Indian Standing Conference
   (London region) 77
White Defence League 75
white privilege 213–14
white riots 73–4
white supremacy 28–9, 183
whiteness 10, 170, 172
   conceptualisation 212–15
WickedSkengman 148–9
Windrush scandal 70–1
Wollstonecraft, Mary 156
World War II 57, 85
Wynter, Sylvia 24, 29–30, 38–9, 40,
   49–50, 54, 168–9

year 2000 103–4
youth violence 124–6, 130–1

Zong (slave ship) 19